2000

DEWEY
RECONFIGURED

SUNY series in the Philosophy of the Social Sciences
Lenore Langsdorf, Editor

DEWEY
RECONFIGURED

Essays on Deweyan Pragmatism

EDITED BY

Casey Haskins
and
David I. Seiple

State University of New York Press

Published by
State University of New York Press, Albany

©1999 State University of New York

Printed in the United States of America

Cover photo from the John Dewey Collection, Special Collections/ Morris Library, Southern Illinois University Carbondale.

For information, address State University of New York Press, State University Plaza, Albany, N.Y., 12246

Production by Diane Ganeles
Marketing by Fran Keneston

Library of Congress Cataloging-in-Publication Data

Dewey reconfigured : essays on Deweyan pragmatism / edited by Casey Haskins and David I. Seiple.
    p.   cm. — (SUNY series in the philosophy of the social sciences)
    Includes bibliographical references and index.
    ISBN 0-7914-4319-1 (hardcover : alk. paper). — ISBN 0-7914-4320-5 (pbk. : alk. paper)
    1. Dewey, John, 1859–1952. 2. Pragmatism. I. Haskins, Casey. II. Seiple, David I. III. Series.
B945.D44D495   1999
191—dc21   99-13704
                                            CIP

10 9 8 7 6 5 4 3 2 1

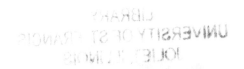

Contents

reflective practices where discussions of large questions about culture, nature, and human problems are responsibly undertaken— for practices, that is, that aim to be critical while forgoing the rhetorical comforts of appeals to timeless and self-evident first principles, and that are in touch with their practical consequences and historical roots. It is this image of philosophical criticism which Dewey did as much as any writer in twentieth-century philosophy to promote and articulate. As he put it in his 1920 work *Reconstruction in Philosophy*, "When it is acknowledged that under disguise of dealing with ultimate reality, philosophy has been occupied with the precious values embedded in social traditions, that it has sprung from a clash of social ends and from a conflict of inherited institutions with incompatible contemporary tendencies, it will be seen that the task of future philosophy is to clarify men's ideas as to the social and moral strifes of their own day."

Such a vision of philosophy's cultural role doubtless came as a breath of fresh air to many during the ideological struggles dominating twentieth-century intellectual and political life through the end of the Cold War. In politics this was a period rife with competing totalizing visions of social justice and reform; in philosophy it was a period rife with competing claims to possession of a final philosophical method, claims eventually to be followed, as we have now seen, by reactionary denials of the very idea of a philosophic method. Dewey is remembered as a passionate opponent of totalizing visions and final philosophic methods of all kinds, even while he advocated the usefulness, especially in modern democratic societies, of what he called the "experimental method" in philosophy. He viewed philosophy not as a dispassionate spectator upon the world—a "mirror of nature" in Richard Rorty's phrase—but as one of various ways in which collective cultural intelligence interacts with its environment. Philosophy's experimental character lies partly in how, like the sciences, it is an essentially empirical discipline. Even more specifically, it lies in a peculiarly reciprocal relationship that always obtains between the interests and actions of any inquiring agency, individual or communal, and the environment or larger world that it investigates. This relationship is reflected in how, first of all, the world sets constraints on any inquirer's interests, which go on, in turn, to shape which questions and hypotheses are taken seriously. The inquirer is then, in turn, moved to introduce new causal input into the world by acting on the findings of the inquiry. In this way thought and action are continuous, just as—from the naturalistic perspective that Dewey made a staple of the pragmatist tradition—are intelligence and nature.

This conception of philosophy continues to wear well for the generation coming of age as we enter a new century. That century has scarcely begun, but what is clear already is that this generation's experience is shaped, more than was the experience of its predecessors, by a sense that human values and problems are local and not global in origin, and resist catch-all political classifications like "marxist" and "capitalist," or philosophical classifications like "positivist," "relativist," and "realist." For academic intellectuals, this conception of philosophy speaks particularly to an atmosphere in which many doctrines associated with the protean end-of-the-twentieth-century phenomenon of postmodernism are shown to be not particulary *post*modern at all, if not also to carry consequences inviting yet further, "post-postmodern" forms of critique. A familiar case in point is the ongoing modern and postmodern struggle to explain human values. If—as some forms of cultural critique associated with postmodernism are often supposed to suggest—all human values are cultural constructs, does it follow that they are not real? Some postmodern critiques make it tempting to answer "no." But a characteristically pragmatic response to such a question is to ask whether communal confidence in values that are at once real *and* local in origin is not a live hypothesis, or indeed an existential necessity, in a world as manifestly shaped by cultural plurality as it is by the scientific outlook.

Dewey's own answer to this question—an answer that continues to bear scrutiny today—was a programmatically resounding "yes." Of course, one can agree with that answer and still not regard oneself as a pragmatist, Deweyan or otherwise. But it should also be kept in mind that the label "pragmatism" no longer names a single fixed theory. It was Dewey's hope, indeed, that many of the doctrines that had come to be associated with the label in his lifetime would eventually be absorbed into the common sense of modern democratic communities, or "naturalized." In any case, "pragmatism" is best understood today as the name of a self-reinterpreting tradition, a tradition which has never lacked its passionate critics as well as supporters. Dewey himself, who rejected the idea that any philosophical outlook or inquiry is ever finished and was continually defending his own ideas in public debate, would be quick to note that this is all to the good. For the test of the value of any teaching in a self-examining democratic culture can only in the end occur through the give and take of critical conversation. These essays, we hope, offer suggestive examples of how the critical conversation over the themes of Deweyan pragmatism can continue to shape the experience of a new century.

The essays fall loosely under two headings. One group, including the essays by Tiles, Campbell, Fesmire, Haskins, and Anderson, emphasizes Dewey's ideas as he understood them. Another group, including the essays by Kestenbaum, Colapietro, Gatens-Robinson, Boisvert, Shusterman, and Conway, presents critical interpretations of Deweyan themes in light of recent debates over the significance and viability of Dewey's ideas.

James Campbell's "Dewey and Democracy" appropriately begins the collection, since it offers an overview of the larger vision of cooperative intelligence which provides the connecting thread for all of Dewey's concerns. Campbell outlines Dewey's account of democracy in three steps, beginning with an examination of Dewey's reconstructive analysis of the general meaning of "democracy." Dewey took this concept to refer not to a settled tradition or set of intellectual principles so much as to an evolving way of life. Democracy, so understood, is not a thing so much as a process whose definition and institutional embodiments are actively constituted and reconstituted by cooperative interaction and inquiry. Campbell turns secondly to democratic practice itself, which Dewey conceived as a kind of dialectic between conservatism and its criticism. It is a commonplace of social life that there arise tensions between various organizational aspects of legal, industrial, educational, political, religious or other practices and the continually shifting historical pressures on human need. One function of democratic institutions as Dewey understood them is to correct for such "institutional lag" by according collective discussion the authority to effect adjustments between "the old and the new" in all areas of life. And nowhere, Campbell notes, did Dewey see this process as more conspicuously needed or displayed than in education, which should aim in a democratic setting to instill habits conducive to creative and adaptive problem solving, and equally to foster habits of cooperation in the course of inquiry.

This last theme of Campbell's essay is continued in Victor Kestenbaum's "The Undeclared Self." Central to Kestenbaum's argument is the idea that the educational process can afford students—in particular college students—opportunities to transform experiences of conflict and alienation into positive occasions for self-formation. The growth of a student's sense of self is in different senses a process of self-discovery and self-reinvention. So understood, it draws on the traditional romantic (and more recently, existentialist) idea that the process of becoming who one is is one of expressive growth. In Kestenbaum's terms, the developmental process is also a process of "self-declaration." This is true in the literal sense that a central rite of passage for the college student is his or her declaration of commitment to a formal field of study. It is also true in the sense that the hurdles of the educational process can move the student towards new, hitherto unimagined, forms of self-recognition, towards fresh opportunities to declare to oneself and others in a performative way who one is and what values one stands for. Kestenbaum concludes with the suggestion that to interpret this thought adequately in the context of Dewey's philosophy of education we need to recall Dewey's earliest writings on education where, still in his "idealist" period, he affirmed the importance of ideals possessing, in a phrase Kestenbaum borrows from William Arrowsmith, an "intangible and invisible" quality.

J. E. Tiles' "The Fortunes of 'Functionalism'" addresses the legacy of Dewey's early psychological inquiries of the eighteen-eighties and nineties. This work would set the stage for all of his subsequent work and indeed, through the influence of the "Chicago school" of functional psychology, for much academic work in psychology of the coming century. Tiles shows how the functional view of mind that Dewey favored was consistent with, and indeed invited, a broader account of the naturalistic basis for ethical norms. This, in turn, made his approach vulnerable in the early decades of the century of the criticisms of positivists in philosophy (and their behavioristic counterparts in psychology), which drew upon the more traditional resources of mainstream empiricism and which dominated American academic circles between the wars. Having traced this development, Tiles then addresses the more recent (post-World War II) appearance in philosophical psychology of another influential doctrine also styling itself as functionalism. Tiles concludes by examining this doctrine from the standpoint of Dewey's earlier version of functionalism, and takes this as an opportunity to venture critiques of some other doctrines in contemporary philosophy of mind from the standpoint of Dewey's philosophical psychology.

Tiles' essay is followed by Vincent Colapietro's "Embodied, Enculturated Agents." Dewey, in opposition to the legacies of

Cartesian dualism and of the associationism favored by the British empiricists and Kant, maintained that intelligence is, in its most fundamental nature, embodied and social. But if Dewey's programmatic commitments regarding this topic were clear, he was often less than forthcoming about the details. In particular, asks Colapietro, what more exactly does a Deweyan view of the self entail? Acknowledging allegations of the inadequacy of Dewey's thinking on this subject by such critics as John Smith and Richard Bernstein, Colapietro argues that the basic philosophical resources in Dewey's writings for a reconstructed theory of the self are considerable and remain underappreciated. Situating Dewey's views in the context of recent philosophical efforts to avoid reducing selfhood to a single static term of explanation (for example, consciousness, possession of a soul, or membership in a natural kind), Colapietro argues for a more fluid conception of the self as an *embodied, enculturated agency*. This approach, he suggests, avoids the pitfalls of dualism while preserving the biological dimension of experience; most importantly, it leaves room for the historically particular ways in which any self is shaped by the developing ethos of its surrounding community.

Dewey's programmatic insistence upon the social and embodied nature of the self is reflected also in his views on a subject that may at first seem at odds with his pervasively naturalistic outlook: religion. Or, more exactly, religious experience, understood as a potential dimension of all human relations that, as he wrote in *A Common Faith*, "shall not be confined to sect, class, or race." Douglas Anderson begins his "Theology as Healing: A Meditation on *A Common Faith*" by noting that Dewey's purpose in offering a naturalistic reconstruction of such notions as "faith," "God," and "piety" was not to undermine traditional religious practice. Rather his purpose was to make the case that religious sensibility, properly understood, embraces the sizable segment of modern people who find themselves alienated from traditional religious practices no less than it embraces the adherents of such practices. Dewey's short but suggestive text on religion, Anderson suggests, is thus best read as a kind of secular sermon directed especially to "the lost souls of the post-Darwinian era." But Dewey's aim was not to preach the desirability of a fully formed ideal of wholeness as a goal for questing lost souls. Rather, it was to underscore the possibility and significance of such a quest construed as an open-ended experiential, and experimental, process. The most desirable outcomes of this process, properly understood, are provisional forms of harmony between self and world—outcomes which will always be shaped by the particulars of an individual's interaction with a specific cultural and historical environment.

Casey Haskins examines another key element in Dewey's vision of the prospects of the modern self's quest for wholeness in "Dewey's Romanticism." It is well known that Dewey referred frequently to romantic authors and themes in his writings, notably in his discussion of aesthetics in *Art as Experience*. These allusions suggest that he was a kind of romantic himself; but what kind exactly? The specific character of Dewey's romanticism, Haskins argues, is revealed by a comparative reading of *Art as Experience* alongside other central Deweyan texts, including *Experience and Nature, A Common Faith*, and *Reconstruction in Philosophy*. Such a reading must also note the multiple meanings of the term "romanticism." For many, a romantic sensibility connotes, as it did in part for Dewey, a positive vision of a life that aspires to expressive wholeness. But for the young Dewey if also had more troubling historical affinities with nineteenth-century sentimentalizations of alienated individuality, with moral and metaphysical pessimism, and with militant nationalism. Dewey's romanticism is thus, Haskins argues, a reconstructed romanticism which needs to be traced not only through Dewey's writings on art, aesthetic experience, and value, but also through his writings on knowledge and scepticism, ethical development, and the meliorative promise of democratic community.

This last linkage of themes suggests how Dewey's philosophy projects what might be termed an "aesthetics of intelligence." In "The Art of Moral Imagination," Steven Fesmire explores a further expression of this theme in Dewey's ethical theory. His focus is an idea Dewey set forth briefly and suggestively in the *Ethics* but never developed in detail: the idea that when confronted with a problematic situation, a deliberating agent imaginatively surveys possible courses of action in search of one that will integrate competing desires and achieve a new form of harmony in the agent's experience. Not only does the dimension of deliberation Dewey envisaged, Fesmire suggests, involve our ability to forecast imaginatively consequences of our action for ourselves; equally important, it involves our ability to imaginatively rehearse the roles of others whose lives interlace with our own. We need to be able to project ourselves into what we hypothesize as the emerging dramas of the lives of others, all to the end of discovering how those lives stand ethically in relation to our own. To this extent, "immoral"

conduct amounts not to a failure to apply universal rules to a
situation so much as to a failure of moral imagination; and moral
conduct emerges as possessing a creative and aesthetic dimension
that likens it to the activity of an artist.

In a more critical vein, Raymond Boisvert turns, in "The Nemesis of Necessity: Tragedy's Challenge to Deweyan Pragmatism," to
a topic about which Dewey has been traditionally taken to task by
critics: his failure to give due attention to the tragic dimension in
human experience. Dewey's basic pragmatic vision of the natural
and cultural history of intelligence, Boisvert argues, was shaped by
a Baconian optimism about the perfectability of mankind which, in
spirit, was not unlike that which underlay such nineteenth-century
movements as Marxism and Emersonian transcendentalism. This
attitude, Boisvert notes, led Dewey to embrace a conception of moral
progress as roughly analogous to scientific progress. Although this
conception became more qualified in Dewey's later writings, he still
in the end resisted acknowledging the primordial tension between
"mind" and "necessity"—between human powers and reaches of
nature which are residually resistant to the human will. Such a
pairing, central to ancient thought as well as to more recent conceptions of the tragic, does not, Boisvert argues, deserve to be forgotten so readily by modern philosophy. This is particularly true in
a culture like ours which enjoys the benefits of growing technology
in all areas, yet still needs to acknowledge the stubborn realities of
warfare, political injustice, and disease—all evidences of the per-
sistence of extra-human necessity in the human world.

In "The Private and Its Problem: A Pragmatic View of Reproductive Choice," Eugenie Gatens-Robinson addresses a dilemma
haunting the ethics of reproductive choice in postmodern liberal
democracies where the plurality of voices claiming authority in
contestations of rights and duties becomes problematic. On the
one hand, a traditional liberal defense of a woman's right to make
her own choices regarding abortion and other reproductive issues
rests on a distinction between the public realm, where the regulation of individual behavior is legally enforced, and the private
realm, where certain kinds of behavior are an individual's legal
prerogative. But on the other hand, traditional versions of the
public/private distinction are often criticized by feminists because
of how these versions can function to legitimize certain kinds of
repression and coercion of women facing reproductive decisions
(for example, through coercion by family members). And this, in
turn, indicates a need for a critical rethinking of such distinctions.

Here, Gatens-Robinson suggests, a valuable resource may be found in Dewey's critique of traditional notions of the private realm. This critique was rooted in his belief that the deepest challenge of democracy is the challenge to form a *public*, in the sense of the latter term connoting a community of open discourse and face-to-face interaction. Suppose, Gatens-Robinson reasons, the inhabitants of contemporary democratic society could learn to take a new view of dilemmas possessing the form "either privacy-and-freedom-to-choose or no-privacy-and-no-freedom-to-choose." They might, that is, learn to view such dilemmas in terms which would drop stark contrasts between public and private and would speak more flexibly of different relationships to a multivocal conversation about values. It may then be possible to create new strategies for overcoming this particular source of public fragmentation about what kinds of reproductive choices women and men should and should not be allowed to make.

The two final papers, by Richard Shusterman and Daniel Conway, deal with issues emerging in the wake of Richard Rorty's well-known—and, among some Deweyans, contested—recovery of Dewey's ideas for contemporary philosophy. In "Dewey on Experience: Foundation or Reconstruction?," Shusterman critically explores the implications of Dewey's thesis that experience occurs in an immediate, or pre-discursive, form. Against Rorty's claim that this line of Deweyan thought betokens a naive appeal to ideas of pre-linguistic epistemological foundations, Shusterman argues that part of this thesis is well worth saving. Contemporary readers can dispense with the foundationalistic aspects of Dewey's thesis—and up to this point Shusterman agrees with Rorty—while still taking seriously another aspect, one that retains valuable implications for a philosophy of experience. This is the idea that experience is rooted in forms of bodily or somatic awareness that possess an integrity apart from discursive or linguistic consciousness.

In "Of Depth and Loss: The Peritropaic Legacy of Dewey's Pragmatism," Daniel Conway views Rorty's recovery of Dewey in the context of the pragmatic tradition's "peritropaic" character—its way of encouraging critiques of received conceptions of what pragmatism is by pragmatists themselves. Conway reviews various ways in which Rorty, who claims Deweyan inspiration for his views, has nonetheless defended a vision of postmodern liberalism that is unapologetically at odds with aspects of Dewey's own metaphysical naturalism and his critique of liberal individualism. But rather than have us view Rorty simply, with some "self-appointed gatekeepers of Deweydom," as a self-serving exploiter of the

Deweyan legacy, Conway argues that what is more significant about Rorty's writings is how they exemplify the self-critical feature of pragmatism without which Dewey's own work (for example) would have been impossible. Viewed in these terms, Rorty's arguments, distasteful though they may be to some orthodox Deweyans, are not, Conway argues, symptoms of a bogus pragmatism. Rather, they are authentic expressions of the kind of challenge that the pragmatist tradition has continually issued to itself and that was, in the end, congenial to the reconstructive spirit of Dewey's vision of philosophy.

Acknowledgments

We thank *The Philosophical Forum* for permission to reprint Richard Shusterman's "Dewey on Experience: Foundation or Reconstruction?," which originally appeared in that journal's Winter 1994 issue (Vol. XXVI, no. 2).

A special acknowledgment is due David Seiple. The original concept of the volume and the work of commissioning the essays were his, but due to pressing personal commitments he asked me to assume the remaining editorial duties. Some of the chapters—including those by Fesmire, Conway, Kestenbaum, and myself—are descended from papers first delivered at the 1993 annual meeting of the Society for the Advancement of American Philosophy at Vanderbilt University, where David Seiple approached prospective authors with the idea of an anthology. (C.H.)

Note on Citations

References to the writings of Dewey throughout the following chapters, unless specified otherwise, are to the Carbondale comprehensive edition of Dewey's works, which comprises *The Early Works of John Dewey, 1882–1898*. Carbondale: Southern Illinois University Press, 1967–1972. 5 vols. (Abbreviated as "EW."); *The Middle Works of John Dewey, 1899–1924*. Carbondale: Southern Illinois University Press, 1976–1983. 15 vols. (Abbreviated as "MW."); and *The Later Works of John Dewey, 1925–1953*. Carbondale: Southern Illinois University Press, 1981–1991. 17 vols. (Abbreviated as "LW.").

1

Dewey and Democracy

===

James Campbell

I

In any discussion of Dewey and democracy, it is perhaps best to begin with a consideration of the concept itself. Dewey concerned himself during his lifetime with the reconstruction of the full range of political concepts, making throughout three separable claims. Each of these claims is fundamentally pragmatic in nature and stands in need of our ongoing evaluation. The first was that such conceptions are tools to be used in our attempts to settle our social problems, and that they have an *absolute* or *final* meaning only in an abstract or definitional sense. Consequently, the requirements of, for example, a full sense of 'democracy' cannot be settled by recourse to traditions or historical documents. Rather, the adequacy of conceptions of 'democracy' must be evaluated in accordance with our particular situations. His second claim was that the various historically-bound conceptions of political terms that we have inherited once made reasonable contemporary sense. The third claim Dewey was making was that at the present time many of these conceptions—like a conception of 'democracy' that is confined to a narrow political sphere—no longer work to advance the common good. These outdated conceptions owe their continued existence to the fact that there are forces in society—individuals, groups, institutions—that benefit from their continuance.

When we begin to consider what Dewey believed 'democracy' should mean in our contemporary situation, it becomes clear that he sees it as "a word of many meanings" (LW 2:286). It carries these many meanings because democratic life "has to be enacted anew in every generation, in every year and day, in the living relations of person to person in all social forms and institutions" (LW 11:416). We need to remember, he continues,

> that every generation has to accomplish democracy over again for itself; that its very nature, its essence, is something that cannot be handed on from one person or one generation to another, but has to be worked out in terms of needs, problems and conditions of the social life of which, as the years go by, we are a part . . . (LW 13:299; cf. 87; EW 3:203).

Because of our ongoing social evolution, our conception of democracy "must be continually explored afresh; it has to be constantly discovered, and rediscovered, remade and reorganized . . . " (LW 11:182).

One basic choice we need to make is between focussing broadly upon "democracy as a social idea" or narrowly upon "political democracy as a system of government" (LW 2:325). Dewey's emphasis was, as I have suggested, on democracy as "a mode of associated living, of conjoint communicated experience" as distinct from democracy as "a form of government" (MW 9:93). It is this broader sense of democracy that recognizes "the moral sense of democracy as a way of living together" (LW 14:79). In defense of this moral emphasis, he writes:

> The idea of democracy is a wider and fuller idea than can be exemplified in the state even at its best. To be realized it must affect all modes of human association, the family, the school, industry, religion. And even as far as political arrangements are concerned, governmental institutions are but a mechanism for securing to an idea channels of effective operation (LW 2:325; cf. 11:217).

It would thus be a mistake to regard democracy as "an alternative to other principles of associated life." More than the agnostic claim that no one is likely to have better opinions than the average person, and more than the timorous claim that democracy is simply a device for self-protection from tyranny, democracy should be seen, Dewey writes, as "the idea of community life itself" (LW 2:328; cf. EW 1:240).

In advocating this broader, moral conception of democracy, Dewey placed a great deal of faith in his fellows. "Democracy is a way of life," he writes, "controlled by a working faith in the possibilities of human nature" (LW 14:226; cf. 11:219). This democratic faith includes a faith "in individuality, in uniquely distinctive qualities in each normal human being . . . " (MW 13:297) and "in the capacity of human beings for intelligent judgment and action if proper conditions are furnished" (LW 14:227; cf. 17:400). This inclusion of conditions reminds us of the centrality to all of his thought of the social conception of the individual. His faith in individuality results from his recognition of the moral efficacy "of associated living, of conjoint communicated experience" (MW 9:93), "of pooled and cooperative experience" (LW 11:219). Dewey's work can thus serve as a needed counteractive to the excessive strain of individualistic freedom in some conceptions of democracy. "Cooperation," he writes, "is as much a part of the democratic ideal as is personal initiative" (LW 13:78). He continues,

> the habit of amicable cooperation . . . is itself a priceless addition to life . . . Democracy is the faith that the process of experience is more important than any special result attained, so that special results achieved are of ultimate value only as they are used to enrich and order the ongoing process (LW 14:228–229).

And, with democracy, the possibility of recognizing and overcoming problems in those results is increased. Moreover, because all of this is grounded in a faith, it can be validated or falsified only in the future success or failure of social action, "in *its* works, its fruits" (MW 13:308).

Democracy as a way of life is tested by interactive living. "From the standpoint of the individual," Dewey writes, the democratic idea

> consists in having a responsible share according to capacity in forming and directing the activities of the groups to which one belongs and in participating according to need in the values which the groups sustain. From the standpoint of the groups, it demands liberation of the potentialities of members of a group in harmony with the interests and good which are common (LW 2:327–328; cf. MW 9:129).

Because of its emphasis upon engagement in social life, democracy is "the road which places the greatest burden of responsibility upon the greatest number of human beings" (LW 13:154; cf. 7:359). The level of work necessary to fulfill the responsibilities of democracy makes Dewey's democrats active participants in communal life. "The key-note of democracy as a way of life may be expressed," he continues, "as the necessity for the participation of every mature human being in formation of the values that regulate the living of men together..." (LW 11:217). Without the chance to participate, individuals cannot grow: "human nature is developed only when its elements take part in directing things which are common, things for the sake of which men and women form groups—families, industrial companies, governments, churches, scientific associations, and so on" (MW 12:199–200). If one is to be a "spectator" rather than a "participant," however, that person will assume the attitude of "a man in a prison cell watching the rain out of the window; it is all the same to him" (MW 9:131). Consequently, Dewey holds up to us the goal of developing "the particular kind of social direction fitted to a democratic society—the direction which comes from heightened emotional appreciation of common interests and from an understanding of social responsibilities" that can be gained "only by experimental and personal participation in the conduct of common affairs" (MW 11:57).

With this large scope of democracy in mind, we can briefly consider two particular aspects: the political and the economic. As Dewey writes, "the supreme test of all political institutions and industrial arrangements shall be the contribution they make to the all-around growth of every member of society" (MW 12:186). In the political realm, democracy denotes "a mode of government, a specified practice in selecting officials and regulating their conduct as officials" (LW 2:286). It is a mode of government "which does not esteem the well-being of one individual or class above that of another; a system of laws and administration which ranks the happiness and interests of all as upon the same plane, and before whose law and administration all individuals are alike, or equal" (MW 10:137). In furtherance of these goals several familiar procedures have been developed: "Universal suffrage, recurring elections, responsibility of those who are in political power to the voters, and the other factors of democratic government are means that have been found expedient for realizing democracy as the truly human way of living" (LW 11:218). The political aspect of democracy would also include other sorts of experiments, like attempts to integrate the knowledge developed by experts to help solve our social problems.

In a modern industrial society, the economic side of democracy is equally important because, as Dewey notes in 1932, "political questions are not economic in nature" (LW 7:357). Economic changes since the time of the foundation of our political frameworks have rendered such frameworks to a large extent irrelevant since "economic developments which could not possibly have been anticipated when our political forms took shape have created confusion and uncertainty in the working of the agencies of popular government . . . " (LW 13:107; cf. 11:366–371). In the modern world where so many people "have the minimum of control over the conditions of their own subsistence," he writes, "it is a problem of the future of democracy, of how political democracy can be made secure if there is economic insecurity and economic dependence of great sections of the population . . . " (LW 13:300). Consequently, even from his earliest writings, he maintains that at present "democracy is not in reality what it is in name until it is industrial, as well as civil and political." This "democracy of wealth" (EW 1:246) requires an organized effort by the community, acting through its government, to foster both liberty and equality. In this regard, Dewey sees democracy as "an endeavor to unite two ideas which have historically often worked antagonistically: liberation of individuals on one hand and promotion of a common good on the other" (LW 7:349; cf. 9:103).

This emphasis upon industrial democracy can be seen in Dewey's advocacy of the democratic management of our economic system, of granting to workers "a responsible share in the management of activities" (MW 12:9; cf. LW 5:104). How large and what type of share they would have would have to be determined and redetermined by future individuals facing particular situations. Related to these egalitarian aspects of industrial management, a full sense of the economic element in Dewey's understanding of democracy would also require that the kinds of employment available to workers have meaning in their lives, that there be changes sufficient to give their daily work "large and human significance" (MW 1:16; cf. 12:9; 14:86–87; LW 1:271–272; 5:240; 11:221). The aesthetic and moral aspects of living thus demand that we develop work environments in which workers would no longer have to engage in pursuits "fixed by accident and necessity of circumstance" (MW 9:143), not be "appendages to the machines they tend" (LW 3:124), nor have jobs in which "[p]ersonal judgment and initiative have no organic place" (LW 5:137; cf. 1:271). This democratic reconstruction of working must also develop the workers' positions, and consciousness of those positions, with regard to the social ends of the community. Our goal, Dewey writes, must be that "every person shall be occupied in something which makes the lives of others better worth living, and which accordingly makes the ties which bind persons together more perceptible ... " (MW 9:326; cf. LW 5:105).

II

Up to this point, we have been considering primarily Dewey's discussion of the meaning of the concept 'democracy.' In this section, I would like to focus more on Dewey's consideration of democratic practice. His analysis that emphasized the ongoing reconstruction of our political concepts is matched here by his emphasis on the processive character of social existence and on our need to adapt the various solutions to our past social problems to face new situations. Our various groupings—in the bureaucracies, in industries, in informal clubs and organizations and neighborhoods—will be more adaptive and effective to the extent that they reflect the sense of democracy considered above.

Social institutions are, Dewey writes, "organized modes of actions, on the basis of the wants and interests which unite men" (EW 3:347). Some typical Deweyan examples of institutions based upon this broad characterization would be: customs, economic systems, political procedures, religions, languages, property, legal forms, schools, etc. He writes that the purpose of all social institutions is "to set free and to develop the capacities of human individuals without respect to race, sex, class or economic status," to "educate every individual into the full stature of his possibility," and to bring about "the all-around growth of every member of society" (MW 12:186; cf. EW 5:48; MW 5:431; 9:9; 14:54; LW 7:227). But institutions tend to lag behind: "The force of lag in human life is enormous" (MW 14:77). Religious formulations and business practices, educational systems and family arrangements, all become inappropriate as time passes:

> Industrial habits have changed most rapidly; there has followed at considerable distance, change in political relations; alterations in legal relations and methods have lagged even

> more, while changes in the institutions that deal most di-
> rectly with patterns of thought and belief have taken place
> to the least extent (LW 11:42; cf. 54; 12:82–83; 13:97).

Institutional lag is a constant condition of our social existence,
more or less serious depending upon the particulars of the situation.

When serious lag develops the institutions in question must be
reconstructed, a process which in a democracy of the rich and
participatory sort that he advocated requires ongoing debate and
discussion to bring the outdated institutions more into line with
the social vision by which we choose to live. Our goal, he maintains, "the universal and all-embracing human task," is "the construction of a proper human environment that will serve by its
very existence to produce sound and whole human beings, who in
turn will maintain a sound and healthy human environment..."
(LW 13:336). Dewey sees this ongoing reconstruction as part of the
life of a liberal democratic community. As it developed, this liberal
spirit "implied a new interest in the common man and a new sense
that the common man, the representative of the great masses of
human beings, had possibilities that had been kept under, that had
not been allowed to develop, because of institutions and political
conditions" (LW 11:365). Out of this attempt to set free the possibilities of the great masses of people came what he sees as three
guiding themes of modern liberal democracy.

First of all, in an evolving society where institutions are constantly being strained by their tendency to lag behind, liberalism
is committed to "the mediation of social transitions," to "adjusting
the old and the new" (LW 11:36, 133; cf. 291–292). Liberal democracy attempts to move from the currently-felt problems toward
resolutions that advance the common good. Secondly, in spite of the
fact that liberalism works to adjust and mediate, it should not be
seen as somehow precommitted to minimizing the degree of change.
Rather, liberalism at its best should pursue radical changes in
society, changes that reach down to the roots of our problems. Dewey
writes that "liberalism must now become radical, meaning by 'radical' perception of the necessity of thoroughgoing changes in the set-
up of institutions and corresponding activity to bring the changes
to pass" (LW 11:45). Renascent liberalism must seek out "the causes
of which inequalities and oppressions are but the symptoms," he
writes; and, "instead of using social power to ameliorate the evil
consequences of the existing system, it shall use social power to
change the system" (LW 11:287). Thirdly, liberalism must also be

committed to carrying out these radical changes by peaceful means. As Dewey writes, "democracy can be served only by the slow day-by-day adoption and contagious diffusion in every phase of our common life of methods that are identical with the ends to be reached . . . " (LW 13:187; cf. 11:218, 298).

Those who adopt a revolutionary perspective and defend the inevitability of violence "as the main method of effecting drastic changes" are wrong, he believes, "in view of the vast scope of changes that are taking place without the use of violence" (LW 11:45, 58). Even admitting as he does that the United States has a "tradition of violence" and that force "is built into the procedures of the existing social system, regularly as coercion, in times of crisis as overt violence" (LW 11:46, 45; cf. 294), he still rejects continued reliance upon violence. Part of the basis of his rejection is his belief that the costs of revolution in the contemporary world are too high and the risks too great (cf. LW 9:94; 11:266, 288). In addition, he maintains that, even assuming that revolution was once necessary, those who continue to advocate violence cannot prove that it is still necessary. "Insistence that the use of violent force is *inevitable* limits the use of available intelligence, for wherever the inevitable reigns intelligence cannot be used" (LW 11:55; cf. 58). Rather than seeing violence as an inherent element in the social process, he writes that "what generates violent strife is failure to bring the conflict into the light of intelligence where the conflicting interests can be adjudicated in behalf of the interest of the great majority" (LW 11:56; cf. 5:415). And, to revert to the prior point, Dewey maintains that relying upon the method of violence does little to prepare us for self-rule. Rather, violence is likely to give us new bosses. As he writes, what is accomplished without the growth of democratic participation "will be badly done and much of it will have to be done over" (LW 9:110–111).

Liberal democracy attempts to apply social intelligence to the process of shared living. It is committed, Dewey writes, "to the use of freed intelligence as the method of directing change" (LW 11:41; cf. 3:178). It offers society the possibility of bringing about, without violence, the kinds of fundamental changes that are necessary. We need to abandon our tradition of trusting "the direction of human affairs to nature, or Providence, or evolution, or manifest destiny—that is to say, to accident" and turn instead "to a contriving and constructive intelligence" (MW 10:240). Accomplishing this redirection would require a recognition of the fact, Dewey writes, that "a government of and by the people might be a positive and necessary organ for securing and extending the liberties of the individuals who both govern and are governed, instead of being an instrument of oppression" (LW 11:248). It is possible, he continues, to develop a system of "collective social planning" that would enable us to translate "the general creed of liberalism" into "a concrete program of action" (LW 11:32, 64) and thereby to maintain a greater degree of ongoing democratic social reconstruction.

Reliance upon this kind of social reconstruction follows from a series of assumptions that Dewey makes about social action. One such assumption is that our society can legitimately be spoken of in collective terms like 'the people' or 'the common good,' and not just in terms of individuals, or of personal or group goods. As he writes, when attempting to address our social conflicts we try to discover "some more comprehensive point of view from which the divergencies may be brought together . . ." (MW 9:336). This assumption of a common good is a crucial one, of course, for if we are not a collective unit with collective goods, then the use of a social focus will disproportionately favor those individuals and groups who are successful in defending their particular interests as representing the general welfare. A second Deweyan assumption is that American society remains ultimately a democracy: either the people *are presently in control* or at least they *can assume control* should they wish to do so through means which presently exist. A third assumption is of a basic common sense on the part of the members of the democratic community who are able to distinguish and willing to follow sound advice. He clearly believes that there is "a general disposition on the part of people to listen to good advice and, when it has been shown that it is good advice, to follow it . . ." (MW 10:403). Moreover, this third claim is not just that they will be willing to follow explicit courses of action once enumerated, but also that they will be willing to engage in social inquiry along as-yet-indeterminate paths.

This third assumption makes the job of democratic social reconstruction largely an educational rather than a narrowly-political undertaking. He writes that the work of liberalism is "first of all education, in the broadest sense of that term" (LW 11:42; cf. 44), suggesting that widespread and time-consuming efforts at developing an informed public opinion are not just misdirected actions that would be better replaced by partisan activities aimed at more immediate and practical results. Thus Dewey denies that many familiar activities of contemporary democratic practice—stretching the truth, dwelling upon divisive themes and fostering hostility

towards opponents—are necessary. "Fair-play, elementary honesty
in the representation of facts and especially of the opinions of others" (LW 9:94; cf. 13:117; 14:227), and so on, are aspects of the sort
of intelligent social inquiry that he is advocating. "The security of
democratic ideals depends upon the intelligent use of the method
of combined and unified honest effort to come to consciousness of
the nature of social and political problems and their causes" (LW
11:515).

Dewey does not believe that the process of democratic living
will ever be without conflict; but he does not believe that the cooperative inquiry of the community can be conducted in spite of such
oppositions. Because the circumstances within the society will continue to change, conflicts will continue to occur. "Of course, there
are conflicting interests," he writes, "otherwise there would be no
social problems" (LW 11:56; cf. 7:322–328). This admission should
not introduce despair, however, since controlled conflict can lead to
beneficial results for the society. "Conflict is the gadfly of thought,"
Dewey writes. "It shocks us out of sheep-like passivity, and sets us
at noting and contriving" (MW 14:207; cf. LW 13:125). In particular, when it is approached with the attitude of cooperative inquiry,
social conflict can help us to "bring to clearer recognition the different interests that are involved and that have to be harmonized
in any enduring solution" (LW 13:115; cf. EW 4:210). This, he
maintains, is the method of democratic social reconstruction:

> The method of democracy—insofar as it is that of organized
> intelligence—is to bring these conflicts out into the open
> where their special claims can be seen and appraised, where
> they can be discussed and judged in the light of more inclu-
> sive interests than are represented by either of them sepa-
> rately" (LW 11:56; cf. MW 9:226; 12:189–190).

True democrats, Dewey writes, have faith that the disputes which
are "bound to arise" in society can be settled through "cooperative
undertakings in which both parties learn . . ." Through the fostering of "the habit of amicable cooperation," conflicts can be amelio-
rated (LW 14:228).

Dewey's position is in essence that democracy can be seen as
a kind of cooperative experiment. Those involved are seeking the
common good in a democratic way. The amount of time and effort
required of us to deal with our problems is an irrelevant matter; we
must do whatever is necessary to address these ills, and take as

long as it takes. In the building and furtherance of democratic community, the process of developing shared activity and values held in common is what matters. Our social groups need to develop, he maintains, the kind of long-term focus that he demonstrates in statements like the following:

> (T)he aim is not limited to effecting a decision on some particular restricted issue, but is rather concerned with securing such decisions on special points as will deepen interest, create a more intelligent outlook on all similar questions, and secure a more personal response from all concerned in the future (LW 5:413–414).

Disagreements will occur and mistakes are to be expected; and they must be tolerated because we trust the sincerity and the commitment of our fellows to the common good.

After this exploration of Dewey's analysis of democracy as cooperative inquiry, we can briefly consider challenges to his view. Some of the most serious challenges can be hinted at as follows: 'the people are not *interested* enough to make this method a democratic social reconstruction work' or 'the people are not *intelligent* enough to do it' or 'the people are not *selfless* enough to do it.' The first of these criticisms—that people are too apathetic for cooperative social inquiry—suggests that Dewey offers us a vision of democratic practice that has a hope of working only if it can generate an unrealistically high level of citizen involvement. The second criticism—that people are too stupid for cooperative social inquiry—asks the following sorts of questions: Are the citizens with whom we are familiar smart enough to play such an involved role in their shared lives? Do those who we encounter demonstrate a level of intelligence sufficient to keep pace with the increasing complexity of our social existence? The third criticism—that people are too selfish for cooperative social inquiry—maintains that the people with whom we are familiar are incapable of the level of impartiality that is necessary. The Deweyan response in each case would be to maintain that, although at the present time such criticisms may seem quite persuasive, none of them should be seen as precluding the possibilities to which the democratic practices of cooperative inquiry could lead.

Another line of criticism of Dewey's view is aimed not individually at the members of society for failing to measure up to the demands of his understanding of democracy. Rather, it is aimed at

Dewey's understanding of the possibilities of our democratic practice itself and, in particular, at his underplaying of social power. This criticism contends that individuals, voluntary associations, local groups, and the other aspects central to Dewey's view matter little; political activity in our society is neither *cooperative* nor *inquiring*, it is the exercise of power. Moreover, it may even be that his democratic rhetoric—of open participation in discussions on street corners, and issues being fully and fairly presented in the media—disguises the facts of social power and leaves open-minded and cooperative citizens unprepared for the realistic practice of power politics. While I believe that this is an absolutely essential criticism of any naive liberalism, it is in no way an adequate criticism of Dewey's position. His method admittedly does not fit the normal sort of social situation with which we are currently familiar: his work does not comprise a handbook for contemporary political practice. Dewey's realistic point, however, is that if we ever hope to break out of the problems of our current practice, we need to reconstruct our situation to make more appropriate something like democracy as cooperative inquiry. The political process could then be seen as an educative one in which we all try to grow in our ability to address social problems and in our appreciation of our shared existence. This kind of cooperative learning would be, Dewey asserts, "precisely the type of education a democracy most needs" (LW 5:416).

III

The intimate connection that Dewey sees between democracy and education can be recognized further in such passages as the following: "Democracy has to be born anew every generation, and educaton is its midwife" (MW 10:139). The relationship between the two is a "reciprocal" or "mutual" one, since democracy "is itself an educational principle" (LW 13:294) that makes possible growth through involvement with the problems of society. "Full education comes only when there is a responsible share on the part of each person, in proportion to capacity, in shaping the aims and policies of the social groups to which he belongs" (MW 12:199). This mention of capacity should not suggest a commitment on his part to some system for ranking citizens. It is, rather, a claim that in a democracy citizens must receive an education sufficient to function as adequate critics of proposed choices. Consequently, for Dewey, "the unsolved problem of democracy is the construction of an education which will develop that kind of individuality which is intelligently alive to the common life and sensitively loyal to its common maintenance" (MW 11:57; cf. 12:185; LW 7:364; 13:297).

The effectiveness of social critics in gaining the attention of the larger community will be increased by efforts on the part of the community to prepare an audience for such critical insights. For this reason, a central theme in all of Dewey's work on social reconstruction is the theme of education. If a society hopes to overcome the actual and potential ills that it has inherited from its past and to pass something better on to the future, it must focus on education. Initially, we need to think differently about what the term 'education' is to mean and to determine what it is that our children will need to enable them to face the modern world better prepared to fulfill their roles. We also need to rework our institutional practices for reaching these intended educational goals.

This consideration of the possibilities of education ought not to suggest that Dewey thought improvement was guaranteed. He emphasized, much more than critics tend to realize, the practical limits in the educational process. " 'Education' even in its widest sense cannot do everything," he writes (LW 9:110); and the school, although it is often treated as "the willing pack-horse of our social system" (MW 10:191), is only "one educational agency out of many" (LW 11:414). Schools are "not the ultimate formative force," he continues. "Social institutions, the trend of occupations, the pattern of social arrangements, are the finally controlling influences in shaping minds" (LW 5:102). Still educational reform is essential as a way to break free from the unthinking reproduction of outdated institutions: "while the school is not a sufficient condition, it is a necessary condition of forming the understanding and the dispositions that are required to maintain a genuinely changed social order" (LW 11:414; cf. MW 9:85, 126).

The role of education and of the school in democratic social reconstruction has two distinguishable aspects. The first of these is to help the students become better problem-solvers in the new and difficult situations of our world, to help them learn how to think rather than to simply fill them with whatever we now believe they will need in later life. Rather than turning out students "possessed *merely* of vast stores of information or high degrees of skill in specialized branches," Dewey writes, our goals as educators should be to produce students with "that attitude of mind which is conducive to good judgment in any department of affairs in which the

pupils are placed . . . " (LW 8:211; cf. 327; MW 9:153). The ultimate
goal of education in his work is thus to produce adults capable of
"sound judgments," people who are able "to pass judgments *perti-
nently* and *discriminatingly*" on the problems of human living (LW
8:211). This focus of education on judgment rather than on information or knowledge is part of Dewey's emphasis on *wisdom* rather
than on *intelligence*. Wisdom, he writes, is "a moral term" (MW
11:44) related to evaluation and criticism of choices for a better
future world. And, because of our need for ongoing evaluation and
criticism, he emphasizes the need to foster ongoing inquiry: "The
most important attitude that can be formed is that of desire to go
on learning" (LW 13:29; cf. 8:139). In this way students will be able
to make more sense of their lives at present and make a more-
ordered entry into the future.

The second aspect of education and schooling in democratic
social reconstruction is the importance of helping students learn to
live more cooperatively, to work together to accomplish tasks that
cannot be done individually. Educators thus play a central role in
socializing the student, in "saturating him with the spirit of service" (MW 1:20). Dewey expands this point as follows: "Education
should create an interest in all persons in furthering the general
good, so that they will find their own happiness realized in what
they can do to improve the conditions of others" (LW 7:243). This
goal of "the definite substitution of a social purpose . . . . for the
traditional individualistic aim" (LW 9:180) is particularly important if we hope to satisfy the broader possibilities with which our
social situation has presented us. "In a complex society, ability to
understand and sympathize with the operations and lot of others
is a condition of common purpose which only education can pro-
cure" (MW 10:139).

It will be worthwhile to consider further two elements of Dewey's
call for socialization. First, in his call for saturating the students
with the spirit of service, Dewey is not attempting to eliminate or
prevent the development of individuality. On the contrary, his goal
is to increase individuality by preparing the students to become
"good citizens in the most comprehensive sense of that term." By
this Dewey means developing citizens who are capable of "recognizing the ties that bind them to all the other members of the community" (MW 15:190, 158; cf. LW 11:205–207). Second, although Dewey
calls for the development of "public-mindedness, a sense of public
service and responsibility" (MW 10:183), this public-mindedness is
to be a critical one and in no way the same as a simple-minded

promulgation of the *status quo.* "If our public-school system merely turns out efficient industrial fodder and citizenship fodder in a state controlled by pecuniary interest," he writes (LW 5:102), we are not building good citizens. Education must make the students better able to recognize values and more conscious of the nature of possibilities of social progress. Students must grow in the "ability to judge men and measures wisely and to take a determining part in making as well as obeying laws" (MW 9:127). They must have the ability "to take their own active part in aggressive participation in bringing about a new social order" (LW 9:182; cf MW 8:412).

Dewey believes that these students' abilities to participate and evaluate could be fostered by democratic school procedures. Schools in which all of the decisions are made for students, in which the individuals and collective responsibility of the youngsters is not developed, will not foster an inquiring democratic citizenry. A democratic school, on the other hand, would not divorce the ends of socialization from the means of its attainment. "The only way to prepare for social life is to engage in social life," Dewey writes (EW 5:62; cf. LW 11:222, 254); and, if that social life is to satisfy the human needs "to lead and to follow" (LW 13:286), schools must provide opportunities for both. We must thus attempt to create in our schools "a projection in type of the society we should like to realize, and by forming minds in accord with it gradually modify the larger and more recalcitrant features of adult society" (MW 9:326). In such a community-oriented school, Dewey writes, the child will be stimulated "to act as a member of a unity, to emerge from his original narrowness of action and feeling and to conceive of himself from the standpoint of the welfare of the group to which he belongs" (EW 5:84). By means of providing an education in a school organized along the lines of the "principle of shared activity" (MW 9:18), we could hope for a very different overall impact from an isolating school in which "for one child to help another in his task has become a school crime" (MW 1:11). It would rather make each individual "a sharer or partner in the associated activity so that he feels its success as his success, its failure as his failure . . . " (MW 9:18: cf. EW 5:88) and give rise to shared meanings of the sort that would make fuller democratic community life possible.

Throughout his discussions of education in a democracy, Dewey takes seriously the responsibility of guidance; and, although he recognizes the potential here for manipulation, he rejects the identification of all education that attempts to guide with manipulation. He emphasizes the need to steer between the extreme positions of releasing the students from all control on the one hand and of attempting to bring them under the control of rigid direction on the other (cf. MW 1:90; 2:279–283; LW 5:319–325; 13:8–10). Historically, of course, the tendency of education, especially about values, has been towards the latter, towards indoctrination. The young child begins as a highly plastic individual; but, to many educators, this plasticity has signified, Dewey writes, "not capacity to learn liberally and generously, but willingness to learn the customs of adult associates, ability to learn just those special things which those having power and authority wish to teach." Such a conception of education makes it "the art of taking advantage of the helplessness of the young; the forming of habits becomes a guarantee for the maintenance of hedges of custom" (MW 14:70, 47). He continues that this sort of "external imposition" *is* manipulative and has nothing to do with guidance, which he defines as *"freeing the life-process for its own most adequate fulfillment"* (MW 2:281). Guidance in this sense is "an aid to freedom, not a restriction upon it" (LW 13:46); and he maintains that it is possible for teachers to guide their students through a consideration of what he calls "the underlying social problems of our civilization" (LW 5:102) without being deflected by partisanship from the pursuit of the common good.

Conceived in this way, guidance must rely upon some understanding of what would constitute human fulfillment. Students would not need to be guided if they spontaneously sought their good. And this conception of fulfillment must of necessity be chosen by the teachers, the school board, the PTA and other groups of adults. The only justifiable defense of the goals toward which the teachers and others would guide the students is that these goals are likely to result in the advancement of the common good. The role that the teacher plays in the school is, for Dewey, similar to the role that the expert plays in the larger society; and, although the students are as yet only partially developed, they are learning to fulfill their later role in society as suggesters and evaluators of others' suggestions.

Finally, Dewey's emphasis upon the relationship between democracy and education is not just a point about schooling but about the ongoing education of engaged citizens. He writes that "freedom of thought in inquiry and in dissemination of the conclusions of inquiry is the vital nerve of democratic institutions" (LW 11:375). This emphasis upon the sharing of knowledge in a democracy requires the abandonment of the "purely individualistic notion of intelligence" and of "our ingrained habit of regarding intelligence as an individual possession . . . " (LW 11:38, 47). Such knowledge as our society possesses is gained through the cooperative efforts of human beings living together. "Knowledge cooped up in a private consciousness is a myth, and knowledge of social phenomena is peculiarly dependent upon dissemination, for only by distribution can such knowledge be either obtained or tested" (LW 2:345). For democracy as cooperative inquiry to succeed, communal interaction must take place over the broad range and through the ongoing processes of shared living. For this is what democracy as a way of life is about.[1]

Notes

1. I have developed the themes discussed in this essay further in my volume, *Understanding John Dewey: Nature and Cooperative Intelligence* (LaSalle, IL: Open Court, 1995).

2

The Undeclared Self

Victor Kestenbaum

William Arrowsmith says: "Education is a spiritual enterprise. We deal in intangibles and invisibles, or at least we still profess to do that, whatever else we may do in the name of certifying skills and competencies."[1] My intent in this paper is not to defend Arrowsmith's proposition, or to elucidate it any further, at least not directly. It is to draw out the implications of the idea that students, teachers, and professors "deal in intangibles and invisibles" by elaborating a conception of the self that tells us what kind of being it is who can profit (and not profit) from "intangibles and invisibles." The conception is hardly new—the self is more than it knows, its being transcends its knowing—but it needs reaffirmation. But mere reaffirmation is not sufficient. The idea that the self is not fully specifiable, determinable, or investigable; that its accessible and inacessible aspects are interleaved or concatenated; and that self-realization involves accessible and not so readily accessible dimensions, must be situated in the present moment in public and higher education. In short, I am outlining a moderately romantic, decisively transcendental view of the self, one which is suggested as well as supported by Dewey's philosophy of experience and philosophy of education. What follows, then, is not an analysis of Dewey's philosophical views on experience and education, but rather an attempt to draw out some interpretive possibilities of these views.

At points in the paper it shall undoubtedly appear as if I am attempting to deconstruct the unitary self. I am not. The sources for my reflections on the self are rather more conventional than

Lyotard or Derrida. There are some convergences with Richard Rorty. His essay, "The Contingency of Selfhood,"[2] raises questions which I find interesting and important, but my answers ultimately are rather different from his. With Rorty, I would agree that Dewey had a rather profound sense of the *doppelbodig* or contingent character of reality. However, to permit this to be taken as the main achievement of Dewey is to miss what is deepest and most challenging in his philosophy of experience. I think the main effort of Dewey's pragmatism was something like this: to give the broadest outlines of a philosophy of experience which, beginning with what Peter Berger calls "entrance points in the world of the ordinary," opens to the extraordinary and the transcendent. In other words, where does the earthbound pragmatist, Rorty's de-divinized self, stand to behold the "ethereal things" of imagination and the sublime? Where Rorty underemphasizes the importance of the transcendent and spiritual character of experience in Dewey, I shall underline its importance, possibly even overemphasize it.

What sort of center is the self, giving and receiving meaning according to the expectations and traditions of the professions, liberal arts, and humanities? What sort of self is it which invites self-knowledge? And what sort of self is it that underlies Dewey's conception of education as growth? Nietzsche, in *The Will to Power* defines self as: "the sphere of a subject constantly growing or decreasing, the center of the system constantly shifting. . . . " Can this be because the educable self, compressed by what is accessible and inaccessible in it, compressed by its surface and its depth, cannot be anything else other than "constantly shifting"? Might its education consist of the fusion and difference of the specifiable and nonspecifiable? To think so would be to admit a rather unsettling possibility: that the good, the virtue, of broad ranges of educational influence are in principle inscrutable, or at least not manifest. Deductions about the effects of an educational endeavor can be made on the basis of the specifiable, but the specifiable is not necessarily the home or seat of what occurs most deeply and transformatively.

The self, then, cannot be wholly unlike the "intangibles and invisibles" with which it concerns itself in educational moments. The knowledge which forms a self at its deepest levels cannot be fully revealed and inspected as if it were like any other object, nor is the self that can learn from such knowledge formulable like any other object. Socrates cautions Hippocrates not to think so:

For there is far greater peril in buying knowledge than in buying meat and drink: the one you purchase of the whole- sale or retail dealer, and carry them away in other vessels, and before you receive them into the body as food, you may deposit them at home and call in any experienced friend who knows what is good to be eaten or drunken, and what not, and how much, and when; and then the danger of purchasing them is not so great. But you cannot buy the wares of knowledge and carry them away in another vessel; when you have paid for them you must receive them into the soul and go your way, either greatly harmed or greatly benefited. . . .[3]

Neither the knowledge that feeds the soul nor the soul that is so wonderously fed can be made wholly explicit or manifest. So the central question returns: how shall we think of the self if we are inclined to see education as a "spiritual enterprise," one concerned with "intangibles and invisibles"?

In order to see the self's intersections with "intangibles and invisibles" in a specific context or setting, I should like to focus on a quite familiar occurrence, i.e., choosing or declaring a major in college. On the one hand, there is nothing special about this ex- ample. One might have focused on a high school graduate's choice of a job, the choice to continue to live with one's parents or to get an apartment, the choice between two political candidates, the choice to tell the truth or shade the truth, the choice to end a relationship, and so on. In short, I simply wish to look at the self becoming itself in everyday life. In another respect, though, the very everyday-ness of declaring a major (everyday at least for a college student) makes it an unusually interesting focus for discussing "intangibles and invisibles." Declaring a major is a rather revealing symbol: in a sense that shall become clear as the paper proceeds, we are declar- ing a major throughout our life. What is important, central, worthy of attention and sustained effort? Just how spiritual is the decla- ration of what is major in college and life?

How mundane or modest a matter it is can be gathered from the answer to the question "When should I choose my major?" found in *Peterson's Guide to Four-Year Colleges 1990*:

A major, or field of concentration, as it's sometimes called, is simply a series of courses designed to provide you with a strong background in the academic area you're most attracted to. No more, no less. Most of the time, declaring a major is a simple process. All you have to do is write in your choice on your registration form, and the administration takes it from there.[4]

Make your choice, write it on your registration form, and "the administration takes it from there." Let us put this bit of advice along side the following characterization of today's undergraduates by Helen Lefkowitz Horowitz in her book, *Campus Life: Undergraduate Cultures from the End of the Eighteenth Century to the Present*:

> Few college students ask existential questions about the meaning of life. As they compete for the grades that will get them into professional school, they allow themselves little room to grow and become. College moves them along to a job or a career, but for most it no longer serves to liberate their souls.[5]

I want to suggest that if we have an interest in improving the prospects for an education—and a life—that sees itself as a "spiritual enterprise," then we might try to see what sort of self students are likely to find when they look for themselves by looking for a major. How is public and higher education to think of the self if "we deal in intangibles and invisibles"?

I

Despite persons (friends, counselors, parents, professors), despite paraphernalia (bulletins, catalogs, program and concentration overviews, orientation meetings), and despite common-sense principles ("study what you are really interested in," "major in something useful," "the professors in this department are really well known and respected"), it is likely that we greatly overestimate the extent to which the choice of a major is a considered, rational choice. The principal reason for this is that the self choosing the major is not a particularly stable, determinate, specifiable center, and not simply because the self at the "young adult" stage of its development is that way. The condition is broader, larger than a developmental stage; one might risk calling it ontological. Frithjof Bergmann puts it this way:

> The self crystallizes behind our back. Meanings attach themselves, experience is organized into new structures, and no announcements of the progress are made to us. It happens unobtrusively and in the background. To determine what we feel or want or hope or think is often hard enough, but there are ropes compared to cobwebs when the questions are: Is this feeling truly my own, or is it copied, borrowed from a book, invented or only a wish? Is this what I want, or is it a Pavlovian response, a knee-jerk of the brain? So the lines are blurred and seem to shift, only fragments come into view and then disappear.[6]

We grow, get wiser, meaner, less confident, more compulsive, less interested in astronomy and more interested in computers. These things happen and no announcements are made. The student choosing a major seems to be in precisely this situation, but with one profoundly significant difference. He or she is expected to make an "announcement" of the self's progress. This is called "declaring a major." And here, the problems begin.

In asking a student to declare a major, we are asking the student to declare or announce a self, an actual self and a possible self. The major will be the focus of the student's effort and attention. In what state, though, is the choosing, declaring self, i.e., in what state of mind and being? In what state ought it to be in if its choices are to be "good" ones? A framework for answering these questions is found in one of the classic chapters from *The Principles of Psychology*, "The Stream of Thought." William James says:

> The traditional psychology talks like one who should say a river consists of nothing but pailsful, spoonsful, quartpotsful, barrelsful, and other moulded forms of water. Even were the pails and the pots all actually standing in the stream, still between them the free water would continue to flow. It is just this free water of consciousness that psychologists resolutely overlook. Every definite image in the mind is steeped and dyed in the free water that flows round it. With it goes the sense of its relations, near and remote, the dying echo of whence it came to us, the dawning sense of

whither it is to lead. The significance, the value, of the image is all in this halo or penumbra that surrounds and escorts it—or rather that is fused into one with it and has become bone of its bone and flesh of its flesh. . . . [7]

With the declaration of the major, the student steps into the stream and scoops up a pail or barrel of water and declares: "Here I am, this is me, or at least this is the closest institutional expression of me that I can find." This major or concentration is the institutional equivalent of James' focus, "topic," or "definite image in the mind." Remember, though, that James says the significance or value of the "definite image" is in the "halo" or "penumbra" that suffuses this focus. What is the institutional equivalent of the halo, the "free water of consciousness"? Distribution requirements? General education? Core curricula? How do these keep the "free water of consciousness" flowing? How do we keep the major from becoming all focus and no background?

If the self that declares a major is to a large extent, though certainly not entirely, undeclared—neither pails, pots, nor spoons of water—what can we expect a choice of major to be like for the undergraduate? This can be the undergraduate who has no idea what activates his or her interest and effort, or it can be the undergraduate who is interested in and pulled by a number of interests. In both cases, "interests" and "likes" are the basis for choice; they offer convenient, almost inevitable ways to focus the attention of the student and the advisor. "What are you interested in?" or "What are your pails, spoons, and quarts?" Interests and likes are the signs, the portents, the bones, that student and advisor as hermeneuticists attempt to read or decipher. Students seek to know themselves by knowing their interests and likes. In this respect, we are all more or less like students, most of our lives. We use one part of our self to inspect another part of our self. We make an object of ourselves to ourselves, we make an announcement of our self to our self. In so doing, we personalize the anonymous, undeclared self; we peek in on the self that "crystallizes behind our back." Maybe, too, we learn that the "free water of consciousness" can be only imperfectly known through its pots and pails.

Where does this leave our undergraduate who is declaring a major, announcing a self? In the language of recent literary criticism, one might say that the choice of a college major is usually either over or underdetermined, depending upon how the "moulded forms of water"—likes and interests—are used. In the first case,

students seek to know themselves by treating their likes and interests as if they were a list of topics and headings in a filing system.
It is a big decision, full of the ambiguity and uncertainty that
characterizes most big decisions. What is the student to do? Get
information, a great deal of information, about majors. Make a list
of goals and priorities. Get more information. Make a list of personal traits, likes, dislikes, strengths, weaknesses. Get more information. But the student is not in an enviable position. He is
inexperienced in making consequential decisions; he is under the
eye of parents, relatives, and friends who are interested in what he
has done with his freedom; he is angry and possibly frightened that
such an important decision has no guidelines, no syllabus. The
student wants to know all about the color, the weight, the essential
properties of the pots and pails he or she is considering as a major
in the hope that the unannounced self's pots and pails will be
teased out by these definitions and a perfect marriage made. The
questions posed to oneself in choosing a major, the objectification of
the self in such questioning and choosing, are of course deeply
unsettling to the student. Calls to parents, advisor conferences,
talks with roommates and friends, more calls, more conferences,
more talks. These students give the impression that they really
have been struggling, really trying to look in on the self forming
behind their backs, but very often they simply have been tacking
back and forth between one pot and another pot, one quart and
another quart. Get the right pot and the "free water of consciousness" will be vanquished or at least safely contained. It is hard to
tell how many of these "decision-makers" believe they have reached,
in James's magnificent phrase, "the bottom of being," but we should
not be surprised if the number is quite large.

The situation may be otherwise. Here, the choice of a major is
handled so directly, almost casually, that an observer would barely
notice anything significant going on, and certainly not a struggle of
any kind. For these students, the self and a major are formed
behind their backs with a vengeance. If the work of knowing the
self for the "information processor" is that of a very ambitious but
imperfect rationality, the "direct" choosers are astonishingly relaxed
in their demands on rationality. "Liking" is necessary and nearly
sufficient as a condition for choice. I liked history in high school, I
really like my chemistry course, etc. Certainly these likes may be
"rational," but shunning much reflection on their likes, these students have little sense of what their lies mean beyond their sincerely felt attraction to a subject. Since, as Bergmann says, "only

fragments come into view and then disappear," these students attend to the fragments, note which one seems to have the strongest valence for them, and go with it. There is little attempt to peek in on the self forming behind their backs, little inclination to feel that some aspect of the self, perhaps the contour of the whole self, is at stake. They "just" decide.

Despite the apparent difference or contrast between these two kinds of "choosers," they share something in common. Both set out from the same condition—a self that has crystallized "behind our back." Whereas the decision-maker wishes to overcome the existential condition described by Bergmann by selecting his or her pots and pails with as much deliberation and precision as possible, the valence chooser simply bypasses it, feels an attraction to some pot or barrel, and goes there. It may appear that the overdetermined undergraduate is bringing more to the choice than the underdetermined student, more in the sense that at least he or she has sensed a problem or challenge. Maybe. And perhaps the relaxed students will ultimately make the wiser choice because they have not spent their energy on the hopeless task of making themselves transparent to themselves by engineering a perfect marriage of their "real self" and a "good major." Maybe.

What is the larger, general meaning of this sketch of the undeclared self, i.e., how does this help us to grasp what is at stake when a student declares a major? First, it suggests that the self's choice of a major is, and should be, both a wedge and a bridge between two indefinites—the self and the major. Bergmann says:

> . . . in actual fact we never have a secure and settled sense of what our identity or real self is. It remains elusive and unstable, and is always seen as through a veil. We guess at it, suspect an error, and grope in a new place.[8]

We guess at what our self is, and try to combat this indeterminacy with triumphant moments of rational decisiveness; or, we guess at what our self is, and surrender to this indeterminacy in noncombative moments of simply doing what we like. In both cases we are estranged from the unannounced self, as we must be. This estrangement is not an accomplishment or achievement of the self, it is its condition. This condition can be denied: we can attempt to stare at the undeclared self or we can look away, we can seek to encompass it or bypass it. But such dodges ultimately must fail, for we cannot live with the unannounced self in such artless ways, at

least—or especially—not those persons who value the sort of growth that is both a condition for, as well as outcome of, self-knowledge and self-fulfillment.

And it is here that we perhaps expect too much and too little of education. What is the purpose of public and higher education, we ask, if not to help the student fashion a self, a whole self that has vanquished the diremptive tendencies of reconciliation and estrangement? J. Glenn Gray is very sobering on this point:

> Education does not eliminate these moods of reconciliation and estrangement. These poles between which human life is tossed are inseparable from the human condition. Education seeks rather to use them as a means for fuller self-understanding. Hence, education is something we suffer from before we can profit. Indeed, suffering in many of its forms seems indispensable to the educated person, however unwanted and ultimately undesirable it may be. The educated man must first be estranged before he can know reconciliation; he must be driven into the confines of his own skin, before he can experience that aspect of his being which is a part of the larger world. Or to put it another way, we must first experience the contrast of inner and outer being as a painful reality before any reconciliation is effected. And this does not happen once for all. Most of us never finally heal over this breach. To become fully at home in our world is an unrealizable and vain ideal, dreamed of by certain idealists. But to renew the struggle to achieve involvement and intimacy with this larger natural and human environment is surely the fuller meaning of the educational adventure.[9]

There is much to ponder here. If the student's choice of a major is a wedge driven between two indefinites—the self and the major—then the student ought to "experience the contrast of inner and outer being as a painful reality before any reconciliation is effected." But, unfortunately, students can be too quickly and too easily reconciled to the inherent estrangement involved in choosing a major by either trying to encompass it, treating it as a problem in information processing, or by trying to bypass it by going with the strongest valence, the strongest "like." In both cases the student has less chance of appreciating why "the educated man must first be estranged before he can know reconciliation." Such an experience is a profound instance of educational growth and offers the student a glimpse of the meaning of wisdom.

The second consideration to which our sketch of the unannounced self leads involves the element of chance, precariousness, or fragility. The endless cycling between estrangement and reconciliation does not have a stop or end. These poles, and our movement between them, are "inseparable from the human condition." This cycling is the basis of much that is tragic in life and the basis of much that is triumphant, i.e., when we come as near as possible to being "fully at home in our world." We would miss, however, the depth of the tragic and the triumphant if we saw estrangement and reconciliation as poles that simply alternated with each other. Their relationship is not so external or predicatable because growth is not so predictable. In the midst of our most sublime moments of reconciliation we can be defeated, compromised, soiled. We can be shipwrecked, as Karl Jaspers says, and without warning. And too, we can be lifted up, suddenly and as if by a miracle, from despair and ruin. Estrangement and reconciliation suffuse each other, infect each other, ultimately qualify each other.

The second chapter of Dewey's *Experience and Nature* is titled "Existence as Precarious and Stable." It seems to me that the psychology, social theory, and educational theory Dewey developed throughout his life are embodied in the outlook presented in this chapter. The precarious and the stable he says "are mixed not mechanically but vitally like the wheat and tares of the parable."[10] This intertwining of the precarious and the stable means that uncertainty characterizes all our dealings, involvements, and stances. Our existence is perilous, subject to chance. So, too, is the growth that education properly seeks. "The Self as Precarious and Stable" is not the title of anything that Dewey wrote, but it is certainly the subject of much of what he wrote. And it is just this vital mixture of the precarious and stable self which helps move us in the direction of a deeper realization that in education we deal in "intangibles and invisibles."

The poles of the announced and the unannounced self are not less "vitally" mixed than the stable and the precarious, but we should be careful not to assume a symmetry between the announced and the stable, the unannounced and the precarious. The shadows cast by the undeclared self are delicately, playfully, solemnly present but unannounced. What we know of these shadows and signs cannot be fully calculated and exposed and hence they can wither and die from neglect or inattention. Or, still resisting calculation and revelation, they draw us to them and exhausting us, exhaust themselves. The intersection of the declared and the undeclared self unearths the contingencies and internal vulnerabilities which establish our finitude as well as the capacity for heroic transcendence of our finitude. It is precisely this remarkable blending and blurring of the announced and the unannounced which makes Dewey's conception of education as growth so risky, so Nietzchean.

Can we expect undergraduates to take their education seriously as an opportunity for self-discovery, or, in particular, to be moved by the humanities as heroic ventures into the depths of a largely unillumined soul, when their own experience, exemplified by their choice of a major, denies the precariousness, fragility, of the unannounced self? How shall they respond to, indeed, even recognize, the shadows cast by the undeclared self onto the appearing and accessible self? What shall be their motivation for the pursuit of wisdom? What shall be the meaning of wisdom in an environment where reconciliation follows no prior state of chance, drama, or estrangement? Dewey says: "A purely stable world permits of no illusions, but neither is it clothed with ideals. It just exists."[11] Ideals are born in the dramatic, uncertain union of the announced and unannounced self. Without the union, and without the drama, the world "just exists," without ideals. Without the union and without the drama, a major "just exists," equally barren of ideals.

Our third, and final, general point draws out the meaning of the precarious and dramatic union of the undeclared and declared self. The student's choice of a major ought to be what Gray called "an educational adventure." Choosing a major, and the education to which it leads, ought to be an adventure because the student has grown into a person who reasons, who reasons about the self. However, precisely because, in Gray's words, "education does not eliminate these moods of reconciliation and estrangement," the student realizes that neither does reason. These poles are "inseparable from the human condition." Reason is only partially successful in announcing what the self is up to, in clarifying what Bergmann says "happens unobtrusively and in the background." If the student is not content to encompass or bypass the unannounced self, the prospects for an "educational adventure" exist.

Very few writers have given us a better view of what this adventure looks like than has Nietzsche. In his essay, "Schopenhauer as Educator," Nietzsche says:

But how can we find ourselves again? How can man know himself? He is a dark and veiled thing; and whereas the hare has seven skins, man could skin himself seventy-times-seven times and still not say, "This now is you yourself, this is no longer skin." Besides, it is an agonizing, dangerous enterprise to dig down into yourself, to descend forcibly by the shortest route the shaft of your being. A man may easily do himself such damage that no doctor can cure him. And again, why should it be necessary, since everything bears witness to our being—our friendships and hatreds, the way we look, our handshakes, the things we remember and forget, our books, our handwriting? But there is a way by which this absolutely crucial inquiry can be carried out. Let the young soul look back upon its life and ask itself: what until now have you truly loved, what has raised up your soul, what ruled it and at the same time made it happy? Line up these objects of reverence before you, and perhaps by what they are and by their sequence, they will yield you a law, the fundamental law of your true self. Compare these objects, see how one completes, enlarges, exceeds, transforms the other, how they form a ladder on which you have so far climbed up toward yourself. For your true nature does not lie hidden deep inside you but immeasurably high above you, or at least above that which you customarily consider to be your ego. Your true educators and molders reveal to you the true original meaning and basic stuff of your nature, something absolutely incapable of being educated and molded, but in any case something fettered and paralyzed and difficult of access. Your teachers can be nobody but your liberators.[12]

" . . . It is an agonizing, dangerous enterprise. . . ." Is this not an echo of Socrates' warning to Hippocrates that there is "far greater peril in buying knowledge than in buying meat and drink"? When Platonic peril, Nietszchean danger, and Deweyan precariousness are spread throughout a life, we may think of it in terms of adventure.

What we notice about such a life is not solely its moments or episodes or risk and uncertainty, nor an outlook or stance formulated as a credo praising the "adventurous life." A life which has the look and feel of an adventure makes the less conspicuous claim that what we are and what we know are not symmetrical, or more generally, that being and being known are not equivalent. Can "the fundamental law of your true self" be disclosed through knowledge of those "objects of reverence" that one truly loves, objects whose power is nothing less than to have "raised up your soul"? No, because what I am and what I know do not coincide. To know these "objects of reverence" is to know "what until now have you truly loved"; it is to climb up a ladder "on which you have so far climbed up toward yourself." My being, however, transcends such knowledge: "your true nature does not lie hidden deep inside you but immeasurably high above you, or at least above that which you customarily consider to be your ego." Thus, the necessary premise of any attempt to "find ourselves again" must be that the human being "is a dark and veiled thing." Our being transcends our knowing for, as Karl Jaspers says, "no matter what I think, my own being as a whole is not contained in any thinking or thought."[13] So too, the undeclared self transcends the declared self. A life that perfects these conditions of existence approximates an adventure. An undergraduate life that perfects these conditions approximates what Gray calls an educational adventure and what Dewey calls educational growth.

A choice of major is a fit or match, a bridge between two indefinites—self and major. It is also a wedge between the unannounced self and its possibilities as shaped by a particular major. The choice of a major is a homecoming and an embarking. It estranges and reconciles. The choice of a major—as the beginning of a series of estrangements and reconciliations—is something far more consequential than the choice of a set of courses and graduation requirements. Administratively or institutionally, declaring a major is, as *Peterson's* says, "a simple process." You just "write in your choice on the registration form, and the administration takes it from there." (The unintended, multiple meanings of this sentence would not have been missed by students in the sixties: it evokes the idea of foul-ups in the registration process as well as the various political senses in which an administration "takes" a student's choice.) I have suggested why the choice of a major is not, or at least ought not to be, a "simple process." Is a major a place to form oneself, shall we say, existentially or humanly, or is it a place to define oneself as a pot or pail? These are not mutually exclusive. It is a great mistake, though, to think that they are unproblematically reinforcing. If the student tends towards the former, then the "free water of consciousness" must flow; if the latter, then pots and pails will do. What sort of situation does the undeclared self find in today's public school and college environment? Is there much "free water of consciousness" or is it all pots and pails?

II

To reflect on the proper place of "intangibles and invisibles" in education is not an indictment of the central place of the transmission of knowledge in public and higher education. That there is knowledge that must remain clear of "the shaft of one's being" in order to have its proper place in the world is one of the facts of existence which may occasion an initial estrangement in the student just discovering the discipline and authority inherent in the subject matter of a major. But such estrangement may grow into a kind of reconciliation—self-discipline. Glenn Gray says: "self-discipline is acquired precisely where the material permits no concessions to subjectivity."[14] The "definite images" of transmissible knowledge do not make any particular or necessary claim on the unannounced self, i.e., do not depend upon the unannounced self for their authority, and, vice versa, the unannounced self can make no claim on the "definite images" of transmissible knowledge, that which permits "no concessions to subjectivity." Gray is right when he says that such knowledge "can represent something of the necessary austerity involved in all self-discipline." Of all the contents of consciousness, the "definite images" of transmissible knowledge offer the most resistance to engulfment by penumbral consciousness. They may be "steeped and dyed" by the free water that flows round them, but they are nonetheless specifiable independently of such colorations, they make "no concessions to subjectivity."

What such self-discipline—such "austerity"—might mean to the unannounced self poses a difficult question to defenders of the self-sufficiency of the rational will. If, as Bergmann said earlier, "only fragments come into view and then disappear"; if, as Nietzsche said, the self is "difficult to access"; if, as Arrowsmith said, "we deal in intangibles and invisibles," and if, as Dewey believed, the precarious and stable are vitally mixed, then self-discipline cannot be the sole route "into the shaft of one's being." E.M. Cioran says:

> I live in expectation of the Idea; I foresee it, close in upon it, get a grip—and cannot formulate it, it escapes me, does not yet belong to me: might I have conceived it in my absence? And how, once imminent and vague, to make it

present and luminous in the intelligible agony of expression? What conditions should I hope for if it is to bloom—and decay?[15]

How rational will illuminates the chiaroscuro world of the undeclared self, how, in other words, the austerity of self-discipline metamorphoses into the "agony of expression," is a worthy topic for public school and university curriculum committees and for conferences devoted to the future of public and higher education.

The one part of the curriculum where we have expected more than incidental attention to soul-making or at least self-making is the humanities. The humanities may have their own professionalized pots and pails, but there is also a presumption that they will have an improving, humanizing effect upon the undeclared self not usually expected of a course, say, in intermediate accounting. If all the great writers and all the great books resident in a high school or college humanities curriculum do not help in this humanizing effort, who or what will? In the great books of the humanities, students have available truly great models, teachers who are greater than any institution's teachers—Plato, Aristotle, Homer, etc. This massive confrontation with greatness, mediated through the skills of a great teacher, will help students discover the bases of their own attempts at greatness.

Inspired by the authority of greatness, curricular pots, pails, and barrels in the form of great books and ideas are sent down the shaft of students and we await reports on the improvement of the soul. If there is little or no evidence of improvement in the state of the soul, we reorganize the curriculum. In the last two decades, there has been much curriculum reorganization.

This certainly is no objection to greatness, particularly as expressed in Whitehead's conviction that "moral education is impossible apart from the habitual vision of greatness." It is an objection to an astonishingly confident assumption in many of the great books proposals, core of common knowledge proposals, "our common heritage" proposals, and other prescriptions for steadying the rocky state of public and higher education, e.g., the assumption that we truly understand how "a dark and veiled thing" makes use of greatness or benefits from greatness. That it often does, I do not doubt. Neither do I doubt that the "shaft of one's being" can be clogged with past greatness, as Emerson noted in "The American Scholar." The objection that the classics are hardly pots, pails, and barrels if properly taught—an objection as easily made as accepted—still does not adequately respond to Karl Jaspers' belief that "no matter what I think, my own being as a whole is not contained in any thinking or thought." When indeed the student is deeply "engaged" with a great text, is it self-evidently the case that the "intangibles and invisibles" with which we deal through it are somehow as nearby as the text or the declared self?

A failure to grasp the intersections of the precariousness and stability intrinsic to the undeclared self will almost certainly lead to a view of greatness which ignores the adventure essential to it. Whitehead says:

> A race preserves its vigor so long as it harbours a real contrast between what has been and what may be; and so long as it is nerved by the vigor to adventure beyond the safeties of the past. Without adventure civilization is in full decay.
>
> It is for this reason that the definition of culture as the knowledge of the best that has been said and done, is so dangerous by reason of its omission. It omits the great fact that in their day the great achievements of the past were the adventures of the past. Only the adventurous can understand the greatness of the past.[16]

Self-realization is not just one encounter-with-greatness away, or a series of such encounters. As greatness meets the penumbral world of the unannounced self, shadows may loom up, echoes may reverberate in unsettling ways, mirages may engulf us. To be engaged with a great book is not a moment of pure illumination which brings the unannounced self to heel, purging it of darkness and lifting the veil. Greatness which has become entangled in the penumbral world of human beings, greatness permeated by the peril involved in "a real contrast between what has been and what may be," is usually something more and less than textbook examples of greatness.

When one deals with what Walter Kaufmann called "life at the limits," a fitting modesty is required. Greatness in these regions involves a dimension of transcendence, what Arrowsmith called "turbulence,"[17] which unsettles as much as it settles and harmonizes. The "intangibles and invisibles" that may be taken "into the soul" are study . . . and fragile. Such mixing and mingling of the precarious and stable is a necessary condition of heroic greatness. And tragedy.

III

The uninvestigable self, what I have been calling the undeclared self, is not, contrary to Kant, beyond experience but rather its center and horizon. The unannounced self underlies appearance but does not itself appear. No wonder that Nietzsche concluded that man is "a dark and veiled thing" and, as a corollary to this, that the basic material of our being is "absolutely incapable of being educated and molded, but in any case something fettered and paralyzed and difficult of access." How can the unannounced self be educated? Our best recent thinkers on higher education—including Henry David Aiken, William Arrowsmith, Jacques Barzun, F.R. Leavis, Michael Oakeshott, Philip Rieff, Harold Taylor—differ on many issues, but on one point I think they might agree: education concerned with what can be received "into the soul" necessarily deals with what Arrowsmith called "intangibles and invisibles." In periods of history aligned to such a spiritual enterprise, the task is difficult. In periods not inclined in this direction, it is virtually impossible.

Our present situation seems to be a turbid mixture of these two tendencies. The university is governed by vocational/professional values, and so predictably "intangibles and invisibles" are in retreat. The antidote? Core curricula, strong and weak versions of the great books, cultural literacy, and so forth. These really are not, however, responses to the professionalization of the student's consciousness, but to its emptying. In public education, our national attention is even more explicitly focused on what our students do not know and cannot do, accompanied by a very unmistakable focus on what is tangible and visible. Do these students know the presidents? Can they write a modestly coherent paper? Can they reason and think? Critically reason and think? These questions inevitably metamorphose into other questions: what should every graduate of a high school know? What should every graduate of college know? Literacy is in, ranging from computer literacy to moral literacy. In other words, what "pailsful, spoonsful, quartpotsful, barrelsful, and other moulded forms of water" should every student possess?

Further, how shall we—parents, students, and educators—be certain that our educational and humanizing efforts are not merely intellectual divertimenti? How shall we assess, evaluate, make sure that students are being held to the "highest standards"? Intellectual rigor and "intangibles and invisibles" are not incompatible but neither is their relationship an obvious one. That fact that "we deal in intangibles and invisibles" is simultaneously a confounding and ennobling condition of education, not an excuse for laxity and indulgence. Still, it must be acknowledged that it is vastly easier to determine what "high standards" might mean with respect to the mastery of pails, pots and barrels than to things which enter "into the soul."

I think matters like this were on Dewey's mind in 1890 when he wrote a short article titled "A College Course: What Should I Expect from It?" In 1890 Dewey was still in his so-called idealistic period. What I shall simply assert here but what I defend elsewhere,[18] is the proposal that Dewey never outgrew his idealistic period. His philosophical achievement is not to be located in his naturalism but in the frontiers along which the natural and the transcendental touch. In the last paragraph of the essay Dewey says:

> But all this is rather intangible, you will say, to one who wishes some definite instructions as to what he should expect from his college course. Undoubtedly; but the kingdom of heaven, in learning as in other matters, cometh not with observation. The general effects, the internal results, those which give the set and fix the attitude of the spirit, are the real effects of the college education.[19]

I do not think that one can understand what Dewey meant by "growth" twenty-six years later in *Democracy and Education* unless one sees its connection to the intangible and the "attitude of the spirit." Bill Arrowsmith would have like the idea of finding such intangibles and invisibles in, of all places, Dewey's pragmatism. He would join Dewey in affirming that the humility occasioned by a proper respect for the unannounced self provides no grounds for a cynical, ironic, or mystical posture with respect to the practices or policies of education. The vision of higher education shared by Arrowsmith and Dewey encourages a more sober and, simultaneously, a more wonderous appreciation of what education purports to do, at least in some settings and circumstances: to promote the examined life and the habits of mind essential to it. Such a vision of education requires a less grudging recognition that the self is not exhausted by the pots and pails surrounding it, whether or not those pots and pails are called majors, disciplines, or professions. The student is involved—and uninvolved—in his or her education as much through the undeclared self as the more apparent, declared self. Dewey and Arrowsmith would agree that precariousness, adventure, and turbulence attend whatever finds its way "into the soul." This is the drama of growth, in education and in life.

So it must be counted as a good for the undergraduate struggling (or not struggling) with the choice of a major to be reminded that as a spiritual enterprise, education deals in "intangibles and invisibles." Such a realization will not make the choice of a major easier, but it will encourage students to stay alert to what choosing a major means for "a dark and veiled thing," a condition of their humanity which some part of their education may speak to, but not eliminate.

(In memory of William Arrowsmith—
"storm the intangible. . . ."
A. R. Ammons)

Notes

1. William Arrowsmith, "The Shame of the Graduate Schools—Revisited," *Proceedings of the Thirty-Sixth Annual Meeting of the Midwestern Association of Graduate Schools*, Radisson-Chicago Hotel, Chicago, Illinois, March 30–31, April 1, 1980, p. 50.

2. Richard Rorty, *Contingency, Irony, and Solidarity* (New York: Cambridge University Press, 1989).

3. Plato, "Protagoras," *The Dialogues of Plato*, Vol. I, trans. B. Jowett (New York: Random House, 1920), p. 86.

4. Susan W. Dilts, ed., *Peterson's Guide to Four-Year Colleges 1990*, (Princeton, NJ: Peterson's Guides, 1989), p. 23.

5. Helen Lefkowitz Horowitz, *Campus Life: Undergraduate Cultures from the End of the Eighteenth Century to the Present* (New York: Alfred A. Knopf, 1987), pp. 3–4.

6. Frithjof Bergmann, *On Being Free* (Notre Dame, IN: University of Notre Dame Press, 1977), p. 85.

7. William James, "The Stream of Thought," in *The Principles of Psychology*, Vol. I (New York: Dover Publications, Inc., 1890), p. 255.

8. Bergmann, op. cit., pp. 84–85.

9. J. Glenn Gray, *The Promise of Wisdom: An Introduction to Philosophy of Education* (New York: J.B. Lippincott Company, 1968), pp. 35–36.

10. John Dewey, *Experience and Nature*, 2nd ed. (1929), *The Later Works*, Vol. 1 (Carbondale: Southern Illinois University Press, 1988), p. 47.

11. Ibid., p. 57.

12. Friedrich Nietzsche, "Schopenhauer as Educator," in *Unmodern Observations (Unzeitgemasse Betrachtungen)*, William Arrowsmith, editor (New Haven: Yale University Press, 1990), pp. 165–66.

13. Karl Jaspers, *Philosophy of Existence*, trans. Richard F. Grabau (Philadelphia: University of Pennsylvania Press, 1971), p. 70.

14. Gray, op. cit., p. 159.

15. E. M. Cioran, *A Short History of Decay*, trans. Richard Howard (New York: Viking Press, 1975), p. 95.

16. Alfred North Whitehead, *Adventures of Ideas* (New York: Macmillan Company, 1933), p. 278.

17. William Arrowsmith, "Turbulence in the Humanities," *Arion: A Journal of Humanities and the Classics*, Vol. 2 (Spring & Fall 1992/1993).

18. Victor Kestenbaum, *Some Unknown But Still Reasoning Thing: John Dewey and the Intangible*, in preparation.

19. John Dewey, "A College Course: What Should I Expect from It?" *The Early Works, 1882–1898: Vol. 3, 1889–1892* (Carbondale: Southern Illinois University Press, 1969), p. 54.

3

The Fortunes of "Functionalism"

═══════════

J. E. Tiles

The modern philosophical doctrine called *functionalism* should not be confused with the older psychological school also known as *functionalism*, which is associated with the work of James, Hall, Cattell, Dewey, Woodworth, and others. There is little, if any, connection between them.

Stephen E. Palmer and Ruth Kimchi (1986)

Functional psychology is not to be identified with that of Angell or the Chicago group of psychologists. There is no functional psychology; rather there are many functional psychologies.

Harvey Carr (1930)

One of the curious tales of the frontier area between philosophy and psychology during the past century is the death and reincarnation of the term "functionalism." Palmer and Kimchi are certainly right about the tenuous connection between the use of the term in the first quarter of this century and what it came to be labeled late in the third quarter. A closer look, however, at the enterprises which have traded under the name "functionalism" will reveal that, although the connection between them is indeed slender, the contrast is instructive. The older "functionalism" turns out,

39

as Carr suggests, not to be cohesive enough to justify the word "school," and Dewey's place in that amorphous band is by no means as clear as some historians would have us believe. Nevertheless, determining where Dewey stands in relation to both the old and the new functionalisms provides a useful way of locating Dewey's approach to the phenomena of mind.

The Older Functionalism

It is important to recall that when Dewey began his career, psychology was still a subdiscipline of philosophy and that he participated in the events that led to psychology's becoming a separate discipline. Psychology was a significant part of Dewey's first teaching responsibilities; his first book was a psychology text and his earliest professional project was to forge an alliance between his own idealism and emerging interest in experimental physiological psychology. As a graduate student, Dewey had encountered experimental psychology in the laboratory which G. Stanley Hall established in the philosophy department at Johns Hopkins. The department which Dewey was given to shape when he moved to the University of Chicago in 1894 included a psychology laboratory directed by the then twenty-five-year-old James Rowland Angell. Among the students who trained in that laboratory, working together for a time on animal experiments (Cohen, pp. 41–43), were Harvey Carr and the man who was to become known as the founder of behaviorism, J. B. Watson.

Dewey claimed that reading James' *Principles of Psychology* initiated the reconstruction of his idealism into a form of naturalistic pragmatism, which he christened "instrumentalism." A number of Dewey's colleagues shared an enthusiasm for the outlook which Dewey was developing and a collaborative publication led William James (1904) to proclaim the emergence of a distinctive school of philosophy at Chicago. Dewey and his colleagues exhibited a certain diffidence about being thought of as a "school," but before long Chicago became known not only as the center for Dewey's brand of pragmatism, but also for an approach to psychology known as "functionalism."

Although Dewey was by no means an innovative experimentalist, psychology did provide the conceptual material in terms of which he rethought his position during the 1890s and the results of his efforts included innovative treatments of the concepts of

emotion (EW 4, pp. 152–188), the reflex arc (EW 5, pp. 96–110) and
effort (EW 5, pp. 151–163). The article on the reflex arc has been
rightly recognized as an important milestone in the development of
Dewey's thought and also, but perhaps with less justice, as an
early manifesto of functionalism.[1]

In a 1933 survey of approaches to psychology, Edna Heidbreder
devoted a chapter to functionalism which traced its trajectory from
Dewey's (1896) article, through a presidential address given by
Angell to the American Psychological Association in 1906, to the
Psychology (1925) of Harvey Carr. Dewey's work, according to
Heidbreder, differed from that of Angell and Carr in that he "necessarily involved the reader in the stress and strain of refashioning
working concepts." Angell wrote at a time when "functionalism was
an established and growing enterprise, one in which youth and
vigor were combined with achievement," while "the work of Carr
represents functionalism when it had settled down and become a
recognized school, and was no longer a renaissance and a reforma-
tion" (pp. 218–219). The story line Heidbreder used has a familiar
form; the torch of revolt against a prevailing orthodoxy ("domination by the Titchenerian, or Wundtian, school," p. 201) was ignited
and passed with an increasingly steady flame from generation to
generation.

A few years earlier Carr had contributed a chapter on functionalism to a collection of statements representing schools and trends
in psychology, which affords a somewhat different perspective. Carr
presents functionalism in its role as the opposition to a program
known as structuralism (a.k.a. existentialism)[2] in a debate which
came to the boil in the first decade of the century.[3] He concludes by
suggesting (pp. 77–78) that the dispute had transmogrified into
one between different forms of behaviorism. Carr, moreover, does
not present functionalism as a revolt against a prevailing orthodoxy but reports without dissent (p. 59) the view of its principal
critic, E.B. Titchener, who treated it as "the dominant psychology
in America which suddenly became conscious of itself, and which
attempted to justify itself as a system with [*sc.* In response to] the
introduction of existentialism." The posture Carr adopts in his replies
to Titchener is that of a person fending off an extremist and Angell's
insistence in his 1906 address on defining functionalism as a broad
church, the fathers of which included Aristotle, Darwin, and Spen-
cer (1907, p. 62), also suggests that the Chicago psychologists preferred to see themselves not as a school but as spokesmen for a
mainstream view.

That functionalism was conceived more broadly than what one might expect of a Chicago orthodoxy is clear from Angell's acceptance that any form of dualism other than epiphenomenalism was compatible with functionalism (1907, p. 83, cp. Carr, p. 61); it is similarly clear from Carr's criticism of functionalism of "the period under consideration" for relying upon that very dualism (op. Cit, p. 76). It is noteworthy that neither Carr's 1930 discussion of functionalism nor Angell's 1907 article mention Dewey's critique of the reflex arc concept.[4] The identity of functionalism as a movement is not tied by these men to Dewey's work but is based rather on its opposition to Titchener's program.

Titchener proposed (Carr, p. 64) that psychology should confine itself to introspective descriptions of the sensory contents of consciousness given only in terms of constituent elements and abstracted from any values, meanings, and functional relations. Although Titchener claimed the authority of the founder of experimental psychology, Wilhelm Wundt, for this methods, they in fact owed far more to the British associationist tradition (from Locke through Hartley to James Mill) and to Mach's brand of positivism.[5] Indeed in Carr's account the dispute appears to be over very general issues which belong to the philosophy of science. Carr's functionalists claimed the right of a science to consider acts of the mind as well as contents; to describe meanings, values, and relations as well as sensory contents (pp. 64–69); to offer explanations (Angell, 1907, p. 67) as well as descriptions. Functionalists wished to claim that respectable science was entitled to make use of the limited teleological perspective sanctioned by Darwin, to consider what service an organ or activity might perform, to take an interest in the relation of psychology to biology and other fields of science, and to seek justification for their findings in their application (pp. 69–71).[6]

From Carr's account, the opposition appears to be between a generous conception of the knowledge sought by a science—that is a concept which places value on explanation and seeks validation through practical results (cp. Angell, 1903, pp. 254–256)–and what may be recognized as a positivist conception of knowledge, one, that is, which couples a narrow conception of what is observable to the insistence that knowledge can take the form only of descriptive reports of observation. Titchener, it must be said, did not see the dispute entirely in terms of general methodology and philosophy of science. He also criticized an account of consciousness which he believed to be endorsed in one form or another by all his functionalist opponents. This is the idea that "conscious activities emerge at the point where reflex acts are found inadequate to meet the needs of particular situations" (p. 535). This issue will be taken up in the next section.

It is certainly the case that whether the debate is over methodological issues or the specific matter of the appropriateness of assigning this general function to consciousness, Dewey obviously belongs in the company of the functionalists. But a position defined only in these general terms leaves room for strange bedfellows. As already noted, Carr felt that dualism had exerted too much influence within functionalist ranks, while Carr in his turn appears (at least to one later observer) to have drifted away from Dewey in a different respect: "In his book, Carr appears almost to have gone back to the concept of the reflex arc that Dewey had rejected in his early statement of the principles of functionalism" (Rucker, p. 72). Functional explanations, even those which assign to consciousness the specific function of guiding action, include many that Dewey would regard as specious. For example, Karl Popper (pp. 341ff.), who thought of consciousness as a "search-light," could be taken as assigning it an action-guiding function in problem situations, although Dewey himself rejected the search-light as an appropriate image for consciousness, (EN, LW 1, p. 235). We need, therefore, to consider carefully the kind of functionalism which Dewey advocated.

Dewey's Functionalism

Three years after Dewey's treatment of the reflex arc concept appeared, he published a discussion of child development in which he underscored the central point of his critique. The problem of child development was "the question whether any continuous function of a typical character can be detected and traced, in its growing differentiations and ramifications, amid all the diversity of phenomena which the infant life exhibits" (MW 1, p. 178). The "working hypothesis" he advanced was "the principle of coordination or of sensori-motor action." One might easily take this as a reiteration of the by then familiar thought that the subject matter of psychology was constituted *au fond* by the connection between sense-stimulus and motor-response (see James 1890 I, pp. 13, 116). But the point here, as in the earlier piece, was to break the hold of a schema which related two distinct things, sense and response, and to draw attention instead to the relationship of similar things.

When Dewey reprinted the critique of the reflex arc concept in 1931 he retitled it "The Unit of Behavior"[7] a way of putting the central point which had already occurred to him by 1899, when he wrote that "In popular language, this unit is an *act*, whether of greater or less complexity" (MW 1, idib.).

The line to be traced by this central point cuts across familiar divisions and this was made abundantly clear in Dewey's original critique: seeing (a light) is not stimulus to a reaching response, if stimulus and response are distinct kinds of things mediated by a nervous system. Seeing is an act; the organism must control its eye movements to focus on the light. Reaching is an act but not a blind act; there is continuous sensory feedback which keeps the hand on its trajectory. Psychologists have to study the co-ordination of acts such as these—the transformation of seeing involving eyes into seeing involving reaching—and how the outcomes of such co-ordinations, both gratifying and distressful, affect the way acts are transformed on future occasions.

Thinking in terms of a schema relating inputs and outputs belonging to different categories may well be appropriate to very simple reflexes, e.g., what happens when the doctor taps just below the patella; but if psychology treats every organism as having a repertoire of responses consisting entirely of an uncoordinated collection of simple reflexes, it will hamstring its investigations. The kind of conceptual move Dewey was urging can be expressed using analogous notions from mathematics.[8] The reflex arc as conceived by traditional psychology has similarities to the abstract concept of a function. The organism can be treated as assigning outputs (behavioral response) to inputs (sensory stimulus) in the way a function assigns a "value" (no more than one) to each of a set of "arguments." Mathematicians have generalized their notion to the extent that it is possible to study functions whose arguments and values are themselves functions. To avoid confusion, functions of this higher-order kind are sometimes called "functors" and it will be beneficial to follow that practice here. A functor assigns one or another function (but no more than one) to each member of a set of functions.

Now consider two mathematicians: one studies the properties of "functions," each of which associates two sets of possibly very different sorts of things; the other studies the properties of "functors," each of which associates two sets of possibly very different sorts of things, except that these sets both consist of functions. Next consider two psychologists: one studies the properties of (physiologically based) mechanisms which associate motor responses with sensory input, the other studies how one such association of motor output with sensory input gives way to a different association of motor output with sensory input (e.g., how responding with a start to a crash of thunder when sitting reading gives way to hardly any response to the next crash as one gazes out the window at the summer storm, or how, after training, a perceptual cue which previously had no impact comes to be sufficient to determine a specific response). What is being suggested here is that if Dewey's 1896 critique of the reflex arc was a manifesto for any kind of functionalism, it should be thought of as a call for psychologists to undertake the second kind of investigation.

This analogy between mathematics and psychology can be used to illuminate a further point. The idea behind the stimulus-response (S-R) schema is that knowledge of the schema together with knowledge of the stimulus should be sufficient to determine the response. (This is the case even when the S-R schema is used in connection with operant conditioning; for a 'trained' organism is supposed to respond reliably to some stimulus.) But how an organism responds to a stimulus depends on its status prior to receiving the stimulus—a point Dewey pressed in his 1896 treatment of the reflex arc in the course of criticizing Baldwin's account of "reactive consciousness" (Arc, EW 5, p. 100). We don't always react with a start to a loud noise; it depends on what we were doing when the noise occurred, "reading a book, hunting, watching in a dark place on a lonely night, performing a chemical experiment" (ibid. P. 101). If instead of treating the occurrence of an event as an input (stimulus) to an S-R schema, we consider it as a new influence falling on a system engaged in activity, we will have to consider how the event is going to transform the ongoing activity, and the nature of the activity will as much determine the response as the event identified as a stimulus.

In effect this means that we cannot treat a loud noise as a stimulus in the same sense as we treat the tap the physician administers to a patient's knee as a stimulus. Writing in 1925, Robert S. Woodworth saw one upshot of the tradition of criticizing the reflex arc concept, which he traced from Dewey through Sherrington and Thurstone, in these terms:

> Instead, then, of thinking of S-R as a unit, we have to think of R alone as the real unit. This unit covers the activity of the peripheral motor organ and of the nerve center which directly controls it. Each R is accessible to several S's, more

accessible to some than to others. Behavior is composed of
R units, Native behavior consists of an assortment of such
R units, which can be elicited by a variety of stimuli, though
not by any stimulus at random. (p. 123)

Woodworth's "R" is "activity of a peripheral motor organ and the
nerve center which controls it"; Dewey's unit extends to activity in
the peripheral sense organs which the controlling (co-ordinating)
nerve centers use to monitor the ongoing activity. Both conclude
that changes in external events must typically be taken as stimuli
to transform units of activity, not to elicit specific motor responses.

It is in the context of this reconceptualization of what is commonly spoken of as a stimulus that Dewey located consciousness
and thereby contributed to the family of functional accounts which
Titchener regarded as untenable. (See end of first section above.)
Dewey's critique of the then current use of the reflect arc concept
(see note 1 above) consisted of an extended meditation on the example of reflex-action provided by the example of an infant reaching for a candle and withdrawing its hand in pain.[9] Dewey's analysis
focused upon the response of the child when it confronted another
bright object after the experience of being burned, and undertook
to show how the child's associations of motor output with sensory
input had been transformed by its previous experience. If another
bright object were to present itself, the original impulse to reach
for a plaything would now have to compete with the distress that
informed the culmination of that time when the seeing-bright-thing
was coordinated with the reaching-for-bright thing. Now the child
confronts the new object uncertain how to constitute it as stimulus:
should it be taken as stimulus to co-ordinate seeing with reaching or
to co-ordinate seeing with redrawing? Dewey here reasons that

> The conscious sensation of a stimulus is not a thing or
> existence by itself; it is that phase of a co-ordination requir-
> ing attention because, by reason of the conflict within the
> co-ordination, it is uncertain how to complete it.... From
> this point of view the discovery of the stimulus is the "re-
> sponse" to possible movement as "stimulus." (Arc, EW 5, p.
> 107)

It is in this tension, Dewey concluded, that the act of seeing is
transformed into "sensation as *possible*, or conscious, stimulus" and
"motion as conscious response emerges" (ibid.).

This suggestion can easily be generalized into the idea that consciousness flickers into being when and only when a conflict interrupts the normal co-ordinations of our actions and vexes us with a problematic situation. No doubt there were vulgar functionalists who offered as doctrine what Titchener attributes to functionalists in general: the idea that "our conscious life is, as a matter of fact, nothing more than a recurrent grappling with problems" (p. 537). But it is far from clear that to suggest that consciousness begins (is first elicited) in this way[10] is to commit oneself to identifying consciousness with the activity of problem solving. Dewey's child is faced with a problem, which is why he/she is temporarily "inhibited by the conflict in the co-ordination" and is held in the activity of seeing "from passing over into further acts until its quality is determined" (EW 5, ibid.). But this is not to maintain that only problems can stimulate a human being to adopt this holding pattern. With a rich enough range of alternatives into which a given act of seeing may be transformed—including a variety of ways of seeing—a more mature human can sustain the holding pattern for long periods and experience, in Titchener's words, "a contemplative as well as an acquisitive awareness" in which we "sun ourselves, as it were, in the full light of consciousness" (p. 537).

Dewey is thus not constrained by his account either to deny that the engine of consciousness can idle as well as aid in the transformation of patterns of co-ordination, or to deny that consciousness itself (that is, attention) can be made subject to a degree of conscious control. It remains plausible nevertheless to regard it as a consequence of the way Dewey located the emergence of consciousness, that to sustain continued awareness an organism must acquire a rich repertoire both of acts and of regular ways of co-ordinating acts. (The latter are habits, instances of the central concept of the framework of social psychology which Dewey laid down in *Human Nature and Conduct*, MW 14.) Titchener appeared bent on resisting the claim that psychology should properly concern itself with anything beyond the introspectively observed contents of consciousness and the structure of those contents. Interest in the way consciousness might function in the life of an organism "duplicated the subject-matter" of psychology in a way that invited outmoded teleological considerations to compromise the scientific status of the results of its investigations (p. 542).

Although Titchener's 1921 survey was part of a controversy more than two decades old and largely spent, Dewey saw a need in 1930 to restate his main criticism of "structuralism," writing that

> Admitting, for the moment, that there are such things as
> conscious processes which constitute "experience" and which
> are capable of direct inspection, it still involves an immense
> leap of logic to infer that direct inspection can disclose their
> structures.[11]

The structure of "immediate qualitative presences" is to be found
rather in the interaction between the organism and its environment (Cnd&Exp, LW 5, p. 220).

Dewey's challenge, and his insistence on how properly to direct
any investigation of the structure of consciousness, called into
question Titchener's implicit identification of mind and consciousness. Both the identification and the challenge came from well-
established traditions. As Kurt Danziger observes, the identification
of mind and consciousness had gone unchallenged in the British
philosophical tradition from Locke until well into the nineteenth
century, while in the German tradition, Leibniz's doctrine of "ob-
scure perceptions" entailed that mind extended further than consciousness. Danziger continues:

> In the present context the importance of Leibniz's position
> derives from the clear implication that if mind is not to be
> equated with consciousness, one cannot expect to discover
> its nature and constitution simply by observing conscious-
> ness. Introspection therefore cannot be regarded as a method
> of unquestionable reliability and fundamental importance.
> (1980, p. 242)[12]

Squarely in the Leibnizian mold, Dewey insisted (in *Experience
and Nature*, LW 1, p. 228) on the importance of sub-conscious
thought. Consciousness operates in a sizable fringe of habitual
responses shaped in important respects by culture (the social environment), of which only a small portion can be brought into the
focus of consciousness at any time.[13] But that limited access can
have a profound effect on the way a conscious organism co-ordinates
its acts.

There are then at least four specific features which distinguish
Dewey's functionalism from other approaches which might claim to
be functionalist. (1) The principal functional unit is an act which
has both sense and motor aspects. (2) What is commonly identified
as a stimulus is not a sensory input but an event bringing about

a transformation in ongoing activity, a transformation which will commonly depend as much on the initial activity as on the character of the event identified as a stimulus. (3) Consciousness emerges when there are conflicting tendencies within the response elicited by a stimulus, i.e., the activity of the organism does not transform smoothly into another activity in response to the stimulus. The perceptual activity of an organism may, for example, go into a holding pattern while it opens itself to more perceptual cues as it struggles to "discover" the stimulus, i.e., to settle on an appropriate motor response. This is where conscious control of a response emerges, and with the development of sufficiently complex habits the holding pattern may itself become subject to conscious control. (4) An individual's mind is not to be identified with that individual's consciousness but with the structure of its activity, the habits by which acts are transformed in one direction rather than another (or are otherwise co-ordinated with one another.)

Failing to take on board any one of the above specific points—identifying mind with consciousness, offering a less subtle account of the function of consciousness, seeking stimuli which fully determine responses, or concentrating exclusively on how to relate (sensory) inputs and (motor) outputs as distinct kinds of things—might be compatible with a kind of functionalism but not the kind which Dewey advanced. Although Dewey's ideas were not neglected, their influence even among those identified as functionalists should not be exaggerated. That Woodworth (who called his own approach 'dynamic psychology') should treat the fundamental point about to conceive the unit of behavior as not part of the "old story" but "more open to debate" (p. 122) suggests that psychologists had not readily assimilated the point. Indeed behaviorism as a movement could almost be defined by its imperviousness to Dewey's message.

Behaviorist Interlude

If by 1930 "functionalism" was regarded as *passé*, a septuagenarian like Dewey could easily recognize the ideological fault lines still dividing psychologists (Cnd&Exp, LW 5, p. 218). Functionalism was supposed to have been supplanted by behaviorism; introspectionism persisted, albeit not in the precise form advocated by Titchener—but the issues were familiar. The principal change could be traced to a product of Dewey's own department, John

Broadus Watson, who had come to Chicago to study philosophy but
found himself drawn toward Angell's laboratory. He summed up
the impression Dewey made on him thus:

> I got something out of the British School of Philosophers—
> mainly out of Hume, a little out of Locke, a bit out of Hartley,
> nothing out of Kant, and, strange to say, least of all out of
> John Dewey. I never knew what he was talking about then,
> and unfortunately for me, I still don't know. (p. 274)

One thing he clearly failed to assimilate was the call to discard the
schema of stimulus and response in favor of the idea of the act as
unit of behavior. Instead Watson appears to have been swept into
positivist currents and, starting from an S-R functionalism, worked
to purge it of the apparatus of interpretive concepts, which had
been the target of Titchener's criticisms.

That behavior conceived minimally in terms of movement was
all that one could, strictly speaking, observe was by no means a
new thought. Dewey himself, writing in 1899, was prepared to
concede that "the only thing that can possibly be observed in another is, as Mr. Warner has brought out with great force, movement."[14] Dewey was content that the observer should fix attention
solely on movements but that left room to appreciate what is "the
important thing with regard to movement, namely, that it is a
reaction whose value lies in its efficiency in completing the circuit
of some act, or, more technically of some coordination, or adjust-
ment." By keeping in mind the question "what mode of action is
now building up?," the observer could dispense with outmoded
"classificatory distinctions of sensations, ideas, purposive volition"
and concentrate on the problem of "the discovery and interpretation of the stimulus which operates in calling out the movement as
response" (MW 1, p. 179).

To many anti-behaviorists, this "proto-behaviorism" in Dewey's
work at the turn of the century would be enough to consign him to
the same perdition as his one-time student Watson, but it is as
important to note what kind of behaviorist Dewey was as it is to
observe the kind of functionalism he advocated. In 1899 Dewey
was trying to pinpoint what infants do that leads us to identify
stages in the development of their intelligence. In 1930 he was
resisting a narrow framework both of laboratory practice and its
interpretation that would leave no room to apply "conscious" as an
adjective to action. One kind of behaviorism, he observed (Cnd&Exp,

LW 5, p. 221) arises from what takes place in the laboratory coupled with a refusal to refer it to the wider context in which human subjects live. Human behavior tends from a laboratory perspective to be resolved into discrete acts when in fact it cannot be understood apart from the series to which it belongs and which constitutes it as 'conduct' rather than mere behavior (Cnd&Exp, LW 5, p. 222); "a behavioristic theory was bound, logically, to emerge from laboratory procedure. Conscious processes drop out as irrelevant accretions" (Cnd&Exp, LW 5, p. 221).

To infer, as an anti-behaviorist would, that Dewey must be treating "conscious action" as reducible to behavior is to overlook this interpretive framework, which seeks to identify acts organized by habits into structures with a "temporal spread." It is also to overlook his insistence that conduct cannot be reduced to behavior. To infer, as a strict behaviorist would, that Dewey is making an illicit appeal to an inaccessible mental realm, is to ignore Dewey's call to consider a wider temporal perspective and hear him only as seeking a hidden ("cognitive") explanation within the narrow temporal spread defined by the occurrences of the stimulus and the response. The behaviorist and the introspectionist connive at sustaining the same account of the meaning of terms like "conscious," "feeling," "desire"; these terms must refer to aspects of occurrences to which only the (experimental) subject has access. The introspectionist insists that these aspects are essential to understanding human behavior; the behaviorist decides that because they are not salient in canonical instances of scientific observation, the terms must be eschewed altogether. Neither accepts the need or even the possibility of seeking "a specifiable quality of some forms of behavior" (LW 5, p. 227) to which the words "aware" and "conscious" are applied.

Just as it was easy before the First World War to lose sight of the specifics of Dewey's position in the dust stirred up by the controversy between functionalism and structuralism, it was easy in the period between the Wars to overlook the alternative he offered to behaviorism and introspectionism. Behaviorism fed itself on the image of scientific rigor and the prospect of human engineering; introspection offered a glimpse of secrets inaccessible to objective science. The former did not want to acknowledge the gap between the simplicity of its principal conceptual schema and the complexity of the phenomena it aspired to control; the latter did not want to hear that what was disclosed in subjective experience was meaningless unless linked "with modes of behavior identified objectively" (LW 5, p. 230).

Turing Machine Functionalism

What brought about the abandonment of entrenched positions and the digging of new ones was once again a development on the side opposed to introspectionism. To avoid being backed into a corner where they might have to admit the explanatory value of "cognitive" concepts, the strict behaviorists had been inclined to "black-box" what takes place between stimulus and response. That is, they studied correlations but declined to speculate on the mechanisms underlying these correlations. The psychologist's experimental subject was a black-box; the inputs and outputs were objects of legitimate study but the insides were off-limits to a psychologist. It mattered not at all whether the correlation between stimulus and response was mediated physically (physiologically) or mentally (spiritually); the science of behavior could accumulate results without giving the inside of the box the slightest attention.

With the development of computers after the war it became possible to obtain research money to pursue the goal of creating artificial devices which manifested intelligence. It did not go unnoticed that this was a quest which could also be furthered by trying to work out how actual intelligent behavior in living organisms might be explained in terms of internal structures which carried out computations within the power of any digital computer. Behaviorists, who were not prepared to acknowledge the legitimacy of speculating about what happens inside the black-box, began increasingly to look as old-fashioned as the functionalists had come to look between the wars.

Thinking in terms of computers allowed one significant conceptual point to emerge clearly. Those who were familiar both with theoretical work as well as with electronic engineering confronted in a new form the fact that there are a variety of ways to build a machine to perform the same function. Mathematical logicians had provided a number of equivalent concepts describing what an effective computation was. The most popular of these concepts, the Turing machine, was given in terms of a simple abstract computer.[15] A machine which would be able actually to carry out any computation within the power of a Turing machine was realizable in a variety of ways.

Psychologists, who speculated on how a behavioral response might be the outcome of a Turing machine computation performed on a set of inputs which were determined by some stimulus, were thus in a position to distinguish the functional explanations they sought from accounts of the mechanism by which nature had managed to implement such functions. The latter were questions which could be left to physiologists; psychologists were then free to advance hypotheses about "cognitive connections" mediating stimulus and response without needing to invoke "mental", in the sense of spiritual, causes. It became fashionable to profess to being a "cognitive psychologist" while still insisting that all that interested a psychologist took place in the brain. What are referred to as mental states and processes were taken to be nothing other than brain states or processes viewed from the standpoint of their function in the (admittedly complicated) computations that turn sensory inputs into behavioral outputs. This was a form of reductionism, not one which held out the promise of identifying each mental state or event with a physical state or event, but rather one which held that each mental state or event could be identified as a functional *type* of a class of physical states or events. As long as the functions allowed in these explanations were confined to those represented in digital computers, the program was known as "Turing machine functionalism."

When it first emerged this new functionalism differed from its older namesake in concentrating its attention on what Dennett (p. 153–154) called the "sub-personal level." That is, the functions in terms of which it sought to define mental states and processes were all functions of physical components of the organism (human or animal). The functions which interested Dewey and others of his generation were functions of the whole organism—preferably (for Dewey at any rate) functions of the whole organism interacting with its environment. Dennett (ibid.) was prepared to defend a disciplinary demarcation which insisted that psychological theories be sub-personal, while acknowledging that there is a place for ("philosophical") theories of the personal level.[16]

The problem with confining one's attention just to the sub-personal level and trying to account for behavior entirely in terms of the functioning of some kind of computation engine[17] is that this project appears to have no resources to account for psychological phenomena which involve meaning; that is, phenomena which involve signification or representation of any kind. What happens in a computation engine between input and output always bears a contingent relationship to what lies outside. One cannot "look inside" any such mechanism; by confining one's attention to the chain of events which link input to output, one cannot identify anything as representing (bearing a "semantic" relation to) something outside the mechanism. From the inside, one can trace the syntax of internal processes; but that does not determine what, if anything, those processes represent. A psychology which is unable to account for ways in which an organism (especially a human being) can represent the environment to itself would appear woefully inadequate.[18] John Searle has pressed this point, remarking that

> The reason that no computer program can ever be a mind is simply that a computer program is only syntactical, and minds are more than syntactical. Minds are semantical, in the sense that they have more than a formal structure, they have a content (p. 31).

Searle reinforced this point by appeal to his "Chinese room"— a notorious thought experiment in which a Turing Machine is embodied (as it may well be) by a human being who follows rules as thoughtlessly as any machine.[19] In this case a hapless machine embodiment is locked in a room with a Chinese lexicon and rules of syntax—in effect a complete rule book in English for manipulating Chinese characters. Chinese characters are fed into the room and the person uses the rules to compose and output grammatical (and sensible) responses using Chinese characters. If the grammar and dictionary are good enough, Searle argues, the inhabitant of the Chinese room can successfully perform this function without knowing the meaning of a single Chinese word. The conclusion which Searle tries to extract from this argument is that some part of the brain (perhaps by virtue of the special biological stuff of which it is composed) must do what manifestly no computer can do, which is to know what something means.

Searle and the strict Turing machine functionalist thus lock themselves into a dispute over whether component functions of a computer can ever constitute meaningful thought. Neither party to the dispute is open to the possibility that although no component of the system can be said to know Chinese, nevertheless the system as a whole (if its responses are sufficiently flexible and comprehend a sufficient range of linguistic interactions) might be said to know what Chinese means. The functionalist is confined by the sub-personal perspective to seek meaning in sub-personal components or to deny that meaning is a phenomenon which a scientific psychology should address. Searle is constrained by the assumption that minds are "in" bodies in order to look inside the body for a component which does not function as a computer. There is here the same refusal to consider the phenomena of mind in a wider context, a refusal which kept the behaviorist and introspectionist locked in their dispute.

Dewey's view of the new functionalism would most certainly have been that its principal weakness was its sub-personal focus. ("Context and Thought," LW 6, pp. 3–21). It is hardly surprising that important mental phenomena appear to elude its explanatory framework entirely. The phenomena of meaning cannot be properly grasped without reference to the wider environment (especially the social environment) in which the organism functions. This is likely to be true of other psychological phenomena, such as awareness and conscious subjective experience, which appear inaccessible to functional accounts. It is possible, however, that this narrow functionalism which was born of a narrow behaviorism will before long acquire a perspective as inclusive as that of the older functionalism and will include biological and social dimensions in its explanations.

In the aftermath of the heated discussion that was generated by Searle's argument, Robert Van Gulick outlined a functionalist approach to conscious subjective experience which included the principle that "What is required for a system to have intentional states [states which represent or are 'about' something] is that it have states that play the appropriate causal roles in mediating the system's interactions with its environment" (p. 97). Van Gulick was, moreover, prepared to allow that systems can be said to understand the semantic properties of symbols without any conscious subjective experience (p. 98)—in other words to accept the Leibnizian denial of the identity of mind and consciousness. Another self-professed functionalist, Keith Oatley, published in the same proceedings, was prepared to venture so far in the direction of the older functionalism as to propose "that a function [of consciousness] might be in creating new pieces of cognitive structure" (p. 380).

So far there is no sign that the newer neo-functionalists might take on board Dewey's doctrine that the unit of behavior is an act and consider systems which function to adjust and co-ordinate a repertoire of sense-response integrated routines. Perhaps it will take the development of an appropriate machine architecture to provide a model of this kind of system. On the other hand, it might possibly be worthwhile for those who try to exercise a speculative lead over the development of computer architecture to explore the central idea of Dewey's functionalism. It might well point the way to a fruitful piece of engineering and a functionalism that lives up to the promise which its earliest exponents saw in it.

Notes

1. "Dewey's 1896 article, 'The Reflex Arc Concept in Psychology,' is widely credited as the foundation of functional psychology as a distinct movement." See Rucker p. 58. I refer to Dewey's article hereafter as "Arc."

2. Both of these terms were recycled by subsequent intellectual movements, and the advice of Palmer and Kimchi applies to them as much as to "functionalism."

3. Dewey, writing in the same volume as Carr, refers to this "controversy, so active about thirty years ago" (p. 410, LW 5, p. 218). Washburn also assigns "the rising school of functional psychologists" (p. 344) to the turn of the century.

4. In 1903, Angell (p. 251 n. 2)—acknowledging that functionalism was not yet an adequately formulated program—cited the reflex-arc article as well as a piece by Dewey on child development ("Principles of Mental Development as Illustrated in Early Infancy," first published in the *Transactions of the Illinois Society for Child Study* 4 [1899], pp. 65–83, reprinted in MW 1, pp. 175–191, hereafter 'Ear Inf'), along with work by Ebbinghaus, Stout, and Ellwood as illustrations which "will all be found valuable in clarifying the scope of such an undertaking." It is intriguing that when, at the end of this article, Angell indicates the general thrust of functionalism, he cites not the reflex-arc piece but Dewey's earliest ("idealist") programmatic statements published in *Mind* 1886, "The Psychological Standpoint" and "Psychology as Philosophic Method" (EW 1, pp. 122–167).

A further indication that "functionalism" had too loose an identity to constitute a school is that different lists of representatives tend to vary considerably. Compare Angell's list and that of Palmer and Kimchi (quoted at the beginning of this chapter) with that of Titchener writing in 1921, viz. Ladd, Judd, Angell, James, Baldwin, and Dewey. Carr (op. cit., p. 60) declines to offer a list of representatives lest he offend those who did not want to be so identified. It is interesting in this connection that Washburn could recall that, at the time she was working at Cornell alongside Titchener, she had both intellectual affinities for, and a reluctance to be identified with, functionalism, "the child of pragmatism" (p. 345).

5. For a discussion of the very considerable distance between Wundt and Titchener, the positivist roots of Titchener's psychology, and the rise of positivism in European psychology during this period, see Danziger 1979, 1980. Danziger contends (1980, p. 256)

that Titchener, although highly visible, was not representative even of introspectionism.

6. Titchener's resort to the rhetoric of "purity and danger" to promote his methods and disparage the achievements of his opponents, recalls a common sociological phenomenon both inside and outside academic life. See Bloor's discussion of Frege's treatment of a science of numbers, pp. 82f.

7. *Philosophy and Civilization*, New York, G.P. Putnam's Sons, p. 233f. The title in the table of contents contained an extra "y," a happy misprint, making the title "The Unity of Behavior."

8. It may be wise here to acknowledge explicitly that the notion of function which inspired people during the first quarter to this century to call themselves 'functionalists' is not that used in mathematics. It was rather the old homonymous notion found in Aristotle (Greek, *to ergon*) which covers both what a thing characteristically does, its *characteristic activity*, and what *use* that activity may be to the furtherance of that thing or of something else (see Ruckmick). Carr (p. 62), in the course of commenting on Ruckmick, argued that not only did these two uses of the term "function" not represent two different meanings—"The term function is used in exactly the same sense in both cases"—but also that this was the way the term "function" was used in mathematics. With this level of sensitivity, one can hardly expect Carr to have kept alight at Chicago the specific flame Dewey tried to ignite with his criticism of the reflex arc concept. (See Rucker's remark on Carr's use of the reflex arc concept quoted at the end of the previous section.)

9. See James, *Principles of Psychology*, vol. 1, p. 25 for a diagram on which Dewey may well have meditated in arriving at this example. Also see ibid., chapter 4, for an indication of the theoretical importance of this concept in late nineteenth-century psychology.

10. Angell is more explicit, "If the reflexes and the automatic acts were wholly competent to steer the organism through its course, there is no reason to suppose that consciousness would ever put in an appearance" (1908, p. 64). But on the basis of his reading of the 1894–1897 articles on emotion, reflex action and effort, Titchener (n.57) hesitated to attribute "a theory of its [consciousness's] first appearance" to Dewey. Nevertheless Titchener argued there was no alternative to the view found in Angell, if "consciousness is primarily and actively a matter of function, and only secondarily and passively a matter of content" (ibid., p. 536).

11. "Conduct and Experience" (referred to below as "Cnd&Exp") first appeared in *Psychologies of 1930*, edited by Carl Murchison,

Worcester, MA: Clark University Press, 1930, pp. 409–422; this passage is from p. 219 of LW 5. The grudging "for the moment" does not signal a reluctance to admit that there are conscious processes but rather to admit these conscious processes constitute "experience" (in its entirety) and are capable of direct inspection (yielding, by themselves, reliable knowledge).

12. Dewey's second book (1888), a commentary on Leibniz's *New Essays*, discusses Leibniz's denial of "the equivalence of soul and consciousness" (see EW 1, p. 311–312).

13. The relative stability of the shared habits (customs and traditions) which constitute the social environment were to Dewey the concrete embodiment of a Hegelian "objective mind." (See the statement Dewey supplied to his daughters for their biographical sketch in Schilpp, pp. 17–18).

Dewey took over the terms "fringe" and "focus" (e.g., EN, LW 1, p. 227) from James. (*Principles of Psychology*, vol. 1, pp. 258, 281–282) but his use of them was informed by his belief in the connection between consciousness and habit-governed activity—a belief given vivid illustration in his experiences with F.M. Alexander. See Mixon.

14. Francis Warner was the author of several works on child development. Dewey's allusion is to *A Course of Lectures on the Growth and Means of Training the Mental Faculty*, New York: Macmillan, 1890 (Checklist, MW 1, p. 446).

15. Alan Turing's notion is anchored in the concrete image of a device which scans an indefinitely extendable tape one segment at a time, performing an operation on that segment (including possibly leaving it unchanged) and moving it one segment to the left or right. What it does to any segment and how it moves after it operates depends on the state of that segment of the tape (usually there are two such states, full and empty) and on its current internal state (usually one of a possible six.) Strictly, a Turing machine is a set of "instructions" which determine how this apparatus will operate on a tape configuration to change it (thereby "computing" the value of the function its instructions embody). Such a set of instructions takes the form of a set of quadruples which specify (1) for a given state, (2) what is done to the tape, (3) how the tape moves, and (4) which internal state it will be in for the next tape segment.

16. For Dennett, "Ryle and Wittgenstein are the preeminent modern theorists of the personal level. In fact in their different ways they invent the enterprise, by showing that there is work to be done, that there are questions that arise purely at the personal

level, and that one misconceives the questions if one offers sub-personal hypotheses or theories as answers" (ibid., p. 154n). Not only can Dewey claim a share of this credit, he (certainly more than Ryle, if not more than Wittgenstein) can also claim credit for insisting on the need for a super-personal (or social level) of explanation. See below.

17. Architecture which is parallel and distributed provides a basis for a form of functionalism which is arguably not "Turing machine" functionalism (the architecture of which is serial and local). For representatives of the enormous philosophic literature generated by Turing machine functionalism, see Putnam, Fodor, and Block.

18. It is, of course, possible to deny that the phenomena of meaning are matters which can be investigated by objective science. Quine, for example, takes this route.

19. The actual Turing machine operations of scanning and possibly changing a segment of the tape, moving left or right and changing the state of the machine can be performed by a human being, without the system being in any way more or less than a Turing machine. (See Weizenbaum, pp. 51–59). Dennett's phrase "intuition pump" is a far more apt expression than "thought experiment" for this kind of example.

References

Angell, James Rowland. "The Relations of Structural and Functional Psychology to Philosophy." *Philosophical Review.* 12 (1903), pp. 243–271.

———. *Psychology.* New York: Henry Holt, 1904.

———. "The Province of Functional Psychology." *The Psychological Review* 14 (1907), pp. 61–91.

Block, Ned. "Troubles with Functionalism." In *Perception and Cognition: Issues in the Foundations of Psychology.* Edited by C. W. Savage, Minnesota Studies in the Philosophy of Science, Vol. 9. Minneapolis: University of Minnesota Press, 1978, pp. 261–325.

Bloor, David. *Knowledge and Social Imagery.* London: Routledge and Kegan Paul, 1976.

Carr, Harvey. "Functionalism." In *Psychologies of 1930.* Edited by Carl Murchison. Worcester, MA: Clark University Press, 1930, pp. 59–78.

Cohen, David. *J. B. Watson: The Founder of Behaviourism.* London: Routledge and Kegan Paul, 1979.

60 *J. E. Tiles*

Danziger, Kurt. "The Positivist Repudiation of Wundt." *Journal of the History of the Behavioral Sciences* **15** (1979), pp. 205–230.

―――. "The History of Introspection Reconsidered." *Journal of the History of the Behavioral Sciences* **16** (1980), pp. 241–262.

Dennett, Daniel C. *Brainstorms*. Cambridge, MA: MIT Press, 1978.

Dewey, John. *The Works of John Dewey*. In three series: *Early Works 1882–1898* (EW), *Middle Works 1899–1924* (MW), and *Later Works 1925–1953* (LW). Edited by Jo Anne Boydston. Carbondale, IL: Southern Illinois University Press, 1969–1990.

Fodor, Jerry A. "Explanation in Psychology." In *Philosophy in America*. Edited by Max Black. Ithaca, NY: Cornell University Press, 1965, pp. 161–179.

Heidbreder, Edna. *Seven Psychologies*. New York: Appleton-Century, 1933.

Oatley, Keith. "On Changing One's Mind." In *Consciousness in Contemporary Science*. Edited by A. J. Marcel and E. Bisiach. Oxford: Clarendon Press, 1988, pp. 369–389.

James, William. *The Principles of Psychology*. 2 vols. 1890. New York: Dover reprint, 1950.

―――. "The Chicago School." 1904. In *Collected Essays and Reviews*. Edited by Ralph Barton Perry. New York: Longmans, Green, 1920, pp. 445–447.

Mixon, Don. "The Place of Habit in the Control of Action." *Journal for the Theory of Social Behavior* **10** (1980), pp. 169–186.

Palmer, Stephen E. and Ruth Kimchi. "The Information Processing Approach to Cognition." In *Approaches to Cognition*. Edited by Terry J. Knapp and Lynn C. Robertson. Hillsdale, NJ: Lawrence Erlbaum Associates, 1986, pp. 37–77.

Popper, Karl. *Objective Knowledge*. Oxford: Clarendon Press, 1972.

Putnam, Hilary. "Minds and Machines." In *Dimensions of Mind*. Edited by Sidney Hook, New York: Collier Books, 1960.

Quine, W. O. *Word and Object*. Cambridge, MA: MIT Press, 1960.

Rucker, Darnell. *The Chicago Pragmatists*. Minneapolis: University of Minnesota Press, 1969.

Ruckmick, Christian A. "The Use of the Term *Function* in English Textbooks of Psychology." *American Journal of Psychology* **24** (1913), pp. 91–123.

Schilpp, P. A., ed. *The Philosophy of John Dewey*. La Salle, IL: Open Court, 1939.

Searle, John. *Minds, Brains and Science*. London: British Broadcasting Corporation, 1984.

Titchener, E. B. "Functional Psychology and the Psychology of Act: I." *American Journal of Psychology* **32** (1921), pp. 519–542.

Van Gulick, Robert. "Consciousness, Intrinsic Intentionality, and Self-Understanding Machines." In *Consciousness in Contemporary Science*. Edited by A. J. Marcel and E. Bisiach. Oxford: Clarendon Press, 1988, pp. 78–100.

Washburn, Margaret Floy. In *History of Psychology in Autobiography*. Vol. 2. Edited by Carl Murchison. New York: Russell & Russell, 1961, pp. 333–358.

Watson, John Broadus. In *History of Psychology in Autobiography*. Vol. 3. Edited by Carl Murchison. New York: Russell & Russell, 1961, pp. 271–281.

Weizenbaum, Joseph. *Computer Power and Human Reason*. Harmondsworth, Middlesex: Penguin Books, 1984.

Woodworth, Robert S. "Dynamic Psychology." In *Psychologies of 1925*. Edited by Carl Murchison, Worcester, MA: Clark University, 1926, pp. 111–126.

4

Embodied, Enculturated Agents

===========

Vincent M. Colapietro

I

My intention here is to sketch a Deweyan approach to what today is often called human subjectivity.[1] In a book on Charles Peirce,[2] I attempted to show that *his* views on the self were not nearly as inconsistent, incomplete, or incomprehensible as some of even his most sympathetic commentators charged. In this chapter, I want to defend John Dewey against similar charges. One way to execute this task would be to use a traditional conception of the human person (e.g., the Platonic, Aristotelian, Thomistic, Cartesian, or connectionist) as a foil for the Deweyan approach to be sketched here. But this strategy, though undoubtedly illuminating, has drawbacks which should not be underestimated. For one thing, it would simply re-enact one of the more unfortunate tendencies in Dewey's own philosophical project: to exaggerate the differences between his own views and more traditional positions. For another, the convergent position of John E. Smith and Richard J. Bernstein, two authors who are at once sympathetic expositors and penetrating critics of Dewey, provides a more suitable foil: to defend Dewey in this context is best accomplished by setting his position against that of these critics. That both Smith and Bernstein are contemporary philosophers shaped by the philosophical tradition Dewey himself so significantly shaped makes it especially appropriate to consider their critiques. Even so, I will briefly discuss near the end of this paper the Deweyan position vis-à-vis several more traditional approaches to human selfhood. This will help us appreciate more fully than otherwise the continuity between Dewey's naturalistic outlook and the dominant tradition in Western culture; in turn, such an appreciation will assist in appraising the novelty of his outlook. But historical affinities and innovations are for me of secondary importance; rather the philosophical tenability and fecundity of Dewey's position is of primary significance. Neither the tenability nor fecundity of this position will be granted if the criticisms offered by informed, sympathetic expositors go unanswered.

What especially moves me to undertake this defense is, quite candidly, the conviction that the pragmatic approach in general and the Deweyan version in particular are especially helpful in illuminating the nature of subjectivity or selfhood. In expressing this conviction, I am obviously not uncognizant of the fact that two of the most prominent commentators on American philosophy have voiced exactly the opposite judgment. Nor in commending the pragmatic approach do I intend to imply that it is the last word on one of the most intractable of philosophical problems.[3]

All that I hope to accomplish here is to render plausible two suggestions: first, that these criticisms of Dewey are unjust; second, that a pragmatic conception of the human self should constitute, for any responsible inquirer, the *first* word at least. More—indeed, much more—needs to be said about the self than what the classical American pragmatists themselves (Charles Sanders Peirce, William James, John Dewey, and George Herbert Mead) collectively have said; perhaps the sustained effort to articulate a truly adequate conception of human subjectivity would even drive us (as Smith[4] and others have argued) beyond functional psychology and naturalistic metaphysics, beyond an instrumentalist construal of knowledge and a theoretical occlusion of privacy. If painstakingly and honestly undertaken, my sense is that, in fact, we would be driven beyond at least some of these doctrines: in general, we would need to formulate a position far less programmatic and also far less polemical than the one which Dewey himself articulated.

But, leaving aside whither we might be driven by such an experiment in articulation, whence we must set out is arguably just where the pragmatists (most consistently, Dewey and Mead) insist upon—namely, with organisms in interaction with their environment(s).[5] In the case of Homo Sapiens, these organisms are "beings with brains and bowels" (MW 3:96) and, indeed, much else. By virtue of their organic constitution and indelible enculturation, they are "beings who suffer and endeavor" (84). They are beings who suffer because they strive and, in turn, strive because they suffer (90). Of course, our exertions and undertakings are not the sole source of our sufferings, nor is our suffering or anticipation of suffering our only motive for acting. But, whatever else these organisms are, they are "concrete empirical conscious centers of action and passion" (97). It is important to stress that, here, action encompasses more than conscious exertion and passion more than either emotion or suffering in the sense of undergoing something painful. Moreover, what can be conceptually distinguished (action and passion) are ordinarily inseparable: Dewey characterizes the organism as an agent-patient because its life is an acting-undergoing.

Organisms are inseparable from an environment of a more or less determinate character. Hence, we must commence with an incessantly active organism in transformative interchange with a historically charged environment. To characterize *our* environment as historically charged is to elevate one of Dewey's principal insights—namely, that "experience both takes up something from those which have gone before and modifies in some way the quality of those which come after" (LW 13:19)—to its proper place.[6] Culturally as well as personally, the dynamic present *through which* we are moving embodies (primarily in our habits and artifacts) the presence of a largely irrevocable past but, nonetheless, the possibilities of a truly novel future (LW 2:66). But this is to jump ahead of our story. First, we need to consider whether there is indeed a story worth telling.

II

A moment ago, I noted that two of the most prominent commentators on American philosophy have expressed severe criticisms of the Deweyan approach to human selfhood. It is time to consider these critiques. Such a consideration might be viewed as preparing the canvas for the sketch that I in due course will make.

John E. Smith calls attention to "the seeming disappearance of the individual experienc*er* in Dewey's view."[7] According to him,

    ... Dewey's dominantly social interpretation of experience as public fact makes it difficult to locate the individual for whom experience is an actual fact. It is true that Dewey

sought to deal with this problem by means of the doctrine
of pervasive quality and what he called having *an* experience; the aesthetic dimension, it would appear, makes room
for the individual and the private. But even in this context
Dewey retained his suspicion of the private; emotions, he
wrote, 'are not, save in pathological instances, private' [*Art
as Experience* (NY: Capricorn), p. 42], but are occurrences
in the development of experience to some issue or conclusion. This seems to place the most individualized of all
experiences once again in the public context where it falls
under the dominant motive to control events (1961, 102–
103).

Later in this essay, Smith returns to this point, contending that

Dewey went so far in the direction of behaviorism or the
translation of experience into external, public fact and function that the individual experiencer becomes insignificant.
The individual and the private always made Dewey un-
easy; it is not that he denied either, he was too good an
empiricist for that, but he wanted to keep them confined to
a place where they would do no public damage. . . . The fact
that an individual self is always the locus of experience,
that experience, as William James put it, is always
somebody's experience, somewhere and somewhen, is not
taken seriously; as either overt behavior or impersonal public
fact, experience virtually closes with nature, and the individual is forced to abscond into the realm of art (109–110).[8]

As part of his critique, Smith notes that, in 1939 (thus, rather late
in Dewey's life), Dewey himself conceded that the criticism prof-
fered by the psychologist Gordon Allport—namely, that no adequate
theory of human selfhood could be found in his vast corpus—was
just. Dewey tried to explain the absence of such a theory by noting
that, in his desire "to cut loose from the influence of older 'spiritualistic' theories about the nature of the unity and stability of the
personal self (regarded as a peculiar kind of substantial-stuff)," he
failed to show how an adequate account could be provided within
a naturalistic context. To this concession, Smith responds that

even if we admit the inadequacy of the concept of substance, surely the problem of locating the unity and iden-

tity of the self remains. This problem cannot be resolved . . . by a purely functional theory. Every functional theory of the self ends by translating it into activities of a sort only a center of consciousness can perform (110).

Then, at this point in his critique, Smith recalls Dewey's own attempt to clarify his position: ". . . I hold that the word 'subject' if it is to be used at all, has the organism for its proper *designatum*. Hence it refers to an *agency of doing*, not to a knower, mind, consciousness or whatever." To this supposed clarification, Smith responds sharply: "I confess that I fail to follow then I am told that a person is not a consciousness or a knower, but even more fail to understand how any 'agency of doing' can become aware of itself, how it can remember, and how it can become divided within itself." Then Smith asks rhetorically: How are we to understand the divided self "unless we presuppose *an underlying unity and center* of the self?" (110; emphasis added).[9]

In a paper entitled "Is the Self an Ultimate Category?" Smith contends that the self is presupposed by every attempt to translate it into something more basic or irreducible. "If you translate the self into a functioning in order to avoid the embarrassments of a substantial or identical ego, or into a way of relating states [etc.] . . . you will discover that this functioning or relating turns out to be the sort of thing that only a self can perform" (1966, 138). His allegation is that you have, in effect, smuggled the notion of self into your account, albeit in a disguised and thus undetected form. "In order for your proposed substitute to succeed in its role you have to endow your function with the ability to recognize, to acknowledge, to compare [to differentiate], etc. In short you have to presuppose the self" (1966, 138).

Though Smith does not mention Dewey in this connection, it is clear from his other writings that Dewey would be among the targets of this criticism. But what needs to be stressed is not just the polemical thrust but also the constructive suggestion; for, in this text, we catch a glimpse of Smith's own position: the human self, understood as a unique, enduring center of power and purpose, is an irreducible category.[10] Shortly, I will use this position as foil for Dewey's view. But, first, let us hear the judgement of another commentator on Dewey.

Richard J. Bernstein, a commentator who is perhaps even more personally sympathetic to the pragmatic approach than John Smith, is no less critical. In *Praxis and Action*, however, he charges that:

"Despite many important hints, Peirce has failed to work out an adequate theory of the self. Indeed, I believe that this was not only his failure, but the failure of the entire pragmatic movement. We might try to excuse this by recalling the dialectical context in which [American] pragmatism developed. The movement rebelled against the excesses of subjectivism and 'mentalism' characteristic of so much of modern epistemology. This is not really an excuse [i.e., a justification], but a way of calling attention to a pervasive failure of this movement" (1971, 197–198). And, in his book on John Dewey, Bernstein claims that "the weakest part of Dewey's entire philosophy is his analysis of the self" (1967, 176).[11] Like Smith, he recalls Dewey's own acknowledgment of the justice of Allport's criticism. That Bernstein himself does not so much develop as simply issue this charge suggests that he imagines the fairness of the criticism will be immediately recognized by anyone familiar with Dewey's writings.

III

In light of all this, it seems deeply misguided to draw upon Dewey's writings for anything more than scattered hints for how to sketch a compelling portrait of the human self. But my thesis is that there are more resources here than these critics recognize. More specifically, I contend that we can readily find in Dewey's writings not only fruitful suggestions for how to explain human selfhood but also what is arguably a hypothesis comparable to the very strongest ones put forth by other contemporary philosophers (most notably, Maurice Merleau-Ponty's notion of the body-subject and Anthony Kenny's recent discussions of the human self).

At the center of the Deweyan approach to human subjectivity is a robust affirmation of human agency: we are first and foremost agents, beings not so much goaded into activity by external stimuli as always active by our own inherent constitution (see, e.g., EW 5:96–109; MW 14:199–200). The role of stimuli in guiding and, indeed, redirecting conduct is enormous; however, their function is not to provoke an inert being into action, but to assist a dynamic being in more finely and fully reorienting itself toward the scene of some engagement. Such reorientations range from re-positioning the way one is sitting in a chair to re-imaging the manner one is situated in the cosmos. But what need to be stressed at the outset is the general point regarding radical agency: we are *inherently* active beings who inevitably undergo transformations as a consequence of our activities. The ubiquitous presence and, of greater moment, the particular propensities of unique agents require recognition. Experience demands that we attend to the agency through which a function is initiated, sustained, and perhaps modified; and, for Dewey, experience reveals clearly the nature of this agency—"a singular organism, an organism that has been subjected to acculturation [cf. LW 1], and is aware of itself as a social subject and agent" (LW 14:199; cf. Mead).

Let me develop this conception in explicit reference to Professor Smith's severe critique of the Deweyan position. A distinctive feature in Smith's own philosophical vision is the status and role which he accords to the self (see, e.g., 1961, 110–111; 1992, 31). As we have seen above, the concept of the self is, according to him, irreducible: All attempts to reduce the self or person (conceived as a center of intention) to something else—e.g., to a historic route of occasions (Whitehead) or a distinctive kind of organism (Dewey)— *either* do not provide the conceptual resources to explain the distinctive activities of the self *or* do so only by smuggling in (ordinarily under the cover of another name) the notion of the self as a centered and unified being (see, e.g., 1966, 137–138). In short, "[t]he self is presupposed by every supposed translation" (1966, 138).

But in fact all that needs to be assumed here is, in my judgment, continuity, not centeredness or unity. The dynamic continuum or organic life underlies the acquisition and integration of habits; the latter processes enhance the continuity of this life. Is it not possible to explain, on a naturalistic basis, the emergence of a centered and unified self? We can start with the human organism as an enduring source of striving and, thus, as a site of fulfillment and frustration. At the outset, this source is not conscious of itself, nor are its strivings integrated. In the course of its strivings, it acquires the capacity for self-consciousness and, thereby, for self-definition (cf. Peirce, Baldwin, Mead). At this point, Smith's analysis of the self comes fully into play. But this analysis primarily concerns the moral unity of personal agents; and this unity itself presupposes a continuity of striving or endeavor, but in no way explains this continuum.

Smith maintains that: "What makes us one person in the course or history of our lives is the overarching purpose through which we organize and harmonize the lesser desires, purposes and drives that constitute our life" (1992, 189; cf. 1966, 143ff.). Yet what makes the framing and, indeed, revision of such an overarching purpose

possible is an embodied source of continuous endeavor. Even apart
from our conscious purposes and anticipations, the incredibly complex array of exertions, strivings, and withdrawals flowing from
this source bear upon one another. The self-conscious moral unity
of the concrete self grows out of the more or less blind gropings of
an organic agent and, at every turn, the self-defining purpose of
this self depends on such agency for both its articulation (including
its revision) and actualization. The human subject is nothing other
than the human organism; but in the course of experience, this
organism is radically transformed in and through its interactions
with others. While such a self or subject might be described as an
emergent function, it would be far less misleading to characterize
this self as an embodied agent (cf. Smith 1961, 110; see also Dewey
1925, chapter 6). At any rate, the notion of such agency seems to
capture the truth of Smith's insistence that the concept of the self
as a centre of intention is irreducible, while doing fuller justice to
the radical transformations actually undergone by human beings
in the course of acquiring the capacities of self-consciousness and
self-definition (MW 12:198; LW 1:176–187).

Now Smith might of course respond by charging that I have,
under the cover of "embodied agent," smuggled into my own account the very notion of the self which he claims must be assumed
at all points in the discussion. But what I am assuming here is a
being whose unity is, at bottom, a function of its continuity. The
self as an enduring, embodied agent underlies the self as an
overarching, integrative purpose: a being able to project and pursue aims comes, as a result of its projects and pursuits, to assume
the integration of these as *a task* (cf. Smith 1992, 165–168). But,
in its most fundamental sense (in its metaphysical as distinct from
moral sense), the self can no more be defined in terms of such a
task than it can be defined in terms of a function, for the execution
of the task assumes an agent capable of devoting itself to the task.
Thus, for me, what is presupposed at every turn is not the unity
of an overarching purpose, but the continuity of organic agency.

Above, I noted that human organisms are *inherently* active
beings who inevitably undergo transformations as a consequence of
their activities. "Experience" is Dewey's term for the transformative process in and through which human beings acquire their
distinctive capacities and forge their unique identities. Perhaps the
most significant phase of this transformative process is that in
which the human infant attains a vast array of symbolic competencies, including the self-referential uses of signs and symbols (the

ability to say "mine" and "I"). These uses underlie one of the most distinctive features of the human subject, the feature which might in fact be taken as *the* hallmark of our subjectivity: namely, our reflexivity (LW 14:199). But, for Dewey, the relationship of the self to itself is derivative. The accent falls heavily on what goes on *between* self and world, not on what occurs *beneath* the skin or *within* the recesses of consciousness. But in fact this means that experience is predominantly what goes on *between* one self and other selves: "[f]or human beings, the environing affairs directly important are those formed by the activities of other human beings. This fact is accentuated and made fundamental by the fact of infancy—the fact that each human being begins life completely dependent upon others" (MW 14:60[12]; cf. Arendt). Hence, our experience is first and foremost intersubjective: it is the ongoing, transformative dialogue among irreducibly different yet ineluctably related subjects.

These distinct subjects are (to paraphrase Dewey) singular organisms, ones that have been subjected to acculturation and, by virtue of this acculturation, have attained awareness of themselves as both subjects and agents (LW 14:199). The human self is an acculturated organism whose distinctive activities and sensibilities result from multiple factors. Principally, these activities and sensibilities arise out of the complex intersection of three historical developments: the evolution of the human species, the evolution of the particular culture into which the individual is born (for cultures evolve no less than species), and the unique process of *this* individual being subjected to acculturation in just these ways.[13]

IV

As a means of identifying and, in a preliminary manner, of clarifying the nature of our selfhood, the concept of organism is far from innocent (cf. Smith 1961, 114). It was deliberately proposed by Dewey and Mead as a naturalistic substitute for the spritualistic and mentalistic entities by which traditional philosophy, modern as well as classical, tried to account for the distinctive features of human beings. In other words, the notion of organism was invoked for the purpose of displacing such entities as spirit, soul, mind, consciousness, and even (in a way) self. On more than a few occasions, Professor Smith has quipped that he only belatedly realized that he himself was among the beings encompassed by Dewey's use of "organism." The point of this remark is that we do not ordinarily identify or conceive ourselves as organisms; but this, in itself, is no decisive criticism, for many of our commonplace understandings are arguably misunderstandings (cf. Santayana 1923 [1955], ix).

What especially needs to be appreciated here is that the efforts of the pragmatists, and in particular of Dewey, to substitute organism for spirit, soul, mind, consciousness, and self were *not* thoroughly reductionistic. Dewey is neither Watson nor Skinner. Rhetorically, he even tries to retain the key terms of traditional discourse, including soul and spirit and subjectivity (LW 1:184; LW 14:198–199). Thus, Dewey in his magnum opus, *Experience and Nature*, suggests that: "'(S)oul' when freed from all traces of traditional materialistic animism denotes the qualities of psycho-physical activities as far as these are organized into unity" (LW 1:223). He quickly goes on to note that his use of this term is intended "to call attention to properties that characterize these bodies, not to import a mysterious non-natural entity or force." Whereas soul is used here to denote unity, spirit is used to denote dynamism: "When the organization called soul is free, moving and operative, initial [initiating] as well as terminal, it is spirit . . . . Soul is form, spirit informs" (LW 1:223–224). After proposing that, even within his naturalistic metaphysics, these traditional terms *might be* given a legitimate meaning, he concedes the obvious: "Perhaps the words soul and spirit are so heavily laden with traditional mythology and sophisticated doctrine that they must be surrendered; it may be impossible to recover for them in science and philosophy the realities designated by idiomatic speech" (224).

Here two points need to be stressed. First, "the idiomatic non-doctrinal use of the word[s] soul [and spirit] retains a sense of the realities concerned," namely, the unity and dynamism manifest on the level or plateau of psycho-physical interactions. What is problematic is not the import of the idiomatic expressions but the retention of these words as technical terms in scientific and philosophical discourse. Second, "the realities are there, by whatever names they be called" (224; cf. LW 14:198–199).

Dewey is not unmindful of the fact that the principal terms in which he casts his own "emergent" theory of the human mind are themselves freighted with historical meanings often quite at odds with his philosophical intentions[14] (cf. Derrida). He is quite explicit on this point: "every word that we can use, organism, feeling, psycho-physical, sensation and sense, 'emergence' itself, is infected by the associations of old theories, whose import is [often?] opposite to that here stated" (LW 1:207). In this connection, he offers a fascinating suggestion about one of his own key words:

> Old ideas do not die when the beliefs which have been explicitly associated with them disappear; they usually change their clothes. Present notions about the organisms are largely a survival, with changed vocabulary, of old ideas about soul and body. The soul was conceived as inhabiting the body in an external way. Now the nervous system is conceived as a substitute, mysterious within the body. . . . [T]he nervous system as the set of mental events is narrowed down to the brain, and then to the cortex of the brain; while many physiological inquirers would doubtless feel enormously relieved if a specific portion of the cortex could be ascertained to be *the* seat of consciousness. Those who talk most of the organism . . . are often just those who display least sense of the intimate, delicate and subtle interdependence of all organic structures and processes with one another. The world seems mad with what is specific, particular, disconnected [Cf. Peirce's critique of nominalism]. . . . In terms of a conscious control of inclusive wholes, search for those links which occupy key positions and which effect critical connections is indispensable. But recovery of sanity depends upon seeing and using these specifiable things *as* links functionally significant in a process. To see the organism *in* nature, the nervous system in the organism, the brain in the nervous system, the cortex in the brain is the answer to the problems which haunt philosophy. And when thus seen they will be seen to be *in*, not as marbles are in a box but as events are in a history, in a moving, growing never finished process (224).

This is certainly overly sanguine: the problems which haunt philosophy in this area are not so easily disposed of. Our reaction to this excessive optimism should not prompt us to disregard Dewey's invaluable suggestion: nothing less than the organism in its entirety is the seat of consciousness. I have quoted this passage at length primarily because it shows Dewey's acute sensitivity to the possibility that his own preferred term, one adopted in the hope of avoiding the stultifying dualisms of traditional philosophy, might itself carry within itself dualistic implications.

In a very late manuscript, Dewey observed that: "Philosophers have exhibited proper ingenuity in pointing out holes in the beliefs of common sense, but they have also displayed improper ingenuity in ignoring the empirical things that every one has; the things that so denote themselves that they *have* to be dealt with" (LW 1:374). (We might recall, parenthetically, a similar observation made by A. N. Whitehead: "Philosophy destroys its usefulness when it indulges in brilliant feats of explaining away" [1978, 17].) In reference to our topic, "the things which so denote themselves that they *have* to be dealt with" are what I called a moment ago the manifest facts about human agency; they provide not only the starting point but also the constraining considerations for any responsible inquiry. As Dewey himself puts it, "(T)he objects of gross observation always persist as limiting conditions which give point and meaning to specific determinations" (MW 11:15).

The various classical conceptions of the human person (e.g., the Platonic, the Aristotelian, the Thomistic, and the Cartesian) were designed to explain nothing less than a wide range of such manifest facts. As compelling indications of just what the manifest facts *are*, they are incomparable; as genuine explanations, they are often suggestive, though they have been by and large rejected by the majority of philosophers and scientists today. Of course, this in itself does not establish their untenability; however, it does perhaps go some distance toward creating a presumption against their plausibility—a far greater distance than many contemporary defenders of these traditional conceptions are inclined to admit.

One of my most recent assertions must have seemed odd to at least some readers. A moment ago I claimed that, as compelling indications of just what the manifest facts *are*, the classical conceptions of the human person are incomparable. But it would appear that manifest facts are those very things which do not need to be ingeniously displayed, for they themselves are so insistently present! What this overlooks, however, is the extent to which our theories might blind us to the facts; it also ignores the extent to which we might need the perspectives provided by other theories to overcome our blindnesses.[15]

Let me offer two illustrations of what I mean by such manifest facts. First, Plato's tripartite conception of the human soul is primarily derived from an analysis of the inner conflicts into which human beings are constitutionally thrust. Such conflicts are things which so denote themselves, which so assert themselves, that they have to be dealt with. Second, Thomas's position is designed to account more adequately for, at once, the unity of the person and the activities whereby humans appear to transcend the conditions of materiality. However deep and manifold are the inner conflicts within an individual self, there is a unity underlying these conflicts; however much we are characteristically absorbed in the here and now, our mode of being in the world and also of relating to ourselves shows a marked—an unmistakable—transcendence. Such unity and transcendence are also things which so denote themselves that they have to be dealt with.

Hence, according to Thomas, the human soul is, at once, the substantial form of a natural substance and itself a spiritual substance (albeit only in a qualified sense).[16] These are the subtle means which he has devised to deal with these manifest facts. What tends to get lost in many discussions of this highly nuanced conception is how severely qualified is the sense in which the soul can itself be called a substance. On Thomas's own account, the human soul is just barely a spiritual substance: *qua* spirit it needs the body. What far less often gets overlooked is Thomas's uncompromising insistence upon the unity of the human person. For him, the soul united to the body is more like God than the soul separated from the body; that is, it more fully realizes its nature in conjunction with some determinate incarnation. The implications of this insistence, however, are profound. One of them is that Thomas's vision of the human person is akin to Dewey's conception of the acculturated organism. In general, many of the thinkers within the various traditions of medieval thought were closer to Aristotle's biological conception of the human *psyche* than either later critics such as Dewey himself or even contemporary disciples tend to appreciate. But, given the decidedly otherworldly emphasis of so much medieval thought, Dewey is justified in ignoring the technical respects in which this thought preserves Aristotle's biological conception and, thus, in stressing the profound extent to which it vitiates the main thrust of the Aristotelian vision.

There is, at one extreme, a deep-rooted philosophical tradition that in effect depicts the human self as an angel imprisoned in a body. There is, at the other, a more recent yet nonetheless influential tradition that portrays the self as an organism imprisoned in an environment. The former position makes the body something inessential to our humanity and, in addition, the unity of body and soul something opaque to our understanding. The latter position excludes the resources for explaining the distinctive capacity of human agents to transcend in various ways their actual circumstances; indeed, this position is launched by a militant refusal to acknowledge any transcendent dimension of human agency. Here the refusal to acknowledge the facts of the case absolves the reductionist of the responsibility to provide an explanation of the fact. Though Dewey occasionally veered in the direction of the reductionist extreme, and though Thomas could not help but be closer to the spiritualistic extreme, there is far greater common ground here than either Deweyans or Thomists are likely to suppose.

Traditionally, the spiritual has been equated with the immaterial in an ontological and not merely an operational sense. Indeed, for Thomas, it makes no sense to try to conceive of an immaterial function or activity apart from an immaterial agent. The fact that in the activities (or functions) of thinking, willing, and loving we transcend the conditions of materiality implies, for him, that we are ourselves in part immaterial.

An alternative position would be more insistently naturalistic, without being immoderately reductionistic. Herein, the human organism, precisely because it has been so radically transformed by its participation in semiotic processes, is itself a spiritual substance in a perfectly intelligible (even if unavoidably metaphorical) sense.[17] Such a being is fully equipped to feel awe, wonder, reverence, piety, gratitude, and mystery—in sum, to feel those emotions or to acquire those attitudes traditionally associated with a religious sensibility (see, of course, *A Common Faith*). Arguably, there is not necessarily anything insincere or inauthentic in turning to some of the traditional forms as indispensable means for expressing these distinctively religious emotions or spiritual attitudes (cf. Santayana; also Levinson). If we think that a mere animal does not merit the designation of spiritual substance, perhaps that reveals an impoverished understanding of the seemingly miraculous potentialities inherent in the natural world and, in particular, in the human organism. Moreover, there might be religious as well as philosophical reasons for identifying ourselves with the temporally continuous yet ultimately mortal embodiment of our agency. One reason would be that the cultivation of distinctively religious attitudes would not require any violation of our rational integrity; another would be that the religious outlook would be linked with a courageous effort to confront squarely our own mortality, rather than with the incredible promise of escaping the absolute finality of our own personal existence. However that may be, there are in my

judgment strong philosophical reasons for taking the human organism as uniquely transformed by human culture to be the most
legitimate referent of the human self. Thus, in the very context in
which he conceded that the criticisms of the psychologist Gordon
Allport "are just" (LW 14:38), a point stressed by Smith in his own
criticism, Dewey suggests that: "Some at least of the criticism of
my theory of experience might have been averted if I had set forth
my socio-biological psychology so as to show how and why, on the
negative side, many philosophical ideas, still put forth as fundamental and as all but axiomatic, represent uncritical acceptance of
psychological theories formed two centuries ago . . ." (LW 14:38–
39). He admits that it would also have been helpful had he, upon
the positive side, shown how and why "a sound psychology provides
a basis for a theory of the nature of experiencing, and of its different modes and their connections with one another" (39). The failure to undertake in a sufficiently detailed and systematic way either
this negative or positive task reflected what he came to see as an
erroneous assumption: "I now see how far contemporary philosophy
[i.e., philosophy in 1939] is from having appropriated and digested
the main principles set forth even in the psychology of William
James" (39). Hence, in "The Vanishing Subject in the Psychology of
James," an essay written around the same time as the text from
which I have been quoting, Dewey himself stressed that: "Philosophy will not be emancipated to perform its own task and function
until psychology is purged, as a whole and in all its special topics,
of the last remnant of the traditional dualism" (LW 14:167). James's
Principles both perpetuates the traditional dualism and provides
the resources for undermining it. On the one hand, there is in
James's work "official acceptance of epistemological dualism" according to which a *mental* "subject" defines the subject matter of
psychological investigation; on the other, "James's analysis of special topics tends . . . to the reduction of the subject to a vanishing
point, save as 'subject' is identified with organism, the latter, moreover, having no existence save in interaction with environing conditions" (LW 14:155). And it is the subject in just this sense that
Dewey highlights in his response to Allport: "(F)rom the standpoint
of a biological-cultural psychology the term 'subject' (and related
adjectival forms) has only the signification of a certain kind of
actual existence; namely, a living creature which under the influence
of language and other cultural agencies has become a person interacting with other persons (concrete human beings)" (LW 14:39).[18]

If this is indeed the first word regarding any truly adequate account of the human self, then we still have much to learn from Dewey—even more than some of his most informed and sympathetic expositors suspect.

V

To return to Smith's trope (though as a means of defending, rather than criticizing, Dewey), the *translation* of the unified, purposive self into embodied, enculturated agency is, I submit, a suggestive reading, immediately plausible and heuristically promising. It is a suggestive reading not only of Dewey's texts, but also of our experience of our own subjectivity. Reflexive agency—agency aware of itself as such—emerges under the pressures and promptings of more mature agents (see, e.g., MW 14:216–217).[19] Such agency is nothing other than experimental intelligence when such intelligence is personally and thus uniquely inflected. Neither scientific investigation nor democratic deliberation is conceivable apart from such personally inflected intelligence. Nor is artistic execution or aesthetic perception. Moreover, the religious dimension of human experience results from the ongoing process of personal inflection, when this process secures the integration as well as uniqueness of the self (*A Common Faith* and *Individualism Old and New*). The self-conscious assumption of responsibility for what one says and does and even feels—indeed, for *who* one is (see, of course, *Theory of the Moral Life*)—interiorizes and transforms the way one has been held accountable by others (MW 14:216–217). The interiorization and transformation of such accountability into personal responsibility lies at the very center of reflexive agency: "To learn to be human is to develop through the give-and-take of communication [and participation] *an effective sense of being an individually distinctive member of a community*; one who understands and appreciates its beliefs, desires, and methods, and who contributes to a further conversion of organic powers into human resources and values" (LW 2, 332; emphasis added). In turn, the very possibility of internalizing and transforming such accountability resides in the remarkable plasticity of the human organism. The distinctive capacities of our biological agency make enculturation possible in the first place; the pressures and promptings of an evolved and evolving ethos help the individual organism transform itself into a reflexive agency.

Notes

1. James Tiles and Kory Sorrell have offered helpful comments on an earlier draft of this paper. For an informative account of the "semantic and ideological space" indicated by the terms *subject* and *subjectivity*, see Kaja Silverman's *The Subject of Semiotics* (NY: Oxford University Press, 1983), p. 126. For readers interested in exploring further the Deweyan approach to human selfhood, see Darnell Rucker's "Selves into Persons: Another Legacy from John Dewey" in *Rice University Studies* (Fall 1980), volume 66, number 4:103–118.

2. *Peirce's Approach to the Self: A Semiotic Perspective on Human Subjectivity* (Albany: SUNY Press, 1989).

3. See Anthony Kenny's *The Self* (Milwaukee, WI: Marquette University Press, 1988).

4. See Smith's "John Dewey: Philosopher of Experience" in *Reason and God* (New Haven: Yale University Press, 1961), pp. 92–114; also *Purpose and Thought: The Meaning of Pragmatism* (New Haven: Yale University Press, 1978), especially chapters 4, 5, and 6.

5. In his *Principles of Psychology*, James suggests that it is far more fruitful to envision minds inhabiting environments "which act on them and on which they in turn react" than "the soul as a detached existent, sufficient unto itself" [Dover Edition, p. 6; cf. MW 14:604–61]. This invites us to take "mind in the midst of all its concrete relations."

In an autobiographical essay entitled "From Absolutism to Experimentalism," Dewey reveals that, "[U]pon the whole, the forces that have influenced me have come from persons and from situations more than from books . . ." But he notes "the great exception" to this claim—James's *Psychology*. Immediately, he adds that this revelation requires explanation, for there are in his judgment "two unreconciled strains in the *Psychology*." On the one hand, there is an underlying subjectivism; on the other, there are fertile suggestions for recovering a biological conception of human agents and, thereby, circumventing the skeptical problematic of so much traditional psychology and, indeed, philosophy. In addition to the subjectivist strain (one manifest in James's tendency to set off a realm of consciousness by itself), then, there is an objectivist strain: it has "its roots in a return to the earlier biological conception of the *psyche*, but a return possessed of a new force and value due to the progress made by biology since the time of Aristotle."

All of this is especially relevant to our topic since Dewey's own conception of subjectivity can be seen as following out fully and boldly the implications of the objectivist strain in Jamesian psychology. For him in fact, "[t]he objective biological approach of the Jamesian psychology led straight to the perception of the importance of distinctive social categories, especially communication and participation [see EN & PC]. It is my conviction that a great deal of our philosophizing needs *to be done over again* from this point of view, and that there will ultimately result in an integrated synthesis in a philosophy congruous with modern science and related to actual needs in education, morals, and religion" (Bernstein [ed.], p. 17; emphasis added). Dewey's philosophical project is perhaps best seen just as this ongoing reconstruction of traditional philosophizing from the approach inspired by James. At the heart of this reconstruction is a reconception of human selves as embodied, enculturated organisms who by virtue of their biological constitution are incessantly active and who by virtue of their cultural inheritances are multivalently communicative.

6. In a late manuscript, Dewey explained that: "When we say that experience is one point of approach to an account of the world in which we live, we mean then by experience something at least as wide and deep and full as all history on this earth, a history which, since history does not occur in the void, includes the earth and the physical relatives of man. When we assimilate experience to history, we note that history denotes both objective conditions, forces, events and also the human record and estimate of these events. Similarly experience denotes whatever is experienced, what is undergone and tried, and also processes of experiencing. As it is the essence of 'history' to have meanings termed both subjective and objective, so with 'experience' " (LW 1:370; cf. 18–19). Later he adds that: "Experience denotes what is experienced, the world of events and persons; and it denotes that world caught up into experiencing, the career and destiny of mankind. Nature's place in man is no less significant than man's place in nature" (LW 1:384). But an important respect in which Dewey's empirical naturalism is also a *historical* naturalism becomes manifest when he insists that: "There are moments of consummation when before and after are legitimately forgotten, and the sole stake of man is in the present. But even such objects are discovered to arise as culminations of processes, and to be in turn transitive and effective. . . . The legitimacy of timeless absorption is no argument in behalf of the legitimacy of timeless objects. Experience is history: and the *taking* of some objects as final is itself an episode in history" (LW 1:385).

7. This charge is, in effect, an echo of one brought against Dewey by Santayana in "Dewey's naturalistic Metaphysics": "In Dewey . . . there is a pervasive quasi-Hegelian tendency to dissolve the individual into his social functions, as well as everything substantial or actual into something relative or transitional. For him events, situations, and histories hold all facts and all persons in solution" (Schilpp [ed.] 1939, 247). Santayana goes so far as to say that, to Dewey, "self-consciousness is anathema" (253). He supposes that Dewey regards such consciousness "as a landscape that paints itself," something thoroughly phenomenal and thus "all above board" (253). But this seems inaccurate and unfair: there is, for Dewey, more to experience than consciousness and, moreover, more to consciousness than self-consciousness.

8. It is instructive to recall here that, in his presidential address to the American Philosophical Association, Dewey himself stressed that "[b]eliefs are personal affairs, and personal affairs are adventures.... [T]he world has meaning as somebody's, somebody's at a juncture, taken for better or worse, and you shall not have completed your metaphysics till you have told whose world is meant and how and what for—in what bias and to what effect" (MW 3, 84; cf. 100). In another context, Dewey goes so far as to assert that: "It is impossible to overstate the significance, the reality, of the relation of self as knower to things when it is thought of as a *moral* relation, a deliberate and responsible undertaking of a self" [Morgenbesser (ed.), p. 106]. Thus, the self conceived either as an abstract ontological condition or as a psychological datum has more often than not proven to be worse than useless; it has obstructed inquiry into what specifically might facilitate inquiry or deliberation. In contrast, the self envisioned as a deliberative agent has significantly aided the cause of "personal rationality or reflective intelligence" (MW 14, 56). Part and parcel of this envisioning is the animating sense of rational agency as a "necessary organ of experimental initiative and creative invention in remaking custom" (MW 14, 56). That is, to characterize the organism as a subject is not merely to stress that the organism is a being "which suffers, is subjected and which endures resistance and frustration"; it is also to bring into focus the fact that the human organism is an enduring center of initiative and innovation (LW 1, 184).

9. It deserves to be noted, even if only in passing, that one of Dewey's most illuminating discussions of the divided self is found in *Individualism Old and New*, a work in political philosophy and social criticism.

10. Two of my colleagues at Pennsylvania State University have written insightfully about the topic of selfhood and personhood, one in a personalist and the other in a pragmatist (quite Deweyan) vein. In "John E. Smith and the Heart of Experience" in *The Recovery of Philosophy in America*, edited by Thomas P. Kasulis and Robert Neville Cummings (Albany: SUNY Press, 1997), Douglas R. Anderson develops some of Smith's insights regarding the self. In "Personalist and Pragmatist Persons" in *The Personalist Forum* (VI, 2), pp. 143–160, and especially in chapter 15 of *Genealogical Pragmatism* (Albany: SUNY Press, 1997), John J. Stuhr develops a more Deweyan position.

11. See Richard J. Bernstein, *John Dewey* (), and *Praxis and Action* (Philadelphia: University of Pennsylvania Press, 1971).

12. At the conclusion of "The Crisis in Education," included as chapter 5 of *Between Past and Future: Eight Exercises in Political Thought*, Hannah Arendt notes that: "What concerns us all and cannot therefore be turned over to the special science of pedagogy is the relation between grown-ups and children in general or, putting it in even more general and exact

terms, our attitude toward the fact of natality: the fact that we have come
into the world by being born and that this world is constantly renewed
through birth" (196). Dewey as a parent and educator was keenly attuned
to what Arendt calls here "the fact of natality"; this attunement deeply
informs his account of subjectivity.

13. In *Toward a General Theory of Human Judgment* (NY: Dover
Publications, 1979), Justus Buchler offers what is, in some respects, a
radical critique of the Deweyan notion of human experience, offering in
place of this notion what he calls "proception": "The interplay of the human individual's activities and dimensions, their unitary direction, constitutes a process which I shall call *proception*. The term is designed to
suggest a moving union of seeking and receiving, of forward propulsion
and patient absorption. Proception is the composite, directed activity of the
individual" (4). Buchler's notion of proception is an attempt, within a naturalistic framework, to do fuller justice to individuality and selfhood than
Dewey or, indeed, any other naturalist has done thus far. A fuller defense
of the Deweyan position than I am able to provide here would have to
confront not only Buchler's criticisms but also assesss the relative merits
of these rival versions of the naturalistic outlook.

14. In an interview translated by Alan Bass and published in *Positions*
(Chicago: University of Chicago Press, 1981), Jacques Derrida suggests, in
reference to the concept of structure, that: "Everything depends upon how
one sets it to work. Like the concept of the sign—and therefore of semiology—it can simulataneously confirm and shake logocentric and ethnocen-
tric assuredness. It is not a question of junking these concepts, nor do we
have any means to do so. Doubtless it is more necessary, from within
semiology [or whatever discursive field one happens to be working], to
transform concepts, to displace them, to turn them against their presup-
positions, to reinscribe them in other chains, and little by little to modify
the terrain of our work and thereby produce new configurations; I do not
believe in decisive ruptures. . . . Breaks are always, and fatally, reinscribed
in an old cloth that must continually, interminably be undone" (24). Dewey's
own philosophical reconstructions, including those pivoting around experience and subjectivity, fit the process described by Derrida. Indeed, Dewey's
own eventual despair regarding his reconstruction of "experience" might
be related to what Derrida says about the interminability of the task. In
a much later manuscript, Dewey confessed that: "Were I to write (or re-
write) *Experience and Nature* today I would entitle the book *Culture and
Nature.* . . . I would abandon the term 'experience' because my growing
realization that the historical obstacles which prevented understanding of
my use of 'experience' are, for all practical purposes, insurmountable. I
would substitute the term 'culture' because with its meanings as now
firmly established it can full and freely carry my philosophy of experience"
(LW 1:361; cf. viii; xii–xvii). But would it have been desirable or even

possible for Dewey simply to junk "experience"? While it is easy to appreciate the frustration which Dewey felt when his concept of experience was so repeatedly and profoundly misunderstood, my own sense is that is was and still is a question of how one sets to work *on* and *with* this and related concepts.

15. Dewey himself makes this point in countless contexts. For example, he points out that: "The excuse for saying obvious things is that much that now passes for empiricism [and, we might add, for common sense] is but a dialectical elaboration of data taken from physiology, so that it is necessary for any one, who seriously sets out to philosophize, to recall to attention that he is talking about the sort of thing that the unsophisticated man calls experience, the life he has led and undergone in the world of persons and things. Otherwise we get a stencilled stereotype in two dimension and in black and white instead of the solid and many colored play of activities and sufferings which is the philosopher's real datum" (LW 1:368–369). In an early essay entitled "Why Study Philosophy?" (EW 4:62–65) he makes a case for the study of philosophy in terms of the need to examine the origins and antecedents of those ideas that determine for us what appears to be obvious (LW 4:62). In the opening chapter of *Experience and Nature*, Dewey makes essentially the same case, acknowledging that: "We cannot achieve recovery of primitive naiveté. But there is attainable a cultivated naiveté of eye, ear, and thought, one that can be acquired only through the discipline of severe thought" (LW 1: 40).

16. This paper originated as a talk given at St. John's University (Queens, NY). While developing Dewey's position in contrast to Thomas' views was originally due to my desire to address an audience in which Thomas would have able and enthusiastic defenders, the contrast has (I hope) merits for other audiences.

17. What most Deweyans will most likely find objectionable about this suggestion is not the attempt to make room for a religious (or spiritual) sensibility, but the attribution of a substantialist ontology to a thinker who was an indefatigable critic of virtually any and every notion of substance. But the attribution of such an ontology to Dewey is certainly not my intention: the historically thick continua designated by uniquely designating expressions are, simply in a manner of speaking, spiritual substances, for they embody what Dewey himself calls Spirit and (in addition) possess inherently the capacity to feel awe, wonder, mystery, etc.

18. In "The Objectivism-Subjectivism of Modern Philosophy," an essay from this same period, Dewey (who is so often militantly anti-subjectivist) asserts that: "The organism is one 'object' among others. However, the function of organic factors is so distinctive that it has to be discriminated. When it is discriminated, it is seen to be so different in kind from that of physical subject-matter as to require a special name. As a candidate for

the name, 'subjective' has one great disadvantage, namely, its traditional use as a name for some sort of existential stuff called psychical or mental. It has, on the other hand, the advantage of calling attention to the particular agency through which the function is exercised: a singular organism, an organism that has been subjected to acculturation, and is aware of itself as a social subject and agent" (LW 14:199).

19. In "The Vanishing Subject of Contemporary Discourse: A Pragmatic Response" in *The Journal of Philosphy* (LXXXVII, 11:644–655) and also in "Purpose, Power, and Agency" in *The Monist* (75, 4:423–444) I have, in ways complementing the emphases of this chapter, treated various aspects of the pragmatic centrality of human agency.

5

Theology as Healing:
A Meditation on *A Common Faith*

═══════

Douglas R. Anderson

In dealing with *A Common Faith*, commentators often fall into some discussion of whether Dewey's use of the term "God" in the text is adequate to our accounts of religious experience. Another standard response has been to ask whether Dewey is actually dealing with experience that is religious or with some other experiential phenomenon such as commitment, hope, or belief.[1] These seem inevitably to constitute a philosophical approach to the text. I do not believe such encounters have proved fruitless, but my aim in the present essay is a bit different. Here I intend to let Dewey's text have its way in hope that I can hear, perhaps better than I have previously done, what Dewey has to say. It may not be quite accurate to call such an approach a "meditation"; yet, in dwelling on and in the text I hope to approximate something like a mood that might rightly be called meditative.

I begin by noting that *A Common Faith* is constituted of the Terry Lectures that Dewey gave at Yale in the early thirties. They were written initially to be read aloud; indeed, they were written to be heard. They are, I think, in Dewey's own way of speaking, sermons of salvation, though not of final salvation. They are meant to involve a redemptive value. Listening to—and hearing—a sermon is, of course, a very different activity from listening to a philosophical treatise. Furthermore, a sermon seeks not a philosophical analysis in response, but an attentive meditation concerning what is spoken—and perhaps action as well. When coming under the sway

of a religious speech, as I intend to do here, it is important to know
something of the intended audience. A letter that Dewey wrote to
Private Charles E. Witzell aboard the "Triton" in 1943 is instructive in this connection.[2] First, we note Dewey's denial of a negative
aim: "It may be a help if I say whom I had in mind in writing the
book. I have taught many years and I don't think that any students
would say that I set out to undermine anyone's faith . . ." (Witzell,
p. 1). Thus, the many denials of preexistent gods, substances, and
telea that Dewey makes should be taken primarily not as attempts
to undermine Christianity and other religions, but as attempts to
partially explain, or at least to describe, to Dewey's intended audience the condition in which they already find themselves. Dewey
reveals his audience in his letter. "The lectures making up the book
were meant for those whose religious beliefs had been abandoned,
and who were given the impression that their abandonment left
them without any religious beliefs whatever. I wanted to show
them that religious values are not the monopoly of any one class
or sect and are still open to *them*" (Witzell, p. 1).[3] The salvific,
redemptive dimensions of the lectures—or sermons—are thus intended. As I proceed, then, I want to keep in mind that Dewey is
not only *talking about* a common faith but is actually trying to
inspire us to have such a faith. The irony is that, contra Santayana,
Dewey's common faith is *not* "a very common faith"; on the contrary, it is uncommon enough to require an appeal from one of the
twentieth century's most important thinkers.

Dewey shared with his predecessor Charles Peirce a deep dis-
taste for theology because of its inherent tenacity and authori-
tarianism. Peirce believed theology doubly dangerous because it
masqueraded as a science while operating in effect as the practice
of damning individuals and excluding them from particular communities. In Dewey's way of thinking this divisiveness of theology
is traceable to religion itself, since "religions hold that the essential
framework is settled in its significant moral features at least, and
that new elements that are offered must be judged by conformity
to this framework. Some fixed doctrinal apparatus is necessary for
a religion" (LW 9: 18–19). What sense then do I make in discussing
A Common Faith through the notion of "theology"? Needless to say,
whatever sense I make must result form a reconstruction of "theology." My aim is to see Dewey's theology as a glimpse into the
nature of human healing. The incentive for this aim is to be found
in Dewey's intentional employment of the vernacular term "God."

He opens the first lecture with an acknowledgment that his use of the term will make enemies in both traditionalist and reform camps. But he insists on the term; that is to say, he insists not that *we* must use it but that *he* must use it. Where there is "God," there may be theology, not perhaps in the traditional sense of a system of texts and doctrines, but in the more aboriginal sense of a story of God's work. The work that Dewey's God seems to be up to when one thinks with the lectures is that of healing—of mending, unifying, and ameliorating.

In thinking back to the letter to Witzell, we can see a purpose in Dewey's employment of "God." His speech is about healing and itself intends to heal; it is not about undermining anyone's faith. In using "God" he offers himself an opportunity to revise belief without shattering it. There is a clear continuity for Dewey between the traditional powers of the Christian God (and other gods) and the unifying function of human experience that he hopes to disclose. A strident atheism, from his perspective, not only breaks continuities with past belief, but reveals itself as cynical and non-constructive. Through his sermon-lectures Dewey hopes to distill from human experience a religious attitude that is unifying and constructive.

This said, Dewey's God stands before us as one thoroughly transformed. No "unseen power" or fixed, arbitrary authority sits at the beginning (or the end) of Dewey's cosmos. His is a God found only *in medias res*, working where human experience meets its own deepest challenges and highest rewards. "It is this *active* relation between ideal and actual to which I would give the name 'God,'" Dewey says (LW 9:34). This active relation constitutes God, in Dewey's ugly way of putting it, as a "function." I say "ugly," yet I do so without a fully pejorative intent. Dewey preaches not about romantic or isolated ideals or states of perfection, but of a power that can reach into the petty strivings of plain human existence and set them aright if only provisionally. I see no harm—indeed, in the ugliness there is a uniquely American charm—in calling such a God a "function" (LW 9:35). "In a distracted age," says Dewey, "the need for such an idea is urgent" (LW 9:35). The active and functional transaction between ideal and actual constitutes Dewey's God; this story of God establishes the theological premises—the place—on and around which the sermons of *A Common Faith* operate. The rest of my meditation will dwell on the pragmatic meaning of this God as function: the unifying of self with universe and, consequently, of self with itself.

Dewey's uplifting speech continues in its dual function, at once talking about God as if one were conducting a philosophy of religion and taking account of God's work, thus theologizing by describing the grounds on which the religious attitude operates. This double way of speaking is also at work in his description of God's function as healing. That is, as we have seen, the healing of estranged, mid-century selves is what drives the lectures; we must suppose, from Dewey's point of view, that something of the divine function is meant to be disclosed in the performances of the lectures as well as in their content.

I employ the word "healing" for several reasons. First, Dewey through the use of medical analogies suggests it. In describing the work of social intelligence as an example of divine work, Dewey makes one such analogy:

> It is possible to trace to some extent these evils [social problems] to their causes, and to causes that are something very different from abstract moral forces. It is possible to work out and work upon remedies for some of the sore spots. The outcome will not be a gospel of salvation but it will be in line with that pursued, for example, in matters of disease and health (LW 9:51).

Second, "healing" bears a sense of its own finitude. The awkward term "wholing" might accomplish the same work I (and Dewey) have in mind. But the notions of "wholes" and "making whole" are too often—mistakenly I think—seen as allied with completion and closure. Healing, on the other hand, is provisional and imperfect, always leaving traces of what is being mended. This squares, as we will see, with Dewey's belief that divine work is ameliorative and not final. And, finally, "healing" captures Dewey's sense that God's work is an ongoing attempt to regain and retain stability and integrity in the face of a precarious existence. Dewey's common faith has to do with each of these dimensions of healing, of making ourselves whole.

The active relation between ideal and actual that constitutes Dewey's God forces us to see the religious dimension of experience in two different though related directions. First, it draws us toward the imaginative ideals that stand on one side of the relationship, placing future constraints on what can be done. Dewey warns us repeatedly, in the vein of R. G. Collingwood, not to confuse imaginative ideals with "fantastic" or "fictional" ideals:

> The idea that "God" represents a unification of ideal values that is essentially imaginative in origin when the imagination supervenes in conduct is attended with verbal difficulties owing to our frequent use of the word "imagination" to denote fantasy and doubtful reality. But the reality of ideal ends as ideals is vouched for by their undeniable power in action (LW 9:29–30).

There lurks in Dewey's account a deep affinity for a kind of Peircean realism of ideals and an Emersonian affection for the freeing power of thought. In thinking on this point, we must remember that Dewey sees a very dramatic sense of life and power in ideals and in their unification—a kind of ideal of ideals. We in part create these ideals, not *ex nihilo*, but under the influence of what current conditions and constraints allow us to see as possible. "The idealizing imagination seizes upon the most precious things found in the climacteric moments of experience and projects them" (LW 9:33). They are our ideals to tend to and their conversion to practice requires that *we* care for them, nurture and cherish them. In the midst of our ongoing instability as human creatures, in our precariousness, these ideals stand before us as worthy of worship. It is their power that offers us real possibilities for our own futures. Dewey repeatedly, in each of his speeches, puts this religious dimension of experience before us:

> all endeavor for the better is moved by faith in what is possible, not by adherence to the actual (LW 9:17).

> Were the naturalistic foundations and bearings of religion grasped, the religious element in life would emerge from the throes of the crisis in religion. Religion would then be found to have its natural place in every aspect of human experience that is concerned with the estimate of possibilities as yet unrealized, and with all action in behalf of their realization. All that is significant in human experience falls within this frame (LW 9:38–39).

Dewey brings us, in a very Jamesian way, face to face with our own possibilities. We may face them with faith or without, but the attitudes of faith and doubt have different practical consequences with which we must be willing to live. Given any time and place, persons are able to maintain a *quaerens* of ideals, a *quaerens* exercised with care and cherishing for the ideals. In this much, Dewey's "God" is real in the way of the God of Peirce; that is, real in the power of ideals and their possibilities, but not *existent* as a being. There is, nevertheless, a crucial existential dimension to Dewey's God, for it is the *actualizing* of ideals that locates God as function, not the ideals taken *in abstracto*.

It has long been a trademark of philosophers to emphasize the importance of purpose in human endeavor. Too often, however, purposes have been read off as fixed *telea* that are either met or not. *A Common Faith* loosens up the nature of purpose. Like Peirce, Dewey sees the actualizing of ideals as developmental; and like Peirce and James, he *sees* purposes in their embodiment. Purposes do not stand out in front of us awaiting some instant of fulfillment. Nor are they merely mental phenomena:

> They have modified institutions. Aims, ideals, do not exist simply in "mind"; they exist in character, in personality and action (LW 9:33).

Dewey's use of "in" here is not metaphorical. A deep sense of purpose is only attained when purpose is lived in its embodiment. Moreover, insofar as they exist *in* character, personality, and action, purposes are dynamic: "Ideals change as they are applied in existent conditions" (LW 9:34). Imagined possibilities meet their specific limitations in practice. Thus, Dewey's God is nothing static; it is the unify*ing*, the heal*ing*, that occurs in the "*active* relation between ideal and actual" (LW 9:34). The religious dimension, which reveals a clear concern for the ideals and their creation, finds its other element of worship in the existential actualizing of ideals: "A clear and intense conception of a union of ideal ends with actual conditions is capable of arousing steady emotion" (LW 9:35).

Finding God in the transaction of ideal and actual makes sense enough. Yet, in its general formulation, this suggestion has a philosophical rather than a religious feel to it. Dewey reveals the "preaching" dimension of his work when he asserts that "a clear idea of that function [of a "working union of the ideal and the actual"] seems to me urgently needed at the present time" (LW 9:35). However, apart from drawing us to a faith in this function, Dewey has promised to keep silent, by and large, about content, about specific ideals and actualizations. A sermon without particularity, without the sharp edge of experiential examples, is in a difficult situation. To stay within my meditation on the text at this juncture, I must recall Dewey's interest in a particular audience or congregation. If we place ourselves in that audience, we can see how Dewey must finesse this point of impasse. We know the conditions of our own religious *quaerens* in the current climate; it is upon *us* that Dewey must rely. The success of his sermon hinges on *our* imaginative powers; we must flesh out the generic faith with elements from our own experiential careers. Ironically, then, it is precisely at this point where Dewey's sermon is about to founder under its own constraints that we—as congregation—are awakened to a common faith. It is Dewey's own faith in a common faith that allows him to move forward without—as he often did—showing us the cash value of it all. In this part of the transaction it is up to the listener to act.

Meditating on this peculiarity of Dewey's text, I find myself with two options: to offer my own experiential reading of the divine function or to work through the general upshot of the function that Dewey describes. To pursue the first option would probably draw out the religious feeling that is so carefully embedded in the text. At the same time, it would serve to narrow the conceptions readers have of Dewey's sense of religiosity and would likely lead to discussions dealing with my specification, leading us away from Dewey's work at hand. Pursuing the second option, however, would leave us, from here on out, always on the brink of losing meditation to the more strictly philosophical feel of the lectures. Still, if we advance as Dewey hopes, with *our* own experiences filling the blanks, we need not lose the contemplative mood. Moreover, I have promised to let the text direct my response, and to choose option one would work against that promise. What, then, in general terms, *is* the upshot of Dewey's God? What can a Deweyan theologian say?

To say anything, I think, I must return to the healing dimension of the divine function. Healing, as I have suggested, has to do not only with a sense of stability in one's environment, but with wholeness. Wholeness adds a positive dimension to our being; it comes in the guise of something we can affirm. Stability, in itself, is more negative in its import, portraying an absence of interference. Wholeness, on the other hand, projects a felt sense of empowerment in addition to the lived results of negative freedom, of being free from a felt precariousness. Wholeness, however, is not a fixed state of being. Rather, it is, on one side, an imaginative ideal in which all of our relations are presented with clarity as in harmony. On its other side, it is an actual feeling of having a place and of movement toward such an ideal. This feeling remains aware of its transitional nature. Dewey makes the first point directly:

> Neither observation, thought, nor practical activity can
> attain that complete unification of the self which is called
> a whole. The *whole* self is an ideal, an imaginative projec-
> tion. Hence the idea of a thoroughgoing and deep-seated
> harmonizing of the self with the Universe (as a name for
> the totality of conditions with which the self is connected)
> operates only through imagination. . . . (LW 9:14).

The actualizing of unifying ideals, in pragmatic terms, is the
only avenue to wholeness open to us. We feel or have felt its effects—if not, then Dewey's sermon must lose its effect on us. The
traditional retreat into the arms of a fixed absolute being, from
Dewey's perspective, reveals itself as self-deception when, instead
of empowering individuals and communities to ameliorate their
conditions, it either takes persons away from active engagement
with the world or leads them to establish exclusionary practices
with unseemly effects. The divine function, on the other hand, heals
through three levels of relation.

The first and most general level we have already encountered:
individuals and communities become adjusted to the projected
environment we call the universe. Through actualizing our ideals—
through purposive conduct—we find an acceptable place and way
of being in the midst of the vastness we project. In short, Dewey's
faith supposes us able, without self-deception, to respond in concrete fashion to Pascal's existential concerns about human finitude.
Not by mere contemplation, but by ameliorative, purposed activities we make ourselves at home in the world.

The second level of relation to which healing applies involves
the adjustments of selves and communities to other selves and
communities. Other selves and communities are, needless to say,
part of the environment as "universe." However, they constitute
special relationships. On the one hand, they present themselves, as
do elements of the physical world, as items and events to which we
must respond. On the other hand, other selves and communities
provide the unique opportunity for communication, shared experience, and cooperation. Thus, the divine function is something we
may have in common with others. This commonness allows us to
develop and expand community and thus empower further the divine
function itself. That is, our power of healing is increased with an
expanded community living in a common faith:

The position of natural intelligence is that there exists a *mixture* of good and evil, and that reconstruction in the direction of the good which is indicated by ideal ends, must take place if at all, through continued cooperative effort (LW 9:32).

It is this second level of healing for which Dewey has always been best known. The development of expansive and inclusive community is at once the result of the divine function on social relations *and* that which further empowers the mending, healing, ameliorating activity of Dewey's God. Here, for Dewey, is the most open and accessible story of God. The divine function here shows its horizontal and vertical dimensions as it knits selves and communities across boundaries and across eras. It also reveals its continuity with Dewey's earlier moralism in *Democracy and Education*:

Ours is the responsibility of conserving, transmitting, rectifying and expanding of the heritage of values we have received that those who come after us may receive it more solid and secure, more widely accessible and more generously shared than we have received it (LW 9:57–58).

Nevertheless, however central the healing of selves in relation to communities is, it is not the last relation with which Dewey deals. What is still at the heart of *A Common Faith*, though it is sometimes overlooked, is a healing in the self's relationship with itself. Dewey makes the point in passing on his way to focusing on the first two levels of relationship:

And it is pertinent to note that the unification of the self throughout the ceaseless flux of what it does, suffers, and achieves, cannot be attained in terms of itself. The self is always directed toward something beyond itself and so its own unification depends upon the idea of the integration of the shifting scenes of the world into that imaginative totality we call the Universe (LW 9:14).

Read in reverse, Dewey's focus on our relationships to the universe and to human communities is intended to show us how the divine function can effect a unifying and healing of the self. Again, his letter to Witzell makes it clear that his sermons are aimed at helping lost or, at least, alienated and destabilized individuals. It also becomes apparent at this juncture that one of the ways he intends to begin this healing process—his own actualizing of an ideal—is to lay the grounds for the individuals in his audience to develop a community. Throughout "The Human Abode of the Religious Function" Dewey presses the importance of community. Though it is of course "philosophical" language in one sense, it is just as clearly performative, religious language in another. If not, the final two lines must sound extremely peculiar. "Such a faith has always been implicitly the common faith of mankind. It remains to make it explicit and militant" (LW 9:58). Dewey, in the manner of Thoreau, would wake us up to bring us back to ourselves. And to bring us back to ourselves, he has found it necessary to take us beyond ourselves.

The healing of the self, in Dewey's triadic set of reciprocal relations, requires healing beyond the self. Indeed, he maintains that amelioration can only really occur when all three levels are addressed. There is no simple dichotomy between changing institutions and changing individual souls; there is no healing without a transactional change in both. Insofar as unifying truly occurs, insofar as mending occurs at all three levels of relationship, the divine function is realizing itself—having its proper effect. This, in Dewey's theology, constitutes the *reality* of God. This God-function, then, permits us in the fullest sense possible to be religious "persons of the world" and not isolated, alienated agnostics.

Conclusion

As I noted earlier, one way that Dewey's sermon-lectures are apt to fail is through the absence of experiential content. We must work to find ourselves in his congregation. Having found our place in the congregation, however, we encounter a second tendency to failure. That is, if we must, as I suggested above, fill in the details of a common faith with our experiential content, we are liable to begin mistaking this content for a common faith. Dewey's sermons could hardly fail more fully on their own terms if this occurs, for then our explicitness and militancy may mean a return to religions and not a move into the clearing of the religious attitude. I end my meditation, therefore, with a reflection on an earlier point—a point that Dewey drives home repeatedly in his speech. God's healing involves the human *quest* for wholeness and not the fixing of the wholeness itself.[4] My experience is no substitute for a common faith; it is simply the place where this faith gets transitionally and provisionally embodied. This is by no means a new thought in the career of human thinking; but in a set of sermons for the lost souls of the post-Darwinian era, it seemed to Dewey to bear repeating.

Notes

1. I must include much of my own work in this description.

2. I came across this letter in William Ernest Hocking's copy of *A Common Faith* in his library in Madison, New Hampshire.

3. Cf. *John Dewey: The Later Works, Volume 14*, ed. Jo Ann Boydston (Carbondale: Southern Illinois University Press, 1989), pp. 79–81. All subsequent references to the *Later Works* will be inserted in the text as LW followed by volume number, colon, and page number.

4. For an extended treatment of this difference in the Christian tradition, see Carl Vaught, *The Quest for Wholeness* (Albany: SUNY Press, 1986).

of romanticism is hardly flattering. Declaring it a source of the pessimism of his age, he describes romanticism as "the attempt to find the satisfactions of life in the enjoyment of intense emotions; in the constant renewal of feeling; in the production of remote and unwonted sentiment." Such remarks may seem odd to those who know Dewey as the author of *Art as Experience*, a book laced with admiring allusions to the likes of Wordsworth, Keats, Shelley, Coleridge, Whitman, and Emerson, and as the defender of a vision of democracy as the social form where human experience most fully realizes its potential to be both means and end—to approximate, in Dewey's favored sense to the term, to *art*. It is virtually impossible to read *Art as Experience*, or for that matter books like *A Common Faith* or *Experience and Nature*, without thinking that Dewey was some kind of romantic. And so he was, to a greater degree than any major American philosopher of the last century. But what kind?

A full answer to such a question would entail sorting through Dewey's entire sprawling corpus—not to mention through the sprawling history of the term "romanticism" itself. It is a term whose applications today range from subjects like aesthetics and hermeneutic anthropology to nationalism and liberalism. As Dewey's friend and critic A.O. Lovejoy argued in a classic study, there is not one romanticism but many.[3] So, given the breadth of the term's applications, not to mention the length of Dewey's corpus, my story will be selective. My larger thesis is that the mature Dewey came to find in the romantic tradition a rich resource for his pragmatic vision of the relation between the self and the natural and social world, and that this justifies our viewing him as a kind of recon-structed—and in his sense of the term, reconstruct*ing*—romantic. To most students of Dewey, the thesis itself should need little ar-gument, but the story of how he came to warrant this description—a story which leads through various Deweyan texts usually not grouped together and which therefore becomes a story about his pragmatism as a whole—does. I begin with some further comments on the sources of the young Dewey's ambivalence towards the idea of romanticism. This will lead to a discussion of his reconstructive treatment of the traditional theme of the relations among mind, knowledge, and the world, as set forth in books like *The Quest for Certainty* and *Experience and Nature*. From there we will turn to *Art as Experience*, which presents Dewey's most distinctive strand of reconstructed romantic argument: the idea that experience is developmental. That idea undergirds his philosophy of art in well-known ways; but it also points in less appreciated ways to a vision of the self as part of a larger whole, naturally and socially speaking, a vision which links the argument of *Art as Experience* with his views on religion and democracy, as set forth in other later books such as *A Common Faith* and *Liberalism and Social Action*. Read together in the right way, these discussions reveal the outlines of a discernibly romantic temper in the mature Dewey's approach to the many-faceted problem he had earlier suggested was exacerbated by romanticism itself: the modern self's choice between pessimism and faith.

Early Ambivalence

In retrospect, it is easy to view Dewey's intellectual development as a sustained effort to recast in naturalistic language an intuition that on all accounts was central to romantic thought: the intuition that experience, borne of conflict, aspires to unity. Its most familiar expression in his mature writing is his campaign against dualisms of all kinds, a campaign in which he would redescribe various distinctions traditionally construed as reflecting "higher" and "lower" realms of being—like spirit versus flesh, theory versus practice, culture versus nature, and art versus science—as developmental continua grounded in the processes of nature. Even before discovering Hegel and Darwin in his twenties, Dewey was drawn to quasi-mystical visions of unity in the writings of such romantic writers as Whitman, Emerson, and Wordsworth. And although he was less impressed by the pantheism of Spinoza than were many English and German romantic writers, he remarks tellingly in the conclusion to his early essay on that subject that an acceptable version of Spinoza's idea that "all things are divine" must "start from the conception of things as they seem to be" and proceed "not by elevating them into God"—which he thought was Spinoza's mistake—but "by bringing God down to them."[4] Some such view must not have been far from his thoughts when, still in his early twenties, he had a mystical experience which he described later as having given him the sense that "everything that's here is here, and you can just lie back on it."[5]

It comes as no surprise that this is the same person who half a century later would describe aesthetic encounters with art and nature as continuous with "the animistic strain of religious experience."[6] But nowhere does the young Dewey use the word "romantic" to characterize his own sensibilities. He had already associated it with the degenerate *mal du siècle* which he found expressed in French writers like Baudelaire, Renan, and Flaubert, and in English writers like Byron; and over the next couple of decades European history would provide additional support for such negative associations. In his 1916 essay "The Mind of Germany," after noting the romantic roots of German nationalism, he writes that "the Romantic spirit [in German philosophy] has deliberately evaded the sifting of emotions and ideas; it has declined to submit them for valuation to the tests of hard and sober fact."[7] These words echo the argument of his 1915 *German Philosophy and Politics*, a selective reading of the Idealist roots of German nationalism which paid particular attention to the role of Fichte's "monistic ethical pantheism" in that history. The book's polemical focus is evidenced by the fact that it scarcely mentions other early nineteenth-century German figures such as Schelling and the Schlegels who, with Fichte, were equally influential in other romantic directions and in whose writings on art, nature, and related topics one detects prototypes of ideas—about which more below—that Dewey would transpose into a more naturalistic idiom in *Experience and Nature* and *Art as Experience*. In his 1922 *Human Nature and Conduct*, Dewey remarks in a critical spirit that the romantic temperament can take the form of rebelliousness borne of frustrated ideals or the form of a naive optimism which assumes a "pre-established harmony between natural impulse and natural objects."[8] Three years later, in *Experience and Nature*, he writes in a similar vein that "Romanticism has made the best and worst of the discovery of the private and incommunicable. . . . In conceiving that this inexpugnable uniqueness, this ultimate singularity, exhausts the self, it has created a vast and somnambulistic egotism out of the fact of subjectivity."[9]

Some of these unflattering references to romanticism were most likely due to Dewey's sense of the word's association with German nationalism in the public imagination. That he himself did go on, sensibly enough, to distinguish between German romantic thought's metaphysical and aesthetic bases and its political uses, however, is borne out by his comment in a 1916 review of George Santayana's *Egoism in German Philosophy*: "(E)ven when Mr. Santayana is pouring forth his vials of scorn upon German subjectivism, one has frequently a feeling that while he came to curse, he is remaining to bless—up to a certain point . . . [ ]. (H)e also sees what his own classic forbears did not see and what it has been the mission of German philosophy and reason to teach—that art after all is itself an achievement of instinct, of vitality and animal bias, under the conditions set by the interaction of instincts with nature and fellowmen. Consequently his criticism is never as complete and sweeping as is that of those writers in the classic tradition who retained unimpaired the belief in the descent of reason and art from on high."[10] Dewey seems to be describing his own sentiments here. Nonetheless, the less than charitable remarks cited above reflect two pervasive themes in his critical assessment of romanticism and of modern thought and practice as a whole which were taking shape in his thinking during these years.

(i) The first of these themes is that modern culture encourages its inhabitants to adopt a peculiarly fragmented attitude toward the nature of value. This attitude is reflected, for example, in the conventional philosophical distinction between intrinsic (or unconditioned) values, and instrumental (or conditioned) values. Such a distinction, as Dewey saw, can encourage the unhappy inference that a thing or practice or experience can be rationally valued for what it *is* or for what it *does* but not both—or the thought, as he would put it in *Theory of Valuation*, that there is no continuity between means and ends. If we try to value an experience or activity only for its own sake, we blind ourselves not only to the impact that the thing valued may itself have on other ends we value, but also to the impact that *our practice of valuing it* has on those ends. Similarly, if we habitually view certain human activities as possessing value only as means to further ends, we may blind ourselves not only to their own untapped potential for affording inherent satisfactions but also to the effect their instrumentalization has on the larger patterns of satisfactions, anticipations, and aversions which characterize our lives. Dewey saw that the error in the romantic tendency to enshrine feeling for its own sake lay in its failure to assume responsibility for the effects of its own adoption and in its failure to assume responsibility for acting constructively to change a social climate against which it was, he claimed, a rebellious response. *Art as Experience*, which appeared in 1934, was a sustained attack on one form in which this valuation of feeling for feeling's sake was being rapidly institutionalized in the modern world. This was the doctrine of art for art's sake, or in Dewey's idiom, the "compartmental conception of art." By this he meant the modern tendency to enshrine fine art as a preserve for the life of the higher feelings in a disenchanted world— making it a "religious rejection of the world" in Weber's sense— and to set it on a metaphysical and institutional pedestal apart from "the everyday events, doings, and sufferings, that are universally recognized to constitute experience."

(ii) About the positive theory of art which emerged from this critique, more presently. But let us turn to a second, and more fundamental, criticism of romanticism implicit in the passage above from *Experience and Nature*. Dewey believed that the romantic attitude encouraged overly compartmental conceptions of the self. To conceive of the self as a solitary repository of feeling obscures what Dewey repeatedly argued is the central feature of all experience, namely, that it emerges out of an ongoing interaction between the individual and its natural and cultural environment. This line of thinking informs *Experience and Nature*'s critique of the "exaggeration" and "isolation" of the ego in modern philosophy,[11] a critique in which Dewey portrayed this idea, as variously articulated by Descartes, Locke, Kant, and others, as a myth which has, in its wide modern acceptance, worked to undermine the coherence of day-to-day experience through contributing to the institutionalization of an invidious distinction between individual and society. This myth encourages modern thinkers to "start out with a naive assumption of minds connected with separate individuals. But developments soon show the inadequacy of such 'minds' to carry the burden of science and objective institutions, like the family and state. The consequence was revealed to be sceptical, disintegrative, malicious."[12]

As this last remark suggests, Dewey numbered scepticism among the dangers of individualism, and by implication of romanticism. His critique of scepticism—what there was of it—provides an instructive example of his view that philosophical criticism is continuous with social criticism. The critique's larger rationale, presented at length in such works as *Reconstruction in Philosophy* and *The Quest for Certainty*, involved redescribing "the problem of knowledge" as a social no less than philosophical difficulty whose diagnosis calls for an understanding of the collective anxiety about living in an unpredictable world, an anxiety which has lent modern secular philosophy's "quest for certainty" its peculiar urgency.[13] Modern philosophy's central mistake, as Dewey saw it, has been to promote epistemic ideals which are not commensurate with the "unfinished" character of experience and inquiry. The challenge to philosophy now is to learn to view those ideals themselves as forms of unfinished inquiry which arose as responses to certain local crises of belief within Western thought. That would provide the deflationary impetus needed for us to abandon our Cartesian habit of describing the phases of these interactions which we call knowing and doubting as happening *in here*, in the inner mental life of the subject, as opposed to *out there*, in the world, and to drop this habit not only in the theory of knowledge, but also in social and political theory, where it is further reflected in the dichotomy between the private sphere of the individual and the common life of the society. We would then find it easier to think of ourselves as simultaneously embodied and encultured parts of the world—which for Dewey means simply "nature"—along with the other parts known in modern philosophy as "objects" and "other minds."[14] This would in turn make it easier for us to accept our experiences of doubt and certainty in our commerce with those human and non-human parts of nature alike as equally normal phases in a larger experiential process that regularly throws us, individually and collectively, into situations that can *themselves*, Dewey liked to say, be doubtful and uncertain.

This line of antisceptical thought also runs, if not always on the surface, throughout *Art as Experience*, for example in the concluding paragraphs of "The Live Creature and Ethereal Things." After approvingly quoting Keats' commendation of Shakespeare as one who was "capable of being in uncertainties, mysteries, doubts, without any irritable reaching after fact or reason," Dewey remarks that "Ultimately there are but two philosophies. One of them accepts life and experience in all its uncertainty, mystery, doubt, and half-knowledge and turns that experience upon itself to deepen and intensify its own qualities—to imagination and art. This is the philosophy of Shakespeare and Keats." Dewey does not explicitly name the other philosophy. But in context it seems clear enough that he means any philosophy that portrays uncertainty and mystery as enemies of intelligence in its quest for knowledge of nature and culture, rather than as ineliminable ingredients in its processes and methods.

Antiscepticism and the "Marriage of Self and World"

The irony about the younger Dewey's criticisms of romanticism, of course, was that they were themselves, as the older Dewey of *Art as Experience* could well appreciate, romantic criticisms. They were directed not at the whole of romantic thinking, however that be defined, but at its more socially despondent, "Byronic" side. This is the side that the critic Morse Peckham has characterized as "negative romanticism,"[15] the side which accepted the Enlightenment image of Mind-as-projector-of-values-onto-purposeless-Nature enough to conclude that since value is not part of the fabric of the outer world as described by science, it is only by taking refuge in the inner life of feeling that we can still hope to find meaning in experience.[16] Here, as in many other connections, it is instructive to compare and contrast Dewey's thinking to Hegel's. Not unlike Hegel, who early in his career suspected that the free subjectivity celebrated by the poets of the *Sturm und Drang* was not as free as it appeared,[17] the young Dewey also sensed that the above romantic reaction against Enlightenment thinking failed to go far enough, and seemed indeed just to reinstate the very dualisms against which it railed. But Hegel had gone on, in Idealist fashion, to install a desensualized Philosophy as the successor to Art in his metaphysical epic of the coming-of-age of Spirit.[18] Dewey's later references to romantic writers and themes, in contrast, reflected his reading not only of Hegel but of Darwin. They had the effect of projecting a view of romanticism as a dialectical phenomenon whose celebration of immediate experience moves through a negative and "sceptical" phase in which the self is absorbed in the particularity of its own feeling to the point of being alienated from the world, into a positive phase in which the world begins to reveal itself through such particularity, thus reconnecting the self to a larger whole. This more dialectical image of romanticism amounts to a this-worldly, naturalized version of Hegel's story of the passage of Spirit through phases of rupture and reconciliation, a story which Hegel intended as a deep philosophical allegory of the *Bildungsromanen* of his day and, more broadly, of the Christian story of the fall and redemption of mankind.[19] It was Hegel's genius to grasp, at a level of unprecedented abstraction, how these stories are all in a sense the same story—a story rehearsed endlessly, and for the most part unconsciously, in Western philosophical debates about mind, knowledge, and the world as well as in our religion, poetry and painting. In Dewey we find a naturalized counterpart of this insight, and we will consider shortly how it led him to a romanticized and naturalized image of social hope.

In his study of American philosophy and the romantic tradition, Russell Goodman points out the centrality of the world-affirming face of romanticism to a tradition linking Emerson, James, and Dewey with recent American philosophers such as Stanley Cavell.[20] Epitomizing this tradition, for Goodman, is the antisceptical theme of "the marriage of self and world," a phrase

echoing some lines from Wordsworth's "The Recluse" which Dewey
surely knew:

> Beauty—a living Presence of the earth
> Surpassing the most fair of ideal Forms. . . .
> [W]aits upon my steps. . . .
> For the disarming intellect of Man,
> When wedded to this goodly universe
> In love and holy passion, shall find these
> A simple produce of the common day.

Dewey might well have used such lines as an epigraph to the
chapter in *Art as Experience* entitled "The Natural History of Form."
There he commends Wordsworth for his ability to incorporate into
his writing a consciousness of what the poet called "the infinite
variety of natural appearances." In Wordworth's writing we find a
clear exemplar, Dewey continues, of the "transition from the conventional, from something abstractly generalized that both sprang from
and conduced to incomplete perception, to the naturalistic—to an
experience that corresponded more subtly and sensitively to the
rhythm of natural change."[21] This remark is in one obvious sense an
allusion to the reconstructive project of *Art as Experience*; but at a
more basic level it also alludes to the conception of nature which
Dewey laid out most fully in *Experience and Nature*. That work
seems, indeed, to have been the pivotal point in the shift from Dewey's
earlier "anti-romantic" phase to the full-blown positive romanticism
of *Art as Experience*. For alongside its criticisms of "romantic" views
of the self, we also find in *Experience and Nature* the remark that

> Poets who have sung of despair in the midst of prosperity,
> and of hope amid darkest gloom, have been the true meta-
> physicians of nature. The glory of the moment and its trag-
> edy will surely pass. . . . [ ]. Thus something unpredictable,
> spontaneous, unformulable and ineffable is found in any
> terminal object. Standardizations, formulae, generalizations,
> principles, universals, have their place, but the place is
> that of being instrumental to better approximation to what
> is unique and unrepeatable. We owe to romanticism the
> celebration of this fact; no fact apparently being fully dis-
> covered and communicated save as it is too much celebrated.
> Aversion to romanticism as a philosophical system is quite
> justifiable; but even an obnoxious system may hit upon a

truth unknown to soberer schemes. Call the facts romantic
or by some sweeter sounding name, and it still remains
true that immediate and terminal qualities (whether or not
called consciousness) form an unpredictable and unfor-
mulatable flow of immediate, shifting, impulsive, adven-
tured finalities, with respect to which the universal and
regular objects and principles celebrated in classic thought
are instrumental.[22]

One detects here more than a casual echo not only of
Wordsworth but of German romantics like Friedrich Schlegel, who
said that "All the sacred play of art is only a distant copying of the
infinite play of the world, that work of art which is eternally refashioning itself"[23]; and also of Schleiermacher, who asked, "Why,
in the province of morals, does this pitiable uniformity prevail,
which seeks to bring the highest human life within the compass of
a single lifeless formula? How can this ever have come into vogue,
except in consequence of a radical lack of feeling for the fundamental characteristic of living Nature, which everywhere aims at diversity and individuality?"[24] Such writers epitomize the intellectual
transformation which Dewey's friend and critic Arthur O. Lovejoy
called the single most significant difference between pre- and post-
1800 thought and the most significant feature of the romantic revolution. This was the movement from "uniformitarian" to
"diversitarian" conceptions of nature and value—or, roughly, from
a view of nature and the sources of human values as governed by
static first principles knowable from a single idealized rational
standpoint to a view of such principles as subject to historical
development and culturally plural interpretation.[25] In recent philosophy we find the same distinction echoed with different emphases in dichotomies like "objectivism versus relativism" in
epistemology and "absolutism versus pluralism" in ethics. Dewey's
own experimentalist reinterpretation of the diversitarian vision took,
of course, many forms, and a more systematic discussion of his
recovery of romanticism could fruitfully pursue this theme as it
shaped his views on, besides metaphysics and epistemology, education, social psychology, politics, science, religion, and art. But enough
has been said now to set the stage for a discussion of Dewey's
treatment of the last item on this list, with particular reference to
two ideas that are articulated more clearly in *Art as Experience*
than in any other of Dewey's writings: the twin themes of the self's
expressiveness and of its *developmental* nature.

Expressivism in *Art as Experience*

What Dewey's philosophy of art inherits from English romantics like Wordsworth and Coleridge, and what they in turn inherited from Germans like Schelling, is the idea that for an age that has watched Reason become mired in dualisms and antinomies as it has tried to know the world as it is in itself, it is not to the scientist or the philosopher that we must ultimately turn for a coherent vision of our experience, but to the artist. For such an age, Art comes into its own to the extent that the idea of mind as the Mirror of Nature comes to be seen as a myth whose practical blessings have, at best, been mixed. We find a seminal expression of this sensibility in Schelling's *System of Transcendental Idealism* of 1800:

> Philosophy was born and nourished by poetry in the infancy of knowledge, and with it all those sciences it has guided toward perfection; we may thus expect them, on completion, to flow back like so many individual streams into the universal ocean of poetry from which they took their source. Nor is it in general difficult to say what the medium for this return of science to poetry will be; for in mythology such a medium existed, before the occurrence of a breach now seemingly beyond repair. But how a new mythology is itself to arise.... that is a problem whose solution can only be looked for in the future destinies of the world, and in the course of history to come.[26]

One finds a comparable emphasis on the centrality of art to human experience—though not, obviously, the same metaphysical backdrop—in *Art as Experience*, which reiterates *Experience and Nature*'s assertion that "[A]rt, the mode of activity that is charged with meanings capable of immediately enjoyed possession, is the complete culmination of nature, and.... science is properly a handmaiden that conducts events to this happy issue."[27] Dewey and Schelling in their different ways both present art as a redemptive force within modern secular culture. In so doing both participate in a tradition of understanding human experience that came to prominence at the end of the eighteenth century and which, with Charles Taylor, I will call *expressivism*.[28] The romantic deposit in *Art as Experience*, which presents an "expression theory of art,"[29] cannot be fully grasped without some reference to this larger understanding, and a few points from Taylor's account are worth reiterating.

The view that human life and activity are in some sense fundamentally "expressive," Taylor notes, is traceable to an early modern tension between two images of the relationship between human beings and nature. One is an essentially Aristotelian image of the human being as part of a single cosmic order graspable by reason—a "great chain of being" in Lovejoy's sense. In the second, more modern image, nature is cast as an Object which is opposed, metaphysically, to the Subject—a subject which, as the Aristotelian paradigm withers away, develops increasingly precise methods of knowing nature while at the same time encountering increasing obstacles to knowing itself as a part of a single encompassing totality. The subject is thus obliged in historically unprecedented ways to define itself. This new need for self-definition is for us now, of course, a familiar feature of what it is to be "modern," finding expression, for example, in the emergent modern ideals of freedom as autonomous action and as individual self-fulfillment. In *Sources of the Self* Taylor remarks that within such an atmosphere

> The modern subject is no longer defined just by the power of disengaged rational control but by this new power of expressive self-articulation as well—the power which has been ascribed since the Romantic period to the creative imagination. This works in some ways in the same direction as the earlier power; it intensifies the sense of inwardness and leads to an even more radical subjectivism and an internalization of moral sources. But in other respects these powers are in tension. To follow the first all the way is to adopt a stance of disengagement from one's own nature and feelings, which renders impossible the exercise of the second. A modern who recognizes both these powers is constitutionally in tension.[30]

This predicament forms the starting point of all modern philosophies of the subject which emphasize the unity of aspects of human nature that tended to be polarized in Enlightenment thinking—soul and body, reason and feeling—as well as of those philosophies which took the further step of valuing the roles of emotion, imagination, and will in experience over that of reason. The nineteenth century would see the emergence of new ways of picturing the self in relation to its inner "expressive" resources, going in one direction, and to its historically situated community, going in another. The political self-conceptions that flourished as a result varied widely, as becomes clear when one considers that Marx and Nietzsche, as well as Dewey's mentor Emerson, all belonged to this dispensation. What all shared was a new sense that the modern individual is thrown back, to an unprecedented degree, upon its own resources when it inquires into what it can know, what it can hope, and what it should do; to such a degree, indeed, that one's individuality itself is actively constituted through the unfolding narrative of events forming one's reflective and volitional history. What one's life *is* is not distinct from, but an emergent product of, what it *means* to that individual. Thus, to return to the theme of a moment ago, the process of self-realization is at the same time also a process of self-definition. To this extent, self-understanding then becomes less an affair of *epistemology*, in the sense of the latter term which connotes an idealized representational activity that abstracts from the self's local perspectives and interests, than of *hermeneutics*. Once this basic approach to understanding selfhood is accepted, it is but a short further step to assert, as Nietzsche went on to do, that one's life is, in a deep metaphysical sense, a kind of artwork.

If one reads *Art as Experience* alongside works like the *Ethics* and *Human Nature and Conduct*, it becomes clear that Dewey subscribed to a version of this line of thought almost as radical in its way as Nietzsche's, though with decidedly more hopeful social implications.[31] It redescribed the substantial selves postulated by more traditional philosophers as unfolding narratives informed by the ongoing interactions between selves and their cultural world, so that life, as Dewey put it, "is no uniform uninterrupted march or flow. It is a thing of histories, each with its own plot, its own inception and movement toward its close, each having its own particular rhythmic movement; each with its own unrepeated quality pervading it throughout."[32] This is essentially an expanded version of the same narrative image of the self that Dewey had years earlier placed at the center of his *Ethics*. He there argued that if a single ideal may fairly claim identification with "the human good," it is the ideal of *growth*. The good person, as he put it, "is precisely the one who is most . . . concerned to find openings for the newly forming or growing self; since no matter how 'good' he has been, he becomes 'bad' . . . as soon as he fails to respond to the demand for growth. Any other basis for judging the moral status of the self is conventional. In reality, direction of movement, not the plane of attainment and rest, determines moral quality."[33] And as with the individual, so too with the community:

experience, whether individual or collective, cannot thrive without the interplay between the old and the new, with a particular accent on the new.

That this view of the primacy of growth is the key link between Dewey's ethics and aesthetics becomes clear when one sees that underlying *Art as Experience*'s theory of fine art is the view that experience is in its nature developmental.[34] To have experience, Dewey holds, is to be capable not only of satisfying basic physical needs and desires but also of finding communicable meanings[35] in the objects and events which constitute one's interactive strivings-in-the-world. Depending on the circumstances under which we encounter or undergo them, we may imaginatively link objects or events with the future: in this case our experience is in an "instrumental" phase. Or, we may attend to such events or objects primarily as qualitative presences in the here and now, in which case our experience is in a "final" phase. These phases may also be co-present, as happens at moments when one's imaginative awareness of an experience's future import, or its role as the consequence of past striving, contributes to that experience's own qualitative intensity.[36] Such moments exhibit a higher degree of development, both phenomenologically and axiologically, than do those in which instrumentality or finality alone predominates. They represent experience's "consummatory" phase. What gives a consummatory experience its special quality is not just the fact of emotional or imaginative intensity but also a felt sense of unity among the phenomenal elements of the experience, as well as between the present moment and other moments in one's past or projected future history.

It is here, in the notion of consummatory experience, that the expressivist theme of self-definition shows itself most distinctively in Dewey's argument. Upon having an experience with marked consummatory quality, I have the sense that my life has achieved enough narrative closure to release my energies for the reassessment of past purposes and the pursuit of new ones; I feel that in some large or small way, my life is literally entering a new "chapter." Dewey intends this not simply as a phenomenological claim about what it is like for me to be the self I am but as an ontological claim. Being neither a Kantian transcendental ego nor a self whose individuating features are otherwise substantially pre-structured (as in Freudian metapsychology), I am continually subject to a process of becoming whose limits are, constraints of biology apart, just the limits of my ability to shed or reconstruct old habits and form new ones. Thus, regardless of how I may picture my identity metapsychologically, my life is literally an adventure, and its shape along any number of dimensions—aesthetic, ethical, and so on—is determined substantially by the consummatory experiences I have.[37]

Some consummatory experiences, in addition, are characterized by an intensified awareness of the qualities of an object. Under such conditions, the experience and the object itself are both *aesthetic*. ("An object is peculiarly and dominantly aesthetic . . . when the factors that determine anything which can be called an experience are lifted high above the threshold of perception and are made manifest for their own sake.") That experiences of this kind can occur in a vast range of human situations including (but not only in) the fine arts, and that they are of great intrinsic and instrumental significance to those who have them, Dewey regards as central data for aesthetic theory. And this brings us, finally, to art itself. Art occurs when a consummatory experience with a marked degree of aesthetic quality leads, through the agency of the subject, to the production of further such experiences not merely for the subject but for others as well:

> Art is a quality of doing and of what is done. . . . Since it
> adheres to the manner and content of doing, it is adjectival
> in nature. When we say that tennis-playing, singing, act-
> ing, and a multitude of other activities are arts, we engage
> in an elliptical way of saying that there is art in the con-
> duct of these activities, and that this art so qualifies what
> is done and made as to induce activities in those who per-
> ceive them in which there is also art. The *product* of art—
> temple, painting, statue, poem—is not the *work* of art. The
> work takes place when a human being cooperates with a
> product so that the outcome is an experience that is en-
> joyed because of its liberating and ordered properties.[38]

The *work of art*, for Dewey, is not an inanimate object but an action. More exactly, it is an interaction between an individual—the artist—and some productive medium, intellectual or material, by which means the artist confers a new order on elements of her experience which were previously felt to be less ordered. This interaction, culminating in the art product (what is conventionally known as the work of art), is the consummation of a specific history of the artist's prior activity, funded by the qualitatively diverse

experiences constituting that history. These reappear in symboli-
cally mediated form as qualitative aspects of the art product, which
then can occasion in an audience an experience that is itself, to
some relevant extent, a reconstruction of the artist's experience.
Art thus amounts not only to a form of *inquiry* in Dewey's sense of
that term, which he would later define in the *Logic* as "the controlled or directed transformation of an indeterminate situation
into one that is so determinate in its constituent distinctions and
relations as to convert the elements of the original situation into a
unified whole"[39]; it is also a form of communication. And although
art is epitomized, in present-day society, in the special compartmentalized cluster of practices we know as the fine arts, there is no
reason in principle why human actions might not become art in "a
multitude of other activities" as well, including our ethical deliberations[40] and our engagement in work outside the fine arts, in
blue-collar work as well as in education, science, philosophy, or
government. Viewed in such general terms, art is not, in Max
Weber's sense, a relatively autonomous "sphere of value" possessed
of its own bureaucratically specific forms of means-ends reasoning[41], as might be claimed about the practices which more narrowly
constitute the "artworld." Rather, it is a potential inherent in all
spheres.

   We may call this broadening of the scope of "art" Dewey's *aestheticism*. It represents his version of a pattern of argument implicit in nineteenth-century writers such as Emerson, Ruskin, and
Morris, although it is most familiar today in connection with
Nietzsche and his poststructuralist followers. Aestheticism in this
sense, which is not to be confused with the term's narrower and
more traditional art-for-art's sake usage, is a dialectical reaction
against traditional aesthetic theory's hierarchical distinction between the fine arts and other areas of cultural production; or between "art" and "life." It consists, first, of dropping the latter
distinction, and second, of investing items traditionally lumped
under the heading of "life" with logical attributes formerly reserved
for the fine arts. This strategy constitutes the more radical face of
Art as Experience's argument against the compartmentalizing tendencies of modern aesthetic theories. I argue more fully elsewhere
that Dewey's larger aim was to find a dialectical way of reconciling
two views of the nature of art which do not sit well together within
the ahistorical framework of traditional aesthetics.[42] One is the
belief that, in present-day society, the fine arts are unique in the
ways they promote shared consummatory experience, and that they

enjoy a certain autonomy in light of that uniqueness. The other is the belief that the most basic philosophical distinction which makes such uniqueness intelligible—the distinction between fine and useful production—is not necessary to our thinking about human affairs, but is rather a convention rooted in the acceptance of certain contingent social conditions which are themselves not in all cases healthy. The general tension between these two approaches to understanding art (and "art") has been described in various ways in modern aesthetics. The most familiar of these descriptions is in terms of the contrasting ideas that the fine arts are *autonomous* as a source of value, and that they are *instrumental*, respectively—where being instrumental implies that the defining value of those practices resides in their promotion of some end or ends that might in principle be promoted through instrumentalities other than art. Dewey's way of negotiating this tension involved, first, describing the aesthetic variety of consummatory experience as an end promoted by our interactions with works of find art but not only by those interactions; and second, suggesting that even though the fine arts provide richer settings for the promotion of such experience than other areas of social practice at the present moment in history, this need not remain the case in a possible social future in which the discontinuities between means and ends pervading present-day institutional life may, for all we know, be lessened.

The kind of dialectical view of art just sketched is not a particularly common one in twentieth-century aesthetics. To see it as a coherent part of Dewey's argument in *Art as Experience*, one needs to be willing to interpret certain portions of that text in accordance with some Hegelian sentiments about the development of culture which Dewey expressed more fully elsewhere.[43] In any case Dewey was consciously walking a delicate line between affirming a compartmentalized division between art and life as two separate spheres of ontology and social practice, as was characteristic of more conventional writing in aesthetics, and completely collapsing the art/life distinction altogether. On the one hand, he agreed with writers like Schiller, Schelling, and Arnold that life is hardly equivalent to art for the vast majority of modern people, whose workaday lives are pervaded with familiar discontinuities between means and ends (what Marx had described as alienation), and that to this extent we all have good reason to prize the fine arts for their ability to offer richer possibilities of experience than do other social practices. Yet he also agreed with writers like Emerson, Ruskin, and Morris that traditional aesthetic theory's habit of exalting "fine" over "useful" forms of production has itself contributed to the legitimization of such discontinuities. For along with its promotion of Arnoldian sweetness and light, the institutionalization of the fine/useful distinction has also functioned to reinforce the undemocratic idea that leisure-class tastes in fine art are somehow inherently "purer" than the tastes of those consigned to lives of "useful" work, when in fact many utilitarian activities—the activities of skilled craftsmen, for example—*can* sustain experiences of artistic quality. It thus does not follow from the contingent fact that the fine arts may in fact at the present historical moment be superior to other areas of everyday "useful" production as sources of art in experience, that this superiority is inherent to fine art practices as such.

Once we understand *Art as Experience* along these lines, it is easy to see how Dewey was in effect elaborating upon various romantic theses about fine art to suggest his own pragmatized version of the romantic theme that life aspires to the character of art. And it becomes clearer how his philosophy of art is continuous not only with his views of the self/world relation discussed earlier, but also with another area of his thinking not touched upon yet: his social philosophy. A key to both connections is *Art as Experience*'s lack of any reference to aesthetic experience, whether it be occasioned through participation in fine art-related activities or in "ordinary life," as a private affair in the inner life of a solitary subject. The self that makes and appreciates art in experience is connected to the world in a variety of metaphysical and social ways. That Dewey thought this way is hardly a surprise, given both his Hegelian roots and his lifelong commitment to the idea that in democracy the expressive aims of human beings come, or at least approximate, to fruition. Democracy, as he put it in an early essay, is "the ultimate, ethical ideal of humanity" in which "the distinction between the spiritual and the secular has ceased."[44] Given his view of traditional aesthetics as overly wedded to a spiritualizing conception of its subject, it seems likely that, even if he never said so in as many words, Dewey viewed *Art as Experience*'s critique of traditional aesthetic dualisms between fine art and life as part of the larger democratic project of overcoming the dualism of spiritual versus secular. If so, *Art as Experience*'s expressivist story about individual experience is clearly not a self-enclosed philosophy of art at all but a continuation of the project of social criticism begun in earlier works like *The Public and Its Problems* and continued in later works like

Liberalism and Social Action—all of which also invoke romantic writers and themes.[45]

Meliorism and the "Tragic Sense of Life"

Since we are on the subject of Dewey's social philosophy, we can scarcely avoid addressing an image of Dewey that still enjoys currency among many of his critics. This is the image of Dewey as a romantic social optimist who, like Marx and other progressive critics of disenchanted modernity, engaged in millenarian prophesies of an expressive utopia that would emerge in human history after a period of conflict and repression. Dewey did, indeed, flirt with this theme in a few writings, notably in the conclusion to his 1920 *Reconstruction in Philosophy*:

> [W]hen the liberating of human capacity operates as a socially creative force, art will not be a luxury, a stranger to the daily occupations of making a living. . . . [ ]. And when the emotional force, the mystic force one might say, of communication, of the miracle of shared life and shared experience is spontaneously felt, the hardness and crudeness of contemporary life will be bathed in a light that never was on land or sea. [ ]. Poetry, art, religion are precious things. They cannot be maintained by lingering in the past and futilely wishing to restore what the movement of events in science, industry, and politics has destroyed. They are an out-flowering of thought and desires that unconsciously converge into a disposition of imagination and as a result of thousands and thousands of daily episodes and contact. . . . [ ]. But while it is impossible to retain and recover by deliberate volition old sources of religion and art that have been discredited, it is possible to experience the development of the vital sources of a religion and art that are yet to be. . . . [ ]. When philosophy shall have cooperated with the course of events and made clear and coherent the meaning of the daily detail. . . . practice and imagination will embrace. Poetry and religious feeling will be the unforced flowers of life.[46]

Another such passage, somewhat soberer in tone, occurs at the end of a work that appeared fourteen years later, *A Common Faith*:

History seems to exhibit three stages of growth. In the first stage, human relationships were thought to be so infected with the evils of corrupt human nature as to require redemption from external and supernatural sources. In the next stage, what is significant in these relations is found to be akin to values esteemed distinctively religious. This is the point now reached by liberal theologians. The third stage would realize that in fact the values prized in those religions that have ideal elements are idealizations of things characteristic of natural association, which have been projected into a supernatural realm for safe-keeping and sanction.[47]

Through passages like this, *A Common Faith*—which appeared the same year as *Art as Experience* (1934)—may be read as putting a more historically inflected spin on *Reconstruction in Philosophy*'s unabashed reference to a future in which "poetry and religious feeling are the unforced flowers of life." Readers of Hegel will recognize in the second passage a structural echo of Hegel's tripartite account of Spirit's development through religious, artistic, and finally philosophic phases of consciousness, an account that in turn echoed the tripartite millenarian visions of history that were commonplace in writers like Schiller, Fichte, and Schelling.[48] All such visions exemplify the romantic theme of a final historical integration of forces and energies that existed in opposition at earlier periods. They exemplify what M.H. Abrams aptly terms the romantic theme of the "spiral return." According to this theme, human beings at some point in our mythic past lost our original relation to a primordially benign state of affairs, whereupon we undertook to recover that relation, not in its original form, but in a form which is in some sense higher or more developed.[49] Modern romantic versions of the spiral return plot, Abrams notes, amount to secularized variants on the older Christian story of the fall and redemption of mankind, in which what is lost in this world is regained in the next. In his own naturalistically reconstructed version of the spiral return myth, Dewey—like Marx and other post-Hegelian socialist critics—reinterprets otherworldly redemption as redemption in a not-yet-realized stage, which may or may not actually get realized, in the history of *this* world.

For this mythic view Dewey clearly offers nothing in the way of serious argument. But once its role in his writings is acknowledged, various themes from the texts we have considered take on a new cohesiveness. It becomes clear, for example, that much of the aestheticist language of *Art as Experience* is most naturally read as descriptive less of present-day, everyday life than of an as yet unrealized social future. It becomes similarly clear why many of *A Common Faith*'s descriptions of the religious phase of experience—which recast the latter in naturalistic terms that make no reference to a deity or other transcendent entity or power—are virtually interchangeable with some of *Art as Experience*'s descriptions of aesthetic experience. Dewey was drawn to the thought, as were many romantic writers before him, that the artistic and religious phases of experience are ideally of a piece with one another and that in a healthy society this will be generally acknowledged. Of course, it is only the better part of sobriety to acknowledge that such an ideal has never been fully realized on a social scale anywhere and that there is no reason to suppose it ever will. Inquiries about the features of a society that would maximize the religious and aesthetic potential of experience thus inevitably have a utopian and hypothetical cast: If a society approximating this religious/aesthetic ideal could exist, what would it be like? Dewey's social and political philosophy projects one kind of modern answer to this question. Central to his answer is the thought that the society that would approximate this ideal most fully in the modern West would be one which crossbreeds a radically naturalized descendant of the idea of Christian redemption to the experimental outlook of modern science, and all of whose members would be encouraged to participate in its development. In a word, it would be a democracy. In giving this theme his own signature, Dewey joined an already strong tradition of late nineteenth- and early twentieth-century American writers including Walt Whitman, Herbert Croly, and William James.[50]

Our discussion has now in a way come full circle. The younger Dewey, we began by noting, saw the defining problematic of the nineteenth century in terms of an opposition between "pessimism" and "faith," an opposition possessing myriad ramifications for more specific problems in modern thought and practice. I am suggesting now that the older Dewey came to regard democracy itself, the social form with the greatest potential for developing an ethos that integrates the scientific, religious, and poetic tempers, as offering, if not a wholesale solution to this problematic, at least a pragmatic approach to it. As a pragmatist, he would have seen the above many-faceted opposition not simply as an intellectual puzzle. More broadly, he would have seen it as a "problematic situation" comprised equally of conflicting ideas and of conflicting habits of individual and collective action—a problematic situation so pervasive and persistent in theory and practice as to make the idea of a definitive solution seem little more than utopian fantasy. And this is fitting, given Dewey's view of democracy as an institutionally embodied *method of inquiry*—a method carrying no presumption of its own final application.[51]

That Dewey understood democracy as unfinished in this sense puts the lie to the cruder version of the claim that he was a naively optimistic romantic about social progress. Not even in his more starstruck moments—as in passages like those quoted above—did he actually predict that democracy would in the forseeable future deliver on the sort of millenarian promise projected by such remarks. But such remarks still, admittedly, sound oddly naive coming from someone who was otherwise an acute critic of the more simplistic social theories of his day, and hence call for some further explanation. Indeed even if, as Sidney Hook argued, Deweyan pragmatism can accommodate a "tragic sense of life," many readers may understandably find this less true of Dewey's own personality. They may sympathize with Raymond Boisvert, who argues elsewhere in this volume, along with numerous distinguished critics, that in the end Dewey "never made the turn toward a tragic sensibility."[52] The nub of the complaint is familiar: Whatever the other merits of Dewey's pragmatic, naturalistic, and romantically tempered vision of the prospects of social life in modern times, that vision's characteristically upbeat tone misses something important about human affairs which is captured by the traditional notion of the tragic.

This complaint is a Rorschach test for how one pictures the subjects and methodology of the human studies. On the side of the complainants, it must be said that even after living through two World Wars, Dewey remained stubbornly resistant to addressing what many of us still, without apology or theology, call the darker side of human existence. At the end of the most indisputably violent century to date, such language seems hardly inappropriate in describing, to cite an obvious example, the ongoing struggle for the recognition of democratic ideals around the world. Here the vision of human nature that Dewey propounded in books like *Human Nature and Conduct* continues to clash with the darker visions of other writers of his generation which still resonate powerfully for many at the beginning of the twenty-first century. (One thinks immediately, for example, of Freud, whose theories of personality and culture drew upon one of the great ancient tragic narratives and also offered what amounted to a reinterpretation of the modern Faustian theme of intelligence at odds with itself.[53]) On Dewey's side, it may be noted that the notion of a "tragic sensibility," like that of romanticism, suffers from a history of multiple, and mutually contesting, usages. For all its seeming indispensability to common sense, the idea of tragedy lacks a single dominant philosophical interpretation and thus fails to translate into a single empirical hypothesis about the way human beings are.[54] To this extent, it behooves those who fault Dewey for avoiding this subject to say more than they have about what exactly that subject is.

But the complaint still unsettles. In fairness to Dewey's critics, might it be possible to recast it in terms that are neutral with respect to the problematically open concept of tragedy? One thing we might say is this: For all Dewey did not say about the limits of civilized intelligence, did he not leave himself open, ironically enough, to a version of the charge of social escapism—in the sense of relying upon a vision of human experience that fails to come to terms with social realities—that he had originally leveled at the romantics? Passages like that quoted earlier from *Reconstruction in Philosophy* suggest that the answer is "yes." But if this answer is meant unequivocally, it raises a problem of chronology; and it is the chronological issue which points, I suggest, to a more nuanced view of Dewey's allegedly untragic optimism. For we need to ask, upon reading such passages, *which* Dewey are we are discussing—early, middle, or late? Dewey's writings spanned a period of over seventy years, and it is interesting to note that the enraptured language of the conclusion to *Reconstruction in Philosophy*—which, appearing in 1920, was for Dewey a young man's book—never really shows up again in his later writings, even in *A Common Faith.* And this for understandable historical reasons. For over the next twenty years, developments like the Depression and Stalinism had ample time to make their mark on the thinking of any intelligent democratic socialist. It thus comes as no surprise that Dewey would offer a soberer description of his social sensibilities when he commented in 1939 that

Democracy is a way of personal life controlled not merely by faith in human nature in general but by faith in the capacity of human beings for intelligent judgment and action if proper conditions are furnished. I have been accused more than once and from opposed quarters of an undue, a utopian faith in the possibilities of intelligence and in

education as a correlate of intelligence. At all events, I did
not invent this faith. I acquired it from my surroundings as
far as far as those surroundings were animated by the democratic spirit. . . .[ ].[55]

Dewey's key word here is "faith," which he used on numerous
occasions when expressing his own form of social hope. But he
never, even in his earlier writings, equated faith with optimism. He
is more explicit on this in the *Ethics*:

The individual whose pursuit of the good is colored by honest
recognition of existing and threatening evils is almost always charged with being a pessimist; with cynical delight
in dwelling upon what is morbid, base, or sordid; and he is
urged to be an 'optimist', meaning in effect to conceal from
himself and others evils that obtain. But . . . optimism of
will . . . is very different from a sentimental refusal to look
at the realities of the situation just as they are. In fact a
certain intellectual pessimism, in the sense of a steadfast
willingness to uncover sore points, to acknowledge and
search for abuses, to note how presumed good often serves
as a cloak for actual bad, is a necessary part of the moral
optimism which actively denotes itself to making the right
prevail. Any other view . . . is next door to brutality, to a
brutality bathed in the atmosphere of sentimentality and
flourishing the catchwords of idealism.[56]

One will, it is true, look in vain here or anywhere else in
Dewey for the dramatic metapsychological vision that lends a book
like Freud's *Civilization and its Discontents* its mythic power. But
these are still hardly the words of a social escapist. Dewey would
elsewhere use the nineteenth-century term "meliorism" to characterize his own mix of optimism of will and pessimism of the intellect, meaning the idea "that at least there is a sufficient basis of
goodness in life and its conditions so that by thought and earnest
effort we may constantly make better things. This conception attacks optimism on the ground that it encourages a fatalistic con-
tentment with things as they are . . . [ ]."[57] Optimism here involves
an intellectual certainty that a good future is, in the short or long
run, in store for us. But given the fallibility of our beliefs and the
precariousness of the world, we are entitled to no such certainty by

anything we might learn from science or philosophy, let alone from traditional religion. To adopt a meliorist outlook is precisely for this reason to forgo those forms of social hope that are rooted in an unwarranted confidence about the course of future history.

But that need not mean that all beliefs about the course of history are unwarranted—a point that returns us to the significance of the notion of faith. "Faith" is a word which, as Dewey noted in A Common Faith, has two levels of usage which modern scientific culture has tended, disastrously, to run together. One connotes belief in a specifically supernatural realm which lacks support from what the modern West has come to accept as ordinary justificatory procedures. The other connotes a certain indispensable action-guiding role which some beliefs, lacking ordinary evidentiary support, will inevitably play within any social setting. (Dewey's position here resonates in obvious ways with William James' nonevidentialist argument in "The Will to Believe.") The bad press given faith in the modern age, as reflected in familiar scientistic critiques of faith as false consciousness (Marx), as childish wish fulfillment (Freud), or as slippage into emotive language (Logical Positivism), is properly directed, from any naturalistic perspective that eschews such narrow forms of scientism, only at the first connotation. It is the second, Dewey maintains, to which modern culture needs to give its reconstructive attention now, since it is only the second which sustains the idea of a genuinely common faith "that shall not be confined to sect, class, or race."[58] "Natural piety," as Dewey calls this naturalized form of religious attitude, is already implicit in a wide range of human practices, "in art, science, and good citizenship." It seems likely that he took the expression "natural piety" from Wordsworth, in whose poem "My Heart Leaps Up" it signifies a stance to the world which embodies continuities between spirituality and nature, and between childlike and adult sensibilities:

> My heart leaps up when I behold
> A rainbow in the sky
> So was it when my life began
> So is it now I am a man
> So be it when I shall grow old
> Or let me die!
> The Child is father of the Man;
> And I could wish my days to be
> Bound each to each by natural piety.

Dewey goes on to comment that our active adoption of a stance of natural piety towards the world

> is not of necessity either a fatalistic acquiescence in natural happenings or a romantic idealization of the world. It may rest upon a just sense of nature as the whole of which we are parts, while it also recognizes that we are parts that are marked by intelligence and purpose, having the capacity to strive by their aid to bring conditions into greater consonance with what is humanly desirable. Such piety is an inherent constituent of a just perspective in life.[59]

Given Dewey's insistence on the inseparability of the drama of the individual life from the larger drama of the life of the community, I suggest that it is in the above sort of meliorism that the core of his own version of romanticism is, in the end, to be found. We have seen now how an important feature of that meliorism, albeit a feature not always evident in Dewey's language, is its acknowledgment of a basic fact: that intelligence often fails, that its life in the world is one of pain and strife at least as much as it is one of success. But Dewey, writing as cultural critic, would add—and here he does part company with a certain quietistic interpretation of the tragic sense of life—that it is especially when intelligence fails that new forms of active and unsentimental striving are most needed.[60] Having lived a life which spanned the publication of Darwin's *Origin of Species* and the early years of the Cold War, he could appreciate in old age how the twentieth century remained haunted by social problems he had long ago identified as at once causes and symptoms of the darker side of romanticism. Foremost among these problems are the more extreme forms of expressive individualism and nationalism, each a distinct threat to the health of societies aspiring to the ideals of liberal democracy. To such phenomena an all-too-familiar response, in Dewey's day as in our own, is indignation followed by slippage into a resigned sense that the ill in question cannot be changed, as if it were a necessary feature of social reality.[61] Dewey was struck by how easy it was even for his own educated, liberally minded peers to slide from indignation to fatalism in this manner and to view the slide itself as natural and inevitable when in fact it issues, as he was convinced, from specific, contingent, and remediable forms of enculturation.

It was that fatalistic strand of modern liberal democratic thought, more than any other, that Dewey wished to change. In this context, his critical legacy amounts not to a finished theory of culture—something he would have regarded as oxymoronic—so much as a philosophical image of what democratic culture might struggle to become. It is an image of how to make existential sense of a natural and cultural world that the inhabitants of the nineteenth century were already describing with phrases like "the death of God" and "the death of poetry"—phrases soon to be joined by others like "the culture of narcissism," "the death of the subject," "the end of philosophy," and indeed "the death of tragedy." But Dewey was convinced that even for the secular mind, a deep metaphysical trust in the world is still possible, and it is this sort of trust that he had in mind in speaking of "natural piety." Like Wordsworth's poem where that phrase first appeared, Dewey's image of his culture also represents the possibility of a certain kind of human growth. It hints at an aesthetic, spiritual, and ethical form of adulthood towards which modern individuals and societies might grow—or, in Abrams' sense, "return"—if we learn to do without the naively optimistic and fatalistic beliefs which continue to fuel the deepest social problems of our times. To this extent Dewey's cultural image expresses what he was convinced is the sanest case for individual hope, and the only remaining case for large-scale social hope, in the modern world. Of course we are talking only of an image; but then romanticism, and social hope, are all about images. If Dewey's version of romanticism retains any resonance at the beginning of yet another century riven by the problematic of pessimism and faith, it surely lies in this cultural image's continuing reinterpretation.

Notes

1. I thank Nina Pelikan Straus, Vincent Colapietro, David Seiple, and the members of the 1996–1997 Fellows' Seminar at the Princeton University Center for Human Values for comments on earlier versions of this essay.

2. "The Lessons of Contemporary French Literature," *The Early Works of John Dewey* 3:36. I will hereafter follow the usual practice of abbreviating passages quoted from the Carbondale Edition of the Early, Middle, and Later Works of John Dewey with the letters "E", "M", and "L", respectively. Citations will include the title of a publication unless it is already cited in the text.

3. A. O. Lovejoy, "On the Discrimination of Romanticisms," in *Essays in the History of Ideas* (The Johns Hopkins University Press, 1948). In a

related vein Dewey once wryly remarked, in commenting on the fantasies of risk and accumulation which drive the modern business world, "different romanticists rarely understand one another," a remark that, in post-Cold War Europe, has a poignancy which Dewey's own generation could scarcely have anticipated. See "The Collapse of a Romance" (1932), LW 6:69. In one sense acknowledged by philosophers since Plato, the problem of defining "romanticism" is just a particular case of the problem of definition in general, which involves the imposition or discovery of unity among diverse applications of any term.

4. "The Pantheism of Spinoza," *The Journal of Speculative Philosophy* (July 1882, XVI), reprinted in EW 1. Dewey was apparently unaware of Johann Gottfried Herder's Leibnizian-derived interpretation of Spinoza as a philosopher of immanence, not a pantheist, which enjoyed considerable influence among nineteenth-century German romantic writers. Nor, apparently, was he aware that one such writer, Friedrich Schleiermacher, had in 1799 put forward a view of religious experience as an aestheticized awareness of the individual's place in the Universe, a view which the young Dewey, one imagines, would have found particularly congenial.

5. Reported in Max Eastman, *Great Companions* (London: Museum Press Limited, 1959), p. 185.

6. *Art as Experience*, LW 10:36. See also chapter one of *A Common Faith*, which appeared in the same year (1931) that Dewey gave the lectures that would become *Art as Experience*.

7. MW 10:231.

8. See MW 14:114 and 176, respectively.

9. LW 1:187.

10. "The Tragedy of the German Soul" (1916), reprinted in MW 10, pp. 304–9.

11. LW 1:174 Similar protests against the egoistic extremes of some romantic writers can be found in an array of later modern writers, beginning with Hegel and continuing through twentieth-century historians of ideas like Arthur Lovejoy and Isaiah Berlin.

12. LW 1:174.

13. For further discussion of the significance of the theme of anxiety which connects Dewey's critique of traditional epistemology with more recent developments in analytic philosophy, the critical theory of the Frankfurt school, and poststructuralism, see Richard Bernstein's discussion of "Cartesian anxiety" in *Beyond Objectivism and Relativism: Science, Hermeneutics, and Praxis* (University of Pennsylvania Press, 1983).

14. For more on Dewey's view of the self see Vincent Colapietro, "Embodied, Enculturated Agents," this volume.

15. "Towards a Theory of Romanticism," in Morse Peckham, *The Triumph of Romanticism* (University of South Carolina Press, 1970). Peckham's implicitly dialectical model was in part a response to Lovejoy's (op. cit.) argument that "romanticism" refers to no one thing. Peckham never discusses Dewey at length in his writings, although he does describe his own views about the larger significance of romanticism for modern culture as "pragmatic." Like Dewey, Peckham cites Byron (or a received image of Byron) as the preeminent exemplar of "negative" romanticism among nineteenth-century literary figures, and Wordsworth and Shelley as exponents of the positive variety.

16. Ironically, some twentieth century logical positivists would commit the mirror image of this error by propounding "emotivist" theories of value which affirmed the primacy of "the cognitive" in human intelligence while depriving emotion or feeling of normative significance.

17. On this point see Jürgen Habermas, "Hegel's Concept of Modernity," in *The Philosophical Discourse of Modernity* (MIT Press, 1990), pp. 31ff.

18. "The spiritual," Hegel wrote in this connection," is distinguished from the natural . . . in that it does not continue a mere stream of tendency, but sunders itself to self-realization. But this position of severed life has in its turn to be overcome, and the spirit must, by its own act, achieve concord once more. . . .[ ]. The principal of restoration is found in thought, and thought only: the hand that inflicts the wound is also the hand that heals it." In G. W. F. Hegel, *The Logic of Hegel*, trans. William Wallace (Oxford, 1902), pp. 54ff.

19. See Peckham, op. cit.; also M. H. Abrams, *Natural Supernaturalism: Tradition and Revolution in Romantic Literature* (Norton Publishing Co., 1971), chapter IV. For more on the significance of the fall-and-redemption theme, see section IV below.

20. Russell Goodman, *American Philosophy and the Romantic Tradition* (Cambridge University Press, 1990). Goodman's theme of the marriage between self and world draws in particular on Stanley Cavell's explorations of the affinities between external world scepticism and solipsism, understanding these as the problems, respectively, of trusting beliefs we would like to be able to hold about the world in general, and of trusting beliefs we would like to be able to hold about one another. Goodman's approach to these themes usefully brings out how various American philosophers have shared with Romantics like Emerson, Wordsworth, and Coleridge a healthy respect for day-to day experience, and in so doing shows how all in their different ways were at work transforming what

Dewey termed the quest for certainty into what Cavell calls the quest for the ordinary. In this connection Goodman also mentions Cavell's Harvard colleague Hilary Putnam; he might also have added to the list Richard Rorty. See especially Rorty's *Achieving Our Country: Leftist Thought in Twentieth Century America* (Harvard University Press, 1998).

21. LW 10:158.

22. LW 1:97.

23. Friedrich Schlegel, *Gespräch über die Poesie* (1800), quoted in Arthur O. Lovejoy, *The Great Chain of Being: a Study in the History of an Idea* (Harvard University Press, 1936), p. 304.

24. F.E.D. Schleiermacher, *Reden* (1799), quoted in Lovejoy, p. 308.

25. Lovejoy, *The Great Chain of Being*, p. 304. Under the heading of the diversitarian conception, Lovejoy includes not only a newly temporalized sense of the plenitude of nature but "the immense multiplication of genres and of verse-forms; the admission of the aesthetic legitimacy of the *genre mixte*; the *gout de la nuance*; the naturalization in art of the 'grotesque'; the quest for local color; the endeavor to reconstruct in imagination the inner life of peoples remote in time or place or in cultural condition; *étalage du moi*; the demand for particularized fidelity in landscape-description; the revulsion against simplicity; the distrust of universal formulas in politics; the aesthetic antipathy to standardization; the identification of the Absolute with the 'concrete universal' in metaphysics; the feeling of 'the glory of the imperfect'; the cultivation of individual, national, and racial peculiarities; the depreciation of the obvious and the general high valuation (wholly foreign to most earlier periods) of originality, and the usually futile and absurd self-conscious pursuit of that attribute" (pp. 293–4).

26. F. W. J. Schelling, *System of Transcendental Idealism*, trans. Peter Heath (University Press of Virginia, 1978), pp. 232–3. The resonance between Schelling's and Dewey's views of the centrality of art to philosophy's subject matter was emphasized by Dewey's student and Columbia colleague John Herman Randall in *The Career of Philosophy* (New York, Columbia University Press, 1965, vol. II). For Schelling, Randall writes, "the world reveals its meaning, not in the purely personal action to which it stimulates him, but in the process of artistic production in which both he and it must cooperate. Hence, though for Schelling as for Fichte it is human experience, the self, that is the key to all understanding, the task of Schelling's self in organizing its world is not to set up an antagonist worthy of the combat, but to work in and with something already able to respond to man and his purposes, something whose impulses he can both imitate and bring to a happy fruition . . . It is the creative activity of the artist's intelligence that is at once the best illustration of the World-Process and its culmination." (pp. 250–1) A few pages later, Randall continues: "In

the artistic attitude lies the fulfillment of the philosopher's long search, the ultimate metaphysical key to reconciling all oppositions in a final synthesis—necessity and freedom, the real and the ideal, the unconscious and the conscious, nature and thought. 'The Self is conscious in its production, unconscious in its product.' This use of the process of artistic creation as the all-inclusive context within which the classic metaphysical oppositions of contingency and necessity, activity and structure, are seen as functional distinctions, is a foreshadowing of much present-day thought: these pages might almost have been written by John Dewey" (p. 261).

27. LW 10:33n; see also LW 1:269.

28. Taylor has pursued the theme of expressivism in a number of books, notably in *Hegel* (Cambridge University Press, 1975) and *Sources of the Self: The Making of the Modern Identity* (Harvard University Press, 1989).

29. As in his reconstructive analysis of "form," Dewey construes "expression" to cover a range of experiences within and without the practices that modern philosophy centrally associates with the aesthetic, i.e., the fine arts. Expression is the culmination of an intelligent creature's basic affective response to its environment, and Dewey pictures such culminations as falling along a developmental continuum. Speaking very generally, expressive behavior occurs when the initial emotionally charged response to a situation is experienced as meaningful and is then further refined into a communicative gesture guided by an intention to transform the initial situation. But not all affective behavior fully fits this description. A simple gush of tears or a cry of joy such as a small child might make is not by itself expressive. Nor, on the other extreme, is behavior which is routinized to the point of simply copying some pre-existing model or following a rule in a mechanical way. Behavior which is fully expressive is aware of convention yet also at the same time inventive; it strikes a balance between the old and the new. (See *Art as Experience*, chapters IV and V.)

30. *Sources of the Self*, p. 390.

31. There are striking resonances between Dewey's and Nietzsche's aestheticizing appropriations of Romantic themes, as well as between their respective expressions of ambivalence toward the Romantic tradition. Both thinkers in their mature writings rejected the dualism of mind and nature implicit in mainstream Idealism and saw such a stance as a secularized carry-over from Christian theology; both were drawn to the idea that values are in some sense a product of human history; and both acknowledged particular indebtedness to Emerson. But there are also important dissonances, not the least of these being that whereas Dewey saw democracy as the most evolved form of social life in part because of the expressive possibilities it affords its inhabitants, Nietzsche fairly despised it.

32. LW 10:42–3.

33. LW 7:3074-8. In *Reconstruction in Philosophy* Dewey remarks in a similar vein that "Honesty, industry, temperance, just like health, wealth, and learning, are not goods to be possessed as they would be if they expressed fixed ends to be attained. They are directions of change in the quality of experience. Growth itself is the only moral 'end'" (MW 12:181).

34. See in particular chapter III of *Art as Experience*, "Having an Experience."

35. Although "meaning" is a central notion in the argument of *Art as Experience*, Dewey is notoriously vague there and elsewhere as to what exactly it entails. He seems to think of *a* meaning not simply as a formal property of a symbol, but as a relation between a phenomenological event and its hermeneutically significant expression, whether that expression occurs only in an individual's imagination, or in more public forms of communicative behavior. This approach to understanding meaning reflects Dewey's general intuition that all the constituents of experience, including the materials of thought, are best understood as parts of developmental processes rather than as static entities.

36. At such moments one has what Dewey, in chapter two, calls "*an* experience." It is instructive to compare Dewey's account of this notion to Wordworth's famous "Spots of Time" section in the *Prelude*, which Dewey undoubtedly knew well.

37. Dewey never develops the implications of this line of thought for ethics in detail. Yet it seems clear that his references in the *Ethics* to moral deliberation as involving "dramatic rehearsal" (in which the agent weighs decisions by placing them imaginatively within alternative hypothetical narratives) presuppose some such view of the agent-as-author-and-interpreter of an unfolding stream of experience. For more on the idea of dramatic rehearsal, see Steven Fesmire, "The Art of Imagination," this volume.

38. LW 10:218.

39. LW 12:108.

40. See note 37.

41. See Weber's 1915 paper "Religious Rejections of the World and their Directions," reprinted in H.H. Gerth and C. Wright Mills, *From Max Weber: Essays in Sociology* (Oxford University Press, 1946). *Art as Experience* may be read as a polemic against the tendency of modern aesthetics to reify the social developments Weber described under the heading of the "Esthetic Sphere" by grounding them in philosophical arguments that presuppose the universal validity of the distinction between "fine" and "useful" art.

42. Casey Haskins, "Dewey's *Art as Experience*: The Tension Between Aesthetics and Aestheticism," *Transactions of the C. S. Peirce Society*, XXVIII, 2 (Spring 1992). See also Haskins, "John Dewey: Survey of Thought," in Michael Kelly, ed., *Encyclopedia of Aesthetics* (Oxford University Press, 1998, vol. 2).

43. I discuss this subject further in "Dewey's *Art as Experience*."

44. "The Ethics of Democracy" (1888); EW 1:248.

45. Thus towards the end of *The Public and Its Problems*, which appeared in 1927, Dewey speaks of an "art of communication" that will facilitate the emergence of a "great community" which "had its seer in Walt Whitman." In *Liberalism and Social Action*, which appeared a year after *Art as Experience* in 1935, he writes similarly that "Liberalism is committed to . . . the liberation of individuals so that realization of their capacities may be the law of their life." He then credits the gradual turn from "individualistic" to "collectivistic" liberalism—what has more recently been known as communitarianism—to the influence of such romantic writers as Coleridge, Carlyle, and Ruskin.

46. MW 12:201.

47. LW 9:48–9.

48. This model is implicit, for example, in the passage from Schelling quoted at the beginning of section III. I discuss the relationship of Dewey's version of this model of his aesthetics in more detail in Haskins (1992).

49. M.H. Abrams, *Natural Supernaturalism: Tradition and Revolution in Romantic Literature* (New York: Norton Publishing Co., 1971). See esp. chapters III and IV. This theme, Abrams notes, shows up not only in the writers mentioned above, in the text but also in English writers like Coleridge and Yeats.

50. On this tradition and its links to later developments in American progressive social thought, see Rorty, *Achieving Our Country*.

51. This is a variant on a point often made in the context of distinguishing Dewey's vision of scientific inquiry from Peirce's: that there is no reason to suppose that science, like nature itself, will ever be "finished." Whereas Peirce took seriously the concept of "finished" inquiry as a regulative ideal for the sciences, Dewey tended to see it as little more than a dignifying flourish on the more modest observation that the scientific method serves the purposes of intelligence in historically unprecedented ways, and that acknowledging this is sufficient for our regarding science as a rational and strongly normative enterprise.

For more detailed discussion of Dewey's social views, see James Campbell, "Dewey and Democracy," this volume.

52. Raymond D. Boisvert, "The Nemesis of Necessity: Tragedy's Challenge to Deweyan Pragmatism," this volume. Boisvert takes issue specifically with Hook's argument in "Pragmatism and the Tragic Sense of Life," a 1960 address to the American Philosophical Association that was later expanded into a book of the same name (The Free Press, 1974).

53. In a related vein, Stanley Cavell, a thoughtful reader of Freud, Dewey, and various Romantic writers already mentioned, characterizes Dewey's "perfectionism" about the prospects of American democratic culture as one which, while appropriately opposed to dogmatically moralistic images of social progress, is lacking in sensitivity to "the height of modernism in the arts, the depths of psychoanalytic discovery, the ravages of the century's politics, the wild intelligence of American popular culture." Cavell's point is well taken and detachable, I think, from his Kant-flavored interpretation of the individualistic ideal he calls "Emersonian perfectionism," an ideal for which readers who favor Dewey's views about nature and the social character of the self may have less use. See Stanley Cavell, *Conditions Handsome and Unhandsome: The Constitution of Emersonian Perfectionism* (University of Chicago Press, 1990), p. 13.

54. I touch on this subject again in note 61 below. On the multiplicity of definitions of the tragic, see Morris Weitz, "Tragedy," in Paul Edwards, ed., *The Encyclopedia of Philosophy* (MacMillan, 1967), vol. 8.

55. "Creative Democracy—The Task before Us"; LW 14:224ff.

56. MW 5:370–1.

57. This passage comes from Dewey's entry under "Optimism" in Paul Monroe, ed., *A Cyclopedia of Education* (New York, 1912–13), MW 7:294. Dewey would have encountered similar sentiments in James, but he may well also have found them in Shelley, who once wrote that "It is best that we should think all this for the best even though it be not, because Hope, as Coleridge says is a solemn duty which we owe alike to ourselves and to the world" (Percy Bysshe Shelley in an 1819 letter to Maria Gisborne, quoted in Abrams, op. cit., p. 447).

58. Dewey's way of understanding faith here resonates with what Bernard Williams calls "ethical confidence," and also with what Gianni Vattimo, drawing on Nietzsche and Heidegger, calls "active nihilism." See Bernard Williams, *Ethics and the Limits of Philosophy* (Harvard University Press, 1985), 170–1; Gianni Vattimo, "Optimistic Nihilism," *Common Knowledge* 1:3 (Winter 1992), pp. 43–4.

59. LW 9:15ff.

60. Here Dewey is in accord with the well-known line in Goethe's *Faust*, where Faust declares before going to Heaven at the play's end that

"Freedom and life are earned by those alone/Who conquer them each day anew."

61. In a related vein, Bernard Williams suggests that the role filled by the notion of "supernatural necessity" in the world-view of Greek tragedy is filled in modern life by the general notion of a "social reality" which "can act to crush a worthwhile, significant character or project. . . .[ ]." Bernard Williams, *Shame and Necessity* (University of California Press, 1993), p. 165. Williams doesn't argue for this point in any detail and presents it simply as an analogy. But even if this is the right way to understand the larger historical context for the fatalistic temper in contemporary liberal thought, that still leaves open the obvious question—a question Dewey, for one, would be quick to raise—whether modern forms of the mythology of necessity deserve our critical respect any more than ancient ones. This brings us back to larger questions of the interpretation of the subjects and methods of human studies, questions which, as Dewey would also be quick to note, remain open for our time.

7

The Art of Moral Imagination

Steven Fesmire

Casey Haskins has observed that nineteenth-century Romanticism left an indelible mark on John Dewey's thought (see Haskins, this volume). Nonetheless Dewey's treatment of imagination diverges in an important respect from that of the Romantics. Their emphasis on the unconstrained, numinous spontaneity of imagination conceals that it is a tool of everyday practical intelligence which derives its structures through interaction with physical, cultural, and interpersonal environments.

Glorification of spontaneous play came at the price of estranging imagination from intelligent mediation of everyday problematic situations. It is in part due to the Romantic legacy that imagination, thus subjectivized, has been marginalized as a subject of study in much twentieth-century philosophy. In contemporary semantics, for example, imagination and its creations (metaphors and the like) are taken to be more elliptical devices that embroider and ornament an otherwise insipid world. At best, our flickering imaginations are thought merely to form the "background" for rational thought, as John Searle proposes; at worst, imagination is thought to be no more than a faculty for forming fanciful images.

In contrast to this tradition, in Dewey's view our capacity for having a conceptually coherent world stable enough to allow some measure of intelligent, deliberate mediation is imaginative through and through. Imagination is very much at the foreground of meaning.

The most important function of imagination from a pragmatic standpoint is that it is our capacity, situated in the present, to take in the full scope of a situation (DE, MW 9:244) and to establish continuity between the actual consequences of past conduct, and the prospective consequences of future conduct. Dewey writes:

> Imagination is the only gateway through which these meanings [derived from prior experiences] can find their way into a present interaction; or rather, as we have just seen, the conscious adjustment of the new and the old *is* imagination (AE, LW 10:276).

Imagination is, Thomas Alexander observes, "the capacity to understand the actual in light of the possible." "It is a phase of activity . . . in which possible activities are envisaged in relation to our own situations, thereby amplifying the meaning of the present and creating the context from which present values may be criticized, thus liberating the course of action itself."[1] The imaginative dimension of experience, far from being an elliptical Romantic orbit, is thus integrated with everyday doings and undergoings.

Dewey's most protracted attempt to formulate an empirically criticizable theory of imagination is his theory of deliberation as *dramatic rehearsal*.[2] Dramatic rehearsal is the reflective, searching phase of any situation (scientific, aesthetic, or moral) involving doubt. In deliberation, we scope out alternative futures and imagine ourselves participating in them. We try on possible actions in an almost interrogative way: Does this scenario mediate between contending values? Does it alter conditions so that relative equilibrium may be reestablished? In a complete deliberation, the imaginative flight continues until we are stimulated to act by a course that appears to harmonize the pressing desires, interests, and needs of the disharmonized scene. Our valuation may then be revised by observation and questioning.

Dewey's theory of imagination provides a framework for accommodating and expanding the work of recent moral theorists exploring the ways human beings actually make sense of tangled circumstances and compose meaningful lives.[3] This essay is an attempt to clarify and develop this framework by articulating a Deweyan theory of moral imagination. My central goal is to articulate what a Dewey-inspired naturalistic empiricism or ecological humanism can do to make "the nature of ordinary judgments upon what it is best or wise to do" (HNC, MW 14:132) more intelligible so that such judgments might be better made.

Dramatic Rehearsal

A synopsis of Dewey's treatment of deliberation as dramatic rehearsal from the 1890s on will serve our more thematic focus on the art of moral imagination. Dewey was deeply influenced by his reading and teaching of William James's *Principles of Psychology* in 1890. James presents deliberation as constituted by two battling impulses: "the impatience of the deliberative state" (i.e., the desire to reestablish equilibrium and continue acting) and "the dread of the irrevocable" (i.e., the hesitancy of carrying an imagined alternative into manifest action). These two motives retard our decisions so that a situation may be reasonably negotiated. A great part of this negotiation "consists in the turning over of all the possible modes of *conceiving* the doing or not doing of the act in point."[4]

In his 1894 *The Study of Ethics: A Syllabus* (EW 4), Dewey proposes that ethical intentions or ends ("what an agent *means* to do") are constituted by mediation of impulses through reflection. This process is beset by difficulties. The perceived satisfaction of following the original impulse may vie with the satisfaction of following the mediating course (a struggle traditionally dubbed "desire versus duty"). Or, the various aims may conflict with one another so that we must either eliminate some or "discover a still more comprehensive aim in which the claims of the conflicting intentions shall be adjusted" (EW 4:251). This is the onset of deliberation, concerning which Dewey writes:

> We are apt to describe this process as if it were a coldly intellectual one. As a matter of fact, it is a process of tentative action; we "try on" one or other of the ends, imagining ourselves actually doing them, going, indeed, in this make-believe action just as far as we can without actually doing them (EW 4:251).

This deliberative process can easily lead one astray. An impulsive idea may have such a hold on us that it is overtly acted upon while we "try it on," even though we may not consciously intend the action (EW 4:251).[5] The proper outcome of deliberation, however, is "decision, *resolution*, the definitely formed plan" (EW 4:252). And a deliberate intention, end, or aim is ethically justifiable only if it gives "attention to all the bearings which could be foreseen by

an agent who had a proper interest in knowing what he is about"
(EW 4:251).

In his 1900–01 lectures on ethics at the University of Chicago,
Dewey began more fully to work out his theory of deliberation.
Deliberation, he observes, "represents the process of rehearsing
activity in idea when that overt act is postponed. It is, so to speak,
trying an act on before it is tried out in the objective, obvious, space
and time world."[6] A situation characterized by opposed tendencies
stimulates us to pursue (in imagination) possible outcomes in order
to make a situation manageable. In this way, the intermediate
steps for reaching those imagined states are defined.

By studying the psychology of tapping into possible avenues
for action, Dewey shows that this process is controlled and guided
by factors in the empirical situation. "The essential thing," as James
insists, "is the process of being guided."[7] Our reflections must help
us determine a workable outcome that will deal with and adapt us
to realities at hand. In place of the authority of Right and Wrong,
Dewey relies on the authority of exigencies and pressures in situations. And imagination is our best tool for negotiating these
pressures.

I turn now to Dewey's more mature treatments of deliberation.
In *How We Think*, the deliberative phase of experience is treated
as a vicarious mode of *acting* when direct action is interrupted. It
is "a kind of dramatic rehearsal. Were there only one suggestion
[for action] popping up, we should undoubtedly adopt it at once"
(HWT, LW 8:200). But when alternatives contend with one another
as we forecast their probable outcomes, the ensuing tension sustains inquiry (HWT, LW 8:200).

Dewey's most extensive discussion of deliberation appears in
Human Nature and Conduct. He writes:

> Deliberation is a dramatic rehearsal (in imagination) of
> various competing possible lines of action. . . . Deliberation
> is an experiment in finding out what the various lines of
> possible action are really like. . . . Thought runs ahead and
> foresees outcomes, and thereby avoids having to await the
> instruction of actual failure and disaster (HNC, MW
> 14:132–33).

That this does not represent a departure from Dewey's earlier view
is supported by his unaltered reprinting of the following passage
from the 1908 *Ethics* in the 1932 *Ethics*:

Deliberation is actually an imaginative rehearsal of various courses of conduct. We give way, *in our mind*, to some impulse; we try, *in our mind*, some plan. Following its career through various steps, we find ourselves in imagination in the presence of the consequences that would follow (MW 5:293 and LW 7:275).

So, having been knocked off of our prior perch, we take an imaginative flight toward prospective perches (often constructed in-flight) and survey the altered conditions that would ensue if we chose that course irrevocably.

The resulting evaluation (that a prospective action may best harmonize factors in a situation) might be called an intuition if by this term one means a naturally conditioned, educated, felt appraisal of probable outcomes of behavior. Intuitions are nurtured for good or ill in the same way that a gestating organism is nurtured or poisoned by its uterine environment.[8] Functionally understood, intuition is a "direct sense of value" (1908 *Ethics*, MW 5:293) provoked by a suggested stimulus to action. An intuition (dubbed a "prizing" in *Theory of Valuation*, LW 13:195) is not an apprehension of a timeless essence that bestows a certificate of certitude. Consequently, it must be entertained subject to revision and correction by ongoing observation and questioning (1932 *Ethics*, LW 7:273).

What is deceptively called intuition is an interactively emergent felt sense with a mainspring in established *habits*: "Immediate, seemingly instinctive, feeling of the direction and end of various lines of behavior is in reality the feeling of habits working below direct consciousness" (HNC, MW 14:26). Dramatic rehearsal, then, is a function of our habits marking out a range of viable courses of action. As Dewey observes, "the more numerous our habits the wider the field of possible observation and foretelling. The more flexible they are, the more refined is perception in its discrimination and the more delicate the presentation evoked by imagination" (HNC, MW 14:123).

Our mostly unconscious horizon of *social* habits tethers our dramatic rehearsals, both disclosing and concealing potential alternatives for conduct. Social habits are shared and stable interpretive structures (e.g., symbol systems, imaginative structures, values, gestures, prejudices) that we inherit as we form personal habits. They enable us to communicate so that we can anticipate and compose the future together. Moral maturation is a process whereby these inherited customs become intelligently reconstructed in light of changing circumstances rather than championed in blind conformity or dismissed in reactionary defiance.

Deliberation is a *dramatic* rehearsal because vying prospects for harmonizing values are intelligible only in the context of the larger narratives of our lives—lives enacted on the same stage as others' lives. To deliberate is to co-author (with environing conditions) a dramatic story. It is not mere application of universal rules to particular instances, nor is it a pseudo-mathematical calculation of means to already coagulated ends.

As a clue to what is story-structured about deliberation, consider the "journey" language in the following description of stories by Paul Ricoeur:

> To *follow* a story is to *move forward* in midst of contingencies and peripeteia under the *guidance* of an expectation that finds its fulfillment in the 'conclusion' of the story. . . . It gives the story an *'end point'*. . . . To understand the story is to understand how and why the successive episodes *led* to the conclusion.[9]

To say that deliberation is dramatic or story-structured means that an experience of deliberation has a beginning, middle, and conclusion just as journeys have starting points, paths traversed, and end points or destinations. Although Dewey employs a wealth of non-journey metaphors to conceptualize deliberation (e.g., organic growth, balance, evolutionary adaptation, scientific experimentation, and the arts), these tend to be overlaid by him (often consciously, for better or worse[10]) as phases along a journey so that the journey metaphor binds the others.

"We compare life to a traveler faring forth" (HNC, MW 14:127). The beginning or starting point is for Dewey an active phase of stable, established habits characterized by equilibrium, adaptation, and harmony. The middle or path traversed is characterized by disrupted habit, disharmony, imbalance, loss of adaptation to surroundings, and competition and disunity among habits and desires. The troubled situation becomes increasingly organized as we are provoked to a reflective phase of deliberation, the active phase of imagination. The conclusion or destination is a consummatory phase of recovered action and stability characterized by reconstructed equilibrium and re-unification of desires.

Just as the good dramatist rigorously imagines her characters thinking, feeling, and acting in ways that will be continuous with their past behaviors, so we act in ways continuous with the established habits that form our characters. And like good dramatists, good moral thinkers compose successive drafts before signing off on the product. A delicately refined moral imagination enables what I shall call a moral artist to configure an action with a rich sense for a maturing situation's possibilities.

Without being over-tempted by Romanticism's severance of imagination from the everyday push and pull of the world, Dewey treats imagination as a capacity, situated in the present, to establish an organic unity or continuity between past and future habits. In this way, Alexander observes, "a continuous process of activity may unfold in the most meaningful and value-rich way possible."[11]

The Art of Deliberation

The avowed method of the naturalistic empiricist (or ecological humanist) is to develop values and standards from within concrete, common experience. Dewey pleads: "The serious matter is that philosophies have denied that common experience is capable of developing from within itself methods which will secure direction for itself and will create inherent standards of judgment and value" (EN, LW 1:41).[12]

Moral philosophy is typically thought to be a transcendental (and not an empirical) discipline that ascertains how we *ought* to deliberate and act. The *facts* about thinking and acting have been deemed marginal concerns for psychologists to address. This has led many moral philosophers to ignore the psychological facts of moral imagination. Dewey's theory of deliberation, in contrast, is put forth as an experimentally warranted, testable, and consequently fallible and revisable theory about the psychological facts of the process of moral decision-making (both for the person-on-the-street and for moral philosophers of whatever stripe). That we *should* deliberate imaginatively is as moot a point as that we should communicate by means of language. Unless we are to leave this capacity to develop haphazardly, empirically responsible moral ideals must accord with and emerge from the stubborn fact that deliberation is imaginative.

To herald ideals independent of an adequate social psychology is to leave unmediated the current tragedy that capacities for moral, political, and legal intelligence have for the most part gone unrealized. We cling to the notion that we should deliberate primarily by applying universal laws of reason, divinely sanctioned moral laws, universal rules, socially contractual rules, natural born rights, God-given rights, or the like, to particular cases. Some of these approaches admittedly have value, but the resulting dissonance between a person's deliberative ideals and the experiential and cognitive realities that she confronts often results in a sacrifice of intelligent direction of conduct in favor of moral contortionism.

I turn now to articulating some ideals for moral conduct that emerge from Dewey's insights into the nature of deliberation. In contrast to traditional standards that proffer moral *governance* (e.g., through some formula, law, universal prescription, or set of *prima facie* duties), a pragmatic ideal must be a method that has offered *guidance* in the past and might continue to do so.[13] In *Logic: The Theory of Inquiry*, Dewey explains that pragmatic standards "are methods which experience up to the present time shows to be the best methods available for achieving certain results, while abstraction of these methods does supply a (relative) norm or *standard* for further undertakings" (LW 12:108).

A pragmatic approach does not eventuate in a set of necessary and sufficient conditions circumscribing all and only right or good actions. Like good methods of farming or surgery, a good method of moral valuation must be experientially grounded by its effectiveness in adapting to problematic situations. Since such a method is checked at every turn by the push and pull of our interactions, it eventuates in judgments that exceed mere emotive preferences. It may indeed be subjectively gratifying to strive for a certain moral ideal, but the pragmatist sanctions one method of valuation rather than another because one is judged to ameliorate experience. The pragmatist treats such sanctioned methods not as immaculate *a priori* truths but as working hypotheses qualified by experimental confirmation or disconfirmation.

I shall take for granted Dewey's view that inquiry into artistic-aesthetic experience is revelatory of the nature of any meaningful experience. "Esthetic experience," Dewey contends in *Art as Experience*, "is experience in its integrity" (LW 10:278). Our *moral* experiences could potentially be as richly developed as are those experiences consummated in peaks of the fine arts.

A caveat: Art is conceived here along Deweyan lines as imaginative social communication through culturally refined interactive skills. It is *not* treated as "the beauty parlor of civilization" (AE, LW 10:346) producing idyllic pleasantries, nor as Romantic spurts of ethereal creativity. This must be borne in mind, since art construed along these latter lines would teach us little about effective moral deliberation.

Approaching morality from the standpoint of aesthetic experience may strike some as, at best, incoherent. Worse, it may appear to be an opening for "anything goes" relativism. Such a judgment is conditioned by our Enlightenment heritage, which teaches that aesthetic and moral experiences are discontinuous. Kant can be held up as a model: Understanding (*Verstand*), according to Kant, is constrained by our universal conceptual structure and has nothing to do with feeling. In understanding, fixed concepts functioning in a purely formal realm enable classification of a presented image in the material realm. An aesthetic judgment, by contrast, has no such determinateness. It is a matter of subjective feeling (albeit "common" or universal feeling, for Kant). With the aesthetic, Kant writes in the *Critique of Judgment*, "the basis determining [the judgment] is the subject's feeling and not the concept of an object."[14] Meanwhile, he writes in the *Grounding for the Metaphysics of Morals* that in a moral judgment "moral concepts have their seat and origin completely *a priori* in reason [*Vernunft*]."[15]

In this context, any attempt to de-compartmentalize the supposedly autonomous spheres of the moral and aesthetic, treating them as distinctive features of a unified field of value, raises a suspicious eyebrow because it seems to subjectivize morality radically.[16] As will be shown, this is not the case.

One of Dewey's greatest contributions to value inquiry was to investigate the continuity between aesthetic experience and everyday life. Contrary to the prevailing view, aesthetic experience is not a pristine flight too far removed from ordinary life to shed light on moral complexities. Far from being a lofty, elite, or contrived ideal, what I call moral artistry simply requires cultivation of what already goes on incessantly. What goes on, as Vincent Colapietro observes, is "the dynamic interpenetration of aesthetic discernment and artistic execution."[17]

To get a clearer idea of what this means it is necessary to elaborate on Dewey's terminology. He writes: "'artistic' refers primarily to the act of production and 'esthetic' to that of perception and enjoyment" (AE, LW 10:53). An artistic-aesthetic experience is a consummated experience of productions (the artistic) and perceptions (the aesthetic). Effective moral deliberations are similarly structured. With moral acts that destroy or divide, there is usually production with a minimum of perception. More inclusive and enduring goals escape notice, eclipsed by obsessive focus on the task at hand (see HNC, MW 14:138). The experience is not aesthetically complete.

One capacity central to wise deliberation is a proficiency aesthetically to recognize and artistically to respond to the way short-term goals are nested in long-term goals. For example, consider a forum in which audience members raise their hands to signal their wish to speak. Someone who is impatient might make his or her views known by simply blurting out a statement without regard for others awaiting an opportunity to speak. The resulting disapproval signifies a tacit communal recognition that an individual's goals are best realized in a community of mutually respecting members. A short-term end (being heard) was in this case actualized only to the detriment of long-term ends. One such long-term goal is to foster conditions in which individuals attain value in their own lives through participation in a community that is (ideally) friendly to the diversity of personal yearnings. More than just bad manners, blurting out a statement in this case indicates an immature moral sensitivity. Instead of contracted perceptions of this sort, what is needed is a cultivated imagination that discerns and enacts communally workable options.

Since we are not disembodied minds insulated from our natural and social surroundings, our wisest moral productions result from responsiveness to others. We require a democratized imagination that aesthetically perceives and artistically responds to a situation's "whole system of desires" (LW 7:197)—that is, to the entire system of pressing exigencies in a troubled situation. Because these conflicting tendencies are not localized and isolated from each other, they must be treated comprehensively or, to borrow an increasingly popular term, *ecologically*. The ecology metaphor highlights that individual parts of a system or situation are intelligible only when understood in their interrelations with other parts of the system. Exigencies must be treated with an inclusive eye to the way they affect values elsewhere in a situation.

An aesthetically complete moral experience, then, strives for an ecological or democratic ideal.[18] Far more than a form of government, Dewey writes in *Democracy and Education*, democracy is "primarily a mode of associated living, of conjoint communicated experience" (DE, MW 9:93). When interests conflict, the democratic way of life *elicits* differences and gives them a hearing instead of sacrificing them to the alter of preconceived plans. A *democratic imagination* refers our "own action to that of others, and . . . consider[s] the action of others to give point and direction" to our own (DE, MW

9:93). From this expansive field of contact an integrative value may emerge to reconstruct and harmonize conflicting values. Thus, to function at its best, deliberation requires a *social* imagination that brings competing tendencies to successful issue and unites us with others.[19] So, we can learn about moral thinking by paying attention to artistic thinking without collapsing into subjectivism.

To approach this from a different perspective, consider moral deliberation in relation to Dewey's conception of aesthetically complete experiences in *Art as Experience*. For deliberation of any sort to be brought to a resolution, it must develop so as to have a form that expresses coherently the conflicts that originally set the problem for inquiry. When a single experience becomes sufficiently demarcated from other experiences to be called *an* experience (as when we say "Now that was an experience!"), a coherent story may be told, from commencement to culmination, about a problematic situation. Dewey calls such individuated experiences "*an* experience" or "consummatory experience."[20] Consummatory experience is exemplified by the artistic-aesthetic experience of deliberately consummated productions and perceptions.

These insights into democracy and artistic-aesthetic experience can be merged in order to comprehend the potential or moral deliberation. Moral deliberation is a communal experience rather than an isolated act. The moral life is a co-operation of self with others, marked by responsiveness to the lives fulgurating in a situation. As communal, then, deliberation realizes its full capacity through a socially responsive or democratic imagination that perceives paths of mutual growth. As an experience, deliberation, like any other coherent human experience, realizes its fullest potential through being aesthetically complete. So, dramatic rehearsal is at its best when executions and perceptions attain to a democratic ideal. A moral experience, then, is brought off well only when we deal perceptively and artistically with the entire system of pressing exigencies in a troubled situation, such as conflicts of long-range and short-range ends, along with pressing needs, desires, and ends of our own and of others, as well as contingent events, and the like.

Refinements of the Theory

The moral artist, like the prototypical artist, must have a finely textured sensitivity to recurrent themes of everyday life and to the potential of the present. We fail morally primarily because our range of creative prospects becomes contracted.

Unfortunately, in much of our experience imagination is contracted. This poses a problem for morality when it abridges reflection. Abbreviated deliberations constrict possibilities for resolving moral problems and render actions impulsive. Consequently, a rich imagination in present activity is as much a moral requirement as it is an artistic requirement.

Often this contraction of imagination results from attachment to preestablished ends. Morality, like art, requires process-orientation rather than product-orientation (a failure of Benthamite utilitarianism).[21] As long as we are not hypnotized by the swirling confusion around us, attention to the insistent present makes situations more manageable. When mindfulness to the particulars of the present is sacrificed, the quality of the product suffers.

Products emerge as present conditions are transformed in light of latent possibilities. A Zen garden, for example, takes on its form through the alternating appreciations and productions of garden*ing*. Exactly what form the product will take is unknown prior to raking the sand and arranging the stones. A predetermined garden would make gardening a drudgery and the garden poor and artless. The moral analogue is that thinking of ends as set and predetermined impoverishes our imaginative survey of alternative futures. This leads to insensitive and unperceptive moral actions.

In contrast to the moral accountant (such as the Benthamite seeking a net gain of pleasures), the moral artist does not subordinate the present to a remote outcome (see HNC, MW 14:185). In *Experience and Nature*, Dewey defines art with respect to "the relation of means and consequence, process and product, the instrumental and consummatory. Any activity that is simultaneously both . . . is art" (EN, LW 1:271). In just the way that process and product (means and consequences) are fused in the imaginative art of the aforementioned gardener, they are fused in the art of morality. Cultivating moral artistry meets the moral demand for a rich imagination, without which life is barren of constructive prospects.[22]

This plea for cultivating rich imaginations exhorts moral theorists to focus on the aesthetic. The aesthetic "is no intruder in experience from without, . . . it is the clarified and intensified development of traits that belong to every normally complete experience" (AE, LW 10"52–53).[23] Sequestering the aesthetic from everyday deliberations, far from celebrating imagination, is a recipe for moral sterility, fragmentation, and alienation. Imagination cannot be democratic in such straits, so it eventually turns (as it historically has turned) either to radically individual pursuits or to the promotion of authoritarian control.

Our *moral* experiences could potentially be as developed as are those experiences consummated in the peaks of the fine arts. This is a realizable ideal for which to aim, and it escapes the time-worn irony of "grounding" ideals in an illusory transcendent realm. It is an ideal we can strive for to consummate and revivify meaning and value.

A further issue warrants attention. Dewey's ecological, democratic, and artistic-aesthetic moral ideal is personified by a moral artist whose aesthetically funded imagination enables sensitivity to the social bearings of action. But given the traditional association of art with the idyllic, impractical, and pleasant, bringing the aesthetic to bear on morals might be taken to imply that moral reflection is invariably a pleasant affair that consummates in delightful outcomes. (In order to focus on a more substantive issue, I shall simply pass over the indefensible belief that aesthetic experience is always pleasurable.) Surely an adequate moral theory must respond to the inherent ambiguities of moral judgment, to the genuineness of moral conflict, and to the pitfalls often encountered in even the best of decisions.

In contrast with most traditional moral ideals, an artistic-aesthetic ideal does not need to explain away tragic conflicts of interest when they arise.[24] Universalist moral philosophies have taught that human reason is capable of sifting through an *apparent* competition of values to discover the single Right channel for action that will satisfy all rational agents. This is based on a pre-Darwinian assumption of an ideal universe in which all "legitimate" desires (those in accord with "duty") can blossom into action simultaneously. The specter of this idealistic assumption does not haunt Dewey's theory. To discover an integrative value among competing values is an ideal for which to strive. But success is not vouchsafed. It would be naive to suppose that the mediation of intelligence can always discover a utopian channel for all the contending desires in a moral situation. Real incompatibles—irreducible tragic conflicts—emerge.

Theoretical strategies designed to purify moral reasoning of attention to practical conflicts promote stupidity by constricting imagination. An adequate moral theory must respond to the tragic dimension of experience in a way that neither embitters us nor leaves us with an impotent, overly narrowly focused moral schema.

What is needed is twofold: (1) to wrest the complete meaning from tragic situations so that we are better prepared for future events, and (2) to transform crippling conditions that may yield to reconstruction so that the future might not merely repeat the past.[25] Imagination expands our focus beyond a confused and dizzying present so that we can reflect and act in ways that may eventually bring about more desirable conditions.

Conclusion

Contemporary moral theories that ignore imagination are irresponsible. This applies equally to theories of the aesthetic that follow the tendency of Romanticism to divorce imagination from practical intelligence. Such tendencies leave morality's most valuable resource wafting in a capricious breeze.

Our capacity for dramatic rehearsal can become an artfully controlled and developed instrument. With this instrument, not only do we forecast consequences for ourselves, but also, as George Herbert Mead observes, we dramatically play the role of others whose lives interlace with our own.[26] We place ourselves in the emerging dramas of others' lives to discover an action that will meaningfully continue their life-dramas alongside ours.

Morality is primarily a matter of cultivating habits of refined moral perceptiveness, creativity, expressiveness, and skill—habits more readily associated with an artist than with a calculating accountant or a dispassionate judge. We feel our way skillfully through a tangle of relationships with a discerning imagination for possible paths of interaction through which these strands may be artfully woven. Morally poor conduct is not merely a deficiency in one's capacity rationally to discern and follow settled moral criteria. Rather, much remediable moral failure stems from a mal-developed imagination and botched moral artistry.

Notes

Note: Unless noted otherwise, Dewey citations are from *The Collected Works*, ed. Jo Ann Boydston (SIU Press), indicated by series (EW for *Early Works*, MW for *Middle Works*, and LW for *Later Works*), volume, and page number.

1. Thomas Alexander, "John Dewey and the Moral Imagination," in *Transactions of the Charles S. Peirce Society*, 1993, 29, No. 3 (1993) 384.

2. To reconstruct Dewey's theory of deliberation one must look beyond his few overt uses of the term "dramatic rehearsal" (in 1908 *Ethics*, MW 5:293; 1932 *Ethics*, LW 7:275; HNC, MW 14:132–3; *How We Think*, LW 8:200. Also see his correspondence at The Center for Dewey Studies, letter 03525; 1915/5/7,8,9; to Scudder Klyce. For earlier discussions of "imaginative rehearsal," see EW 4:251–52, and John David Koch, ed., *John Dewey's Lectures on Ethics: 1900-1901* (SIU Press, 1991), 141–43, 226–29. Among the few discussions of dramatic rehearsal in the literature on Dewey are: James Gouinlock, *John Dewey's Philosophy of Value* (Humanities Press, 1972), 302–4; Joseph Kupfer, *Experience as Art* (SUNY Press, 1983), 141–70; Victor Kestenbaum's preface to *Theory of the Moral Life* (Irvington Publishers, Inc., 1980), xvii–xviii; Thomas Alexander, "John Dewey and the Moral Imagination," 369–400; Steven Fesmire, "Dramatic Rehearsal and the Moral Artist: A Deweyan Theory of Moral Understanding" in *Transactions of the Charles S. Peirce Society* 31, no. 3 (1995), 568–97.

3. I have in mind such works as Martha Nussbaum, *The Fragility of Goodness: Luck and Ethics in Greek Tragedy and Philosophy* (Cambridge University Press, 1986), Alasdair MacIntyre, *After Virtue* (University of Notre Dame Press, 1981), Mark Johnson, *Moral Imagination: Implications of Cognitive Science for Ethics* (University of Chicago Press, 1993), and Owen Flanagan, *Varieties of Moral Personality: Ethics and Psychological Realism* (Harvard University Press, 1991). For example, Mark Johnson argues in *Moral Imagination* that metaphor is "the locus of our imaginative exploration of possibilities for action" (University of Chicago Press, 1993, 35). That is, courses for thought and action become options for us because a metaphor by which we conceptualize a situation lends itself to these alternatives. Metaphors are part of our mostly unconscious horizon of inherited interpretive structures, enabling us to communicate so that we may envision an uncertain future together. They tether deliberations, both highlighting and concealing alternatives for conduct.

4. William James, *The Principles of Psychology*, Vol. II (New York: Dover), 531.

5. Likewise, James observes: "Now into every one's deliberations the representation of one alternative will often enter with such sudden force as to carry the imagination with itself exclusively, and to produce an apparently settled decision in its own favor. These premature and spurious decisions are of course known to everyone" (PP, II, 530). (Cf. PP, II, 562–65 on being in "some fiery passion's grasp." This is quoted by Dewey in MW 5:188 and MW 14:136.)

6. *Lectures on Ethics: 1900–1901*, ed. Donald Koch (Carbondale: SIU Press, 1991), 226. In the 1900–01 *Lectures*, Dewey observes four ways in which people deliberate: (1) "Some people deliberate by dialogue." (2) "Others visualize certain results." (3) "Others rather take the motor imagery

and imagine themselves doing a thing." (4) "Others imagine a thing done and then imagine someone else commenting upon it" (245). Dewey explores the generic pattern of these ways of deliberating.

7. William James, *Pragmatism* (Hackett), 97.

8. For a discussion of the self as *in utero* "in" the world, see John McDermott, *Streams of Experience* (Amherst: University of Massachusetts Press, 1986), 128–31.

9. Paul Ricoeur, *Time and Narrative*, 1:66. Quoted in Johnson, *Moral Imagination*, 166 (Johnson's emphasis).

10. For example, see HNC, MW 14:127. The extent to which this Source-Path-Goal schema directed and sometimes constrained Dewey's communicated thought merits careful study. As a model for understanding means and ends, processes and products, the journey metaphor has an unfortunate tendency to separate the "means whereby" from the "goal sought." With this metaphor, the end is prototypically thought of as a pre-set destination "down the road." This lends itself to precisely the separation of means from ends that Dewey fought. Perhaps this sheds some light on why Dewey's treatment of means and ends is so often misinterpreted.

11. Alexander, "John Dewey and the Moral Imagination," 386.

12. What is at stake here may be clarified by a glance at the corrosiveness of this denial in our larger culture. The traditional faith in a non-natural spring for values has tended to promote a distrust of *human* intelligence and *human* moral capacities. Mistrusted capacities are seldom effectively understood and developed. Many have internalized a self-fulfilling prophecy by which human beings, believing out of doctrinal faith that they are morally and mentally inept, neglect to cultivate the very imaginative capacities that could make our world a source of hope.

13. The guidance/governance distinction is used by Mark Johnson in *Moral Imagination*.

14. Immanuel Kant, *Critique of Judgment*, trans. W. Pluhar (1790; Hackett, 1987), S. 17, Ak. 231.

15. Immanuel Kant, *Grounding for the Metaphysics of Morals*, trans. James W. Ellington, 3rd edition (Hackett, 1993), 22, Ak. 411. In the *Critique of Judgment* Kant nonetheless probes theoretical links (even analogical mappings) between aesthetic and moral judgments. See Casey Haskins, "Kant and the Autonomy of Art," *The Journal of Aesthetics and Art Criticism*, Winter 1989.

16. Dewey writes in *Art as Experience* that moral experience is different from aesthetic experience in that it is more distinctively "practical" than "emotional" (LW 10:44). On this "aestheticist turn" in value inquiry,

see Casey Haskins, "Dewey's *Art as Experience*: The Tension between Aesthetics and Aestheticism," *Transactions of Charles S. Peirce Society*, Fall 1992.

17. Vincent Colapietro, "Art and Philosophy: A Fateful Entanglement," chapter 3 of *Reason Subjectivity, and Agency: Postmodern Themes and Pragmatic Challenges* (SUNY Press, forthcoming). Quoted from working draft.

18. As Joseph Kupfer explains, "we judge whether our imaginative projection of alternative futures proceeds in an *aesthetically complete way.*" Kupfer, *Experience as Art*, 142.

19. For further discussion of Dewey's democratic credo, see Michael Eldridge, "Dewey's Faith in Democracy as Shared Experience," in *Transactions of the Charles S. Peirce Society*, 32, no. 1 (1996). Also see the ensuing response, in the same issue, by Robert B. Westbrook, "Democratic Faith: A Response to Michael Eldridge."

20. Gadamer's notion of *Erlebnis* in *Truth and Method*, derived from Dilthey, is drawn along lines very similar to Dewey's notion of *an* experience. For a full discussion of the concept of "*an* experience," see *Art as Experience*, chapter 3. Cf. Dewey's Introduction to "Essays in Experimental Logic," MW 10:321–24.

21. In *Human Nature and Conduct*, Dewey critiques the Benthamite metaphor which understands our moral "deliberation upon what purposes to form" in terms of "business calculation of profit and loss" (MW 14:146–49). Happiness is logically "a maximum net gain of pleasures." The metaphor lends itself only to calculating future gain or loss of a fixed end, namely pleasure.

22. This observation runs counter to the common evaluation of Dewey as a product-oriented technophile whose "instrumentalism" is a masterplan for ready-made goals.

23. Dewey leaves no doubt that he intends this paradigm to apply to morals. For example, he wrote of *Art as Experience* in 1950 that the "principle of development" from everyday to "artfully developed" subject matter holds for "morals, politics, religion, science, philosophy itself, as well as the fine arts" (LW 16:397).

24. For more on irreducible tragic conflicts, see Nussbaum, *The Fragility of Goodness*.

25. John McDermott quotes from Dewey's *Experience and Education* in the context of a discussion of tragedy: "We always live at the time we live and not at some other time, and only by extracting at each present time the full meaning of each present experience are we prepared for

doing the same thing in the future. This is the only preparation which in the long run amounts to anything." John McDermott, ed., *The Philosophy of John Dewey: The Lived Experience* (New York: G. P. Putnam's Sons, 1973), xix.

26. See George Herbert Mead, *Mind, Self, and Society* (University of Chicago Press, 1934), chapters 18–20.

8

The Nemesis of Necessity:
Tragedy's Challenge to Deweyan Pragmatism

═══════════

Raymond D. Boisvert

1. Introduction: Tragedy and Necessity

Gary Cooper, as *The Virginian*, finds himself faced with the sort of dilemma that Hegel, focusing on *Antigone* as "the most excellent and satisfying work of art," identified with Greek tragedy (Hegel, 377). Like Antigone, Cooper is forced to choose between two goods, the demands of justice and those of friendship. But *The Virginian* is no tragedy. The nameless character played by Cooper has little difficulty coming to a decision. Frontier justice must prevail. The dilemma was only apparent. There is one correct resolution, and it is swiftly implemented. "Tragedy," the intractability of a situation involving competing claims, has been supplanted by an axiological absolutism which asserts, in the words of Martha Nussbaum, that "in every case there is at most a single correct answer, and the competing candidate makes no further claim once the choice is made" (Nussbaum, 30).

The Virginian, ironically enough, was released in 1929 as American optimism about "single correct answers" and continued progress was about to be tested. Still, the film depicts a certain new world robustness, a refusal to admit, along with Max Scheler, and the tragic is "an essential element of the universe itself" (Scheler, 249). The American myth of exceptionalism is well at work here. Despite the writings of Hawthorne, which should have put to rest the belief in exceptional, unique conditions which would free the

151

new world from such old world problems as adultery, small-mindedness, and fanaticism, popular art continued to view the tragic as illusory.

If this was the attitude of the popular arts during the early decades of the century, what was the attitude of America's intellectuals? Hawthorne, along with Melville, had sounded the call to a different understanding of human life, one more consistent with that of classical tragedians. But the philosophers seem not to have heard. Emerson, though a contemporary, exuded confidence in an ultimate, transcendental oneness. He celebrated the power of will and intellect to transform the very worst of what fate could provide into triumphs of human ingenuity.

Few writers can outdo Emerson in his vivid description of natural constraints, what traditional language called "necessity" or "fate." At the same time, few would as effectively counteract the description by so profusely championing the power of mind and will to effect a liberating transformation. "Fate then is a name for facts not yet passed under the fire of thought; for causes which are unpenetrated" (Emerson, 379). Once thought has penetrated the causes, the fearsome natural forces, like wild animals, can readily be tamed. "The mischievous torrent is taught to drudge for man; the wild beasts he makes useful for food, or dress, or labor; the chemic explosions are controlled like his watch" (Emerson, 380). Mind is a wonderful and powerful force. Under its guidance even the "solid" can become "liquid." Failure is due only to "want of thought" (Emerson, 386–387).

What about those who would reject axiological absolutism? Human life, after all, provides examples of situations where no unified resolution is possible. Belief in the ineluctability and intractability of such cases need not be unusual. For Emerson, though, this belief is superficial and illusory. Fundamentally, all is "Blessed Unity" (Emerson, pp. 389–390). The Virginian was right not to engage in Hamlet-like soul searching. "One way is right to go; the hero sees it, and moves on that aim, and has the world under him for root and support" (Emerson, p. 378).

Emerson's vision cannot therefore be labelled "tragic." His commitment to an all-embracing oneness in which difference and difficulty are ultimately dissolved is incompatible with the view that tragedy is an essential element of the universe itself. But what of later thinkers? What, for example, can we say about Dewey? Here is someone who substituted an unregenerate pluralism for Emerson's monism. Whereas Emerson spoke eloquently of reform, and then retreated into an inner world of thought, Dewey worked in the community.

Surely in his dealings with so many individuals under so many circumstances, Dewey must have begun to feel in the marrow of his bones that combination of factors which form part of the "necessity" so dominantly acknowledged in tragedy: the inevitability of conflict, the evil of unintended consequences, the unfair defeat of the good, the frustration of human aspirations, the ineluctable mixture of good and evil, the lack of control over circumstances. He lived long enough to witness the First World War, the depression, Hooverville shanties, the squalor of immigrant neighborhoods, the Second World War, and the cruelty of Stalinist Russia. His childhood memories included images from the Civil War. Dewey's personal life, too, had been touched by the harsh hand of necessity. Within one decade, two of his sons died of diseases while visiting Europe.

Temperamentally, Dewey was too much of a reformer for even such horrors as these to move him toward a pessimistic acquiescence. But should they not have occasioned a sensibility like the tragic? Tragedy is not, after all, a species of pessimism. Agamemnon, Antigone, and Hamlet are neither passive nor quiescent.[1] Tragedy, in the words of Ricoeur, can only be expressed in dialectical terms. "Without the dialectics of fate and freedom there would be no tragedy" (Ricoeur, 220). Both "fate" and "human action" must be present (Ricoeur, 221). Quiescence is out of the question because tragedy requires and celebrates a faith in the greatness of humans (Krutch, 84).

If these commentators are correct, the impulse of the reform-minded philosopher need not be detached from a sense of the tragic. What is needed, however, is an almost tangible feeling of what, for lack of a more suitable term, I will call "necessity." "Necessity" here is admitted to be a permanent participant in the living drama of human life.

A tragic situation is composed of many elements, which, in proper Wittgensteinian fashion, do not exactly overlap in every case. However, one theme which is repeatedly present is the acceptance of a sphere of activity over which humans have no control. This "necessity" can take various forms. One is that virtue carries within itself the seed of vice. It is Othello's love that makes him vulnerable to murderous jealousy.[2] Another is the unavoidability of conflicting loyalties. Agamemnon must choose between his daughter's life and the success of his expedition. Antigone is torn between loyalty to her brother and loyalty to the state, a loyalty further complicated by her upcoming marriage to the King's son.

A third sort of "necessity" is sheer happenstance. We cannot control what others do, nor what we do every moment of the day. Hamlet does not choose to be the son of a father who is murdered by his brother. Desdemona does not lose her handkerchief on purpose. Nor can she control the deadly course that follows upon this seemingly innocuous event. Finally, having good intentions may be under our control, but the actual outcome of the activities we undertake has a logic of its own. Oedipus seeks to avoid killing his father and marrying his mother. But the very actions he follows are those that lead to the events he most wishes to avoid.

As these examples indicate, the "necessity" associated with tragedy is not to be conflated with "fate" or "determinism." Tragedy requires no cosmic plan in which every event is fated to occur from eternity. The "necessity" involved in tragedy is the unavoidability of certain events. Blindness is an appropriate metaphor for this "necessity." What the characters can neither see nor foresee is what generates the tragic situation. Ricoeur notes how this blindness is related to mythological figures such as Moira, Zeus, and Erinyes. Moira, he says "is the 'portion,' the 'share,' the 'lot' imparted to man beyond his choice; it is the non-choice of choice, the necessity that surcharges and over-determines his acts" (Ricoeur, 215).

Whether Dewey took this necessity into account is questionable. One prominent commentator, Robert Westbrook, has argued for an evolution toward the tragic in Dewey's thought. The "animating ideals of Dewey's ethics" remained fairly consistent after 1908, says Westbrook. However, "there had crept into his work a considerably more chastened, even occasionally tragic, view of experience and a more explicitly modest estimate of the reach of moral philosophy" (Westbrook, 416). My own reading of Dewey will claim that the changes in his formulations are due to an honest empiricism responding to the horrors of his time. They always, however, remained peripheral. In particular, they did not lead to any serious absorption of the "tragic view" into Dewey's thought.

Henry James contrasted Hawthorne and Emerson by claiming that "Hawthorne's vision was all for the evil and sin of the world: a side of life as to which Emerson's eyes were thickly bandaged" (Sewall, 211). As we shall see, Dewey's eyes were not quite so thickly bandaged as were those of Emerson. But in the end, despite the multiple ways in which he went beyond Emerson, Dewey's eyes were covered over by lingering layers of the Emersonian bandage.

Such a thesis is not new. Others have announced it before. Randolph Bourne, for example, complained that the Deweyan philosophy had "no place for the inexorable" (Coughlan, 86). Morris Raphael Cohen made explicit the comparison with Emerson: "Though Dewey would hardly subscribe to Emerson's idealistic Platonism and the doctrine that the over-soul is everything, he shares Emerson's benign attitude in regard to the unconquerable natural ills which have dogged human existence throughout the ages" (Cohen, 1940, 405). Reinhold Niebuhr criticized Dewey as the very embodiment of that American delusion, the belief that scientific methodology extended to social questions would foster an era in which human ills would be definitively resolved (Niebuhr, 1954, 80–81). Even so staunch a supporter as John McDermott has been led to concede a similar limitation. "Unfortunately, he [Dewey] had an undeveloped doctrine of evil, the demonic, and the capacity of human beings *en masse* to commit heinous crimes against other human beings" (LW 11:xxxii).

The one prominent exception to these interpretations is Sidney Hook. In "Pragmatism and the Tragic Sense of Life," Hook attempted to defend the marriage of tragedy and pragmatism as one that is natural and unforced: "As you may have gathered by this time, I have been concerned to show that this pragmatic approach to the moral problem can not only be squared with the recognition of tragic conflicts, of troubles, minor and grave, which dog the life of man in a precarious world, but that it gets its chief justification from this recognition" (Hook, 243). As I will indicate later in this essay, Hook's attempt, though worthwhile, is unsuccessful. No marriage between tragedy and Deweyan pragmatism is possible without a sensitivity to the irrecusable presence of "necessity."

With the exception of Hook, what these commentators are charging is that Dewey has situated himself in that especially modern stream which dismisses ingredients that are central to tragedy. Both George Steiner and Joseph Wood Krutch have argued that modernity so altered the philosophical assumptions which guided human life, that tragedy in a sense continuous with the Greeks was no longer possible. The borderline signalling the discontinuity is a new attitude toward "necessity." The tragic sensibility keeps us rooted in the complex world where our best-laid plans can go awry. "In tragedy, the twist of the net which brings down the hero may be an accident or hazard of circumstance, but the mesh is woven into the heart of life" (Steiner, 128). The opposite of tragedy is not comedy, which combines, with differing results, the same elements of choice and necessity. Comedy and tragedy represent the middle ground on a continuum whose extremes are pessimistic resignation and utopian optimism. During the modern era, it was the latter, utopian enthusiasm, which overshadowed tragedy.

Tragedy is especially important as a counterweight to philosophical *hubris*. It forces us to face the fact that no rational or explanatory grid will match perfectly the abundant, multifarious character of life. Philosophy must incorporate the tragic sensibility, not try to get beyond it. Plato, whose demiurge in *The Timaeus* is limited by necessity, provides a model for conceding the tragic sensibility. For the Greeks and the Medievals, the tug of war between mind and necessity went on within a universe admittedly limited and limiting. The tension between *Nous* and *Anangke* was thought to be woven into the very fabric of things. Pre-modern thinkers, sensitive to limits, were not deluded into thinking that mind would one day decisively overcome necessity.

2. Mind Seeks to Subdue Necessity

That delusion was the dream of modernity. No one announced it better than Machiavelli. *Fortuna*, for him, was what had to be dominated. This was a word with a lengthy Roman history and an embodiment as a prominent goddess. Etymologically the word derived from *ferre*, to bring. It signified, generally, all that was brought, whatever happened to enter into human lives. For the Romans, *Fortuna* was a goddess to be respected. For Machiavelli, however, fortune is no longer a goddess to be respected but a woman to be conquered.[3] Control of her requires one "to beat her and strike her down" (Machiavelli, sec. 25).

This type of conquest and domination of necessity is precisely what tragedy rejects. The tragic sensibility admits the continuous nature of the struggle between mind and necessity. Humans are like ship captains. Sometimes the journey is uneventful. At other times a punishing storm surprises the ship at sea. "Mind" as embodying knowledge, experience, and wisdom must be put to work to survive the challenge. Certain captains go down with their ships, others weather the storm successfully. What all captains know, however, is that necessity has not been decisively conquered. Each time they sail, the dialectic of mind and necessity is renewed.

With Machiavelli, the issue is no longer one of balance between two eternal forces, but a contest between two individuals, male and female. Fortuna is now challenged by *virtu* (from *vir*, man). The new challenge is for the male to make the female permanently submissive. Fortune, says Machiavelli, is like a river on a rampage. Humans can take the attitude that such is their fate and do nothing. Or they can build dams and channels so that the once dangerous flow is diverted into a harmless extra amount of water. "It happens similarly with fortune, which shows her power where virtue has not been put in order to resist her and therefore turns her impetus where she knows that dams and dikes have not been made to contain her" (Machiavelli, sec. 25).

By transforming Fortune from a goddess into a woman, Machiavelli signalled the possibility, foreign to tragedy, that fortune could be held in check. *Fortuna*, demythologized, became mere *natura*, the concatenation of natural forces waiting for the controlling and dominating hand of man. For the philosophers who proudly set forth the machinery of modernity, nature was transformed into a beast who had simply not yet been tamed. Humans, it was thought, would no longer need be prey to its fickle ways.

3. Dewey's Rootedness in the Modern

This kind of optimistic game-plan for dominating nature was most clearly announced in Bacon's *New Atlantis*. Belief in progress signalled the waning of the tragic dimension from life. Three centuries later, this attitude was alive and well. Dewey's fulsome praise for Bacon in *Reconstruction in Philosophy*,[4] for example, would seem to situate him within, if not a purely utopian tradition, then at least one that was overly blind to the workings of necessity. The very problem of "reconstruction" as Dewey defines it, follows exactly the path of mind (science) dominating necessity.

> Put in the language of Bacon, this means that while we have been reasonably successful in obtaining command of nature by means of science, our science is not yet such that this command is systematically and preeminently applied to the relief of the human estate. Such applications occur and in great numbers, but they are incidental, sporadic and

external. And this limitation defines the specific problem of
philosophical reconstruction (MW 12:104).

What is of special note in this citation is that the "limitation"
mentioned is not a limitation inherent in the nature of things, is
not *Fortuna* or *Anangke*. It is, rather, a limitation of human will
and effort. Indeed, a sensitivity to inherent natural limitations is
decidedly underemphasized in *Reconstruction in Philosophy*.

Summarizing the elements of modernity which follow in the
spirit of Bacon, Dewey waxes eloquent about the belief in progress.
"Great store," he says, "is set upon the idea of progress." This
Baconian attitude was adopted by "the great French thinkers of
the later eighteenth century," who "developed it into the doctrine of
the indefinite perfectibility of mankind on earth. Man is capable, if
he will but exercise the required courage, intelligence and effort, of
shaping his own fate. Physical conditions offer no insurmountable
barriers" (MW 12:106–107). Even admitting the fact that Dewey is
in part reporting the beliefs others have held, the reader nonetheless gets the sense that this tendency to set "great store in the idea
of progress" and that "physical conditions offer no insurmountable
barriers" are understood by Dewey to be part of the permanent,
positive legacy of early modern thought.

If such assertions were limited to this one book, they might be
dismissed as aberrations caused by the circumstances of composi-
tion. But these texts are not isolated. They are typical of an attitude that pervades Dewey's writing. In one of his two articles entitled
"Progress," Dewey states once again the belief that scientific advances applied to social issues will usher in an epoch of improvement. Scientific advances, he says, have provided the "preliminary
conditions of progress." What remains as a project is the application of scientific method to the moral sphere. The difference between science and morality is not one of two radically different
realms. "The problem which now confronts us, the problem of
progress, is the same in kind, differing in subject-matter" (MW
10:240).

The fresh memory of World War I should have served as a
powerful counterweight, indicating that matching scientific advance
with moral advance might not be as possible as Dewey thought.
Addressing this issue directly, Dewey indicates just how little his
faith in the realization of social progress had been affected. The
essay begins with a concession of the type that is necessary for a
tragic sensibility. The war revealed that the dream of "uninter-

rupted progress" had been "a fool's paradise" (MW 10:234). There is even room for *Anangke* in a world beyond the dream of uninterrupted progress. "We do not of course wholly control the energies of nature; we shall never wholly do so" (MW 10:237). But the tone of the essay indicates how little this realization had altered Dewey's Baconian bias. He is like a Newtonian physicist forced to accept the Einsteinian revolution, but persisting in viewing it as a minor tinkering with the Newtonian outlook, rather than as the fundamental re-orientation that it is.

A careful reading of the essay reveals why this is so. It defends the "institution of a more manly and more responsible faith in progress than that in which we have indulged in the past" (MW 10:234). What was wrong with the pre-war belief was its assumption that progress would issue automatically. "We confused rapidity of change with advance, and we took certain gains in our own comfort and ease as signs that cosmic forces were working inevitably to improve the whole state of human affairs" (MW 10:234–235). While such a belief may have been puerile, modern man had nonetheless been correct in promising progress allied to science. "While the modern man was deceived about the amount of progress he had made, and especially deceived about the automatic certainty of progress, he was right in thinking that for the first time in history mankind is in command of the possibility of progress" (MW 10:237).[5]

Assuming the possibility of progress in morality to be analogous to progress in technology, Dewey makes what we now know to be a questionable distinction between civilized people and "savages." "Civilized man has not a better endowment of ear and eye than savage man; but his social surroundings give him more important things to see and hear than the savage has, and he has the wit to devise instruments to reinforce his eye and ear—the telegraph and telephone, the microscope and telescope" (MW 10:238–239). Such antiquated anthropology, seeing earlier peoples as "primitive" and "savage," is seemingly counterbalanced by the admission that "there is no reason for thinking that he [civilized man] has less natural aggressiveness or more natural altruism—or will ever have—than the barbarian" (MW 10:239). But a careful reading of the essay reveals that such an awareness had not penetrated to the marrow of Dewey's bones.

What are we to make of the great moral systems of the past? What would Dewey say about the social fabrics woven by the Confucian, the Judaic, or the Stoic world views? Their success, he seems to say, was merely accidental. "We cannot too much insist on the fact that until men got control of natural forces civilization was a local accident" (MW 10:236).[6] Revealing the degree to which the lessons of World War I had not penetrated deeply enough into his thinking, Dewey asserts blithely that backsliding can now be kept in check. "We have now a sure method. Wholesale permanent decays of civilization are impossible" (MW 10:237).

Of course, Dewey could not predict the butchery of another world war, its genocidal horrors, and its bloody, cruel aftermath in Stalinist Russia. But, examining the evidence we have, it appears that qualifications to his belief in moral progress as analogous to scientific progress were minimal. Because Dewey's philosophy was rooted in experience, it does contain some formulations which attenuate somewhat his position, preventing it from being naively optimistic. In *Experience and Nature*, for example, he admits that "the sacred and the accursed are potentialities of the same situation" (LW 1:43). Such an attitude, if taken to heart, would make one susceptible to the tragic sensibility. But, in Dewey's case, such admissions, made because he is a good empiricist, are recorded but not deeply felt. The best that can be said is that, as he aged, Dewey's qualifications of his views became more prominent. Never, though, did these qualifications occasion a paradigm shift away from his Baconian faith.

A good example of this is an essay published just prior to Dewey's ninetieth birthday. The article is entitled "Philosophy's Future in Our Scientific Age, Never Was Its Role More Crucial." In it Dewey makes the sorts of admissions and qualifications required by the tragic sensibility. After asserting, typically, "that the methods developed and the conclusions reached in natural science constitute the most decisive factor in life as it is now lived all over the world," he continues in a more sobering vein. "There is probably no case in which the good achieved by the intervention of science has not been offset by some evil; while, on the other side, it may be doubted if even the worst of these evils does not have an attendant benefit" (LW 16:373). Such an observation can easily lead an interpreter to think that Dewey was revising his position. Westbrook, as we have seen, comes to such a conclusion. However, the rest of the essay does not support such an interpretation.

Despite his growing sensitivity to the complexities involved in "progress," and despite the explicit admission just cited, Dewey never made the turn toward a tragic sensibility. Later in the article, he reverts to the familiar fusion of science and social/moral questions:

It is for the philosophers today to encourage and further methods of inquiry into human and moral subjects similar to those their predecessors in their day encouraged and furthered in the physical and psychological sciences: in short, to bring into existence a kind of knowledge which, by being thoroughly humane, is entitled to the name *moral* (LW 16:375).

The Baconian element is here attenuated, but is still present. Moral progress and scientific progress are isomorphic.[7] Just as measurable advance has been made in the sciences, so it will be in the moral sphere. In Kuhnian terms, Dewey came more and more in contact with anomalous instances, but his adherence to the long-held paradigm never wavered.

If what I am arguing is correct, Dewey belongs to the tradition of thinkers whose outlook is consistent with what George Steiner called "The Death of Tragedy." Tragedy, let us recall, is not opposed to comedy. One of the very last lines in *The Symposium* describes Socrates as arguing that "authors should be able to write both comedy and tragedy: the skillful tragic dramatist should also be a comic poet" (Plato, 223D). *Fortuna* and *Anangke* play a role in comedy as well as in tragedy. There are forces outside the control of utilitarian reason [a Puck, an Oberon, or a Titania], but such forces need not lead to an inextricable crisis for the protagonists. Whereas tragedy indicates that we all have within us the nobility, the greatness to confront and stand up to the evil forced upon us by *Fortuna*, comedy indicates how even the nobles, the admired, share in our foibles.

What is opposed to both comedy and tragedy is modernity's belief that careful planning, mind, will once and for all bring humans to eliminate the vagaries of *Fortuna*. The nineteenth century, a time when faith in progress reached a sort of apogee, was especially inimical to tragedy. Steiner begins his analysis by quoting a nineteenth-century thinker: "Marx repudiated the entire concept of tragedy. 'Necessity,' he declared, 'is blind only in so far as it is not understood'" (Steiner, 4).[8] Tragedy, by contrast, assumes an entirely different perspective. "Tragic drama arises out of precisely the contrary assertion: necessity is blind and man's encounter with it shall rob him of his eyes, whether it be in Thebes or in Gaza" (Steiner, 5). The Utopian attitude would have us be akin to Plato's prisoner who escapes from the cave. In the sunlight of midday, all is clear. Mind is like perfect vision. The Forms come into sharp focus. An intelligent blueprint for guiding life is possible. What tragedy announces, however, is that humans do not, as a rule, have access to the realm of Forms. We spend our time in the cave. There is much to which, despite our best laid plans, we are blind. The tragic hero is "blindsided" by events over which s/he has no control.

What we find, therefore, is that the tragic and the comic exist on a continuum whose extremes are populated by utopian optimism and quiescent pessimism. The middle is characterized by belief that the problems afflicting humans, problems like murder, incest, adultery, jealousy, unfettered ambition, and parent-child conflicts, will always be with us. There is no planned community that will eliminate them. They, together with unforeseen events and unexpected challenges, form part of the "necessity" which is our permanent companion.

The modern period, the time from Machiavelli to H. G. Wells, was an epoch especially fascinated by the ability of mind to dominate necessity. As such it sounded the death knell of tragedy. "It is the triumph of rationalism and secular metaphysics which marks the point of no return. . . . The modes of imagination implicit in Athenian tragedy continued to shape the mind until the age of Descartes and Newton. . . . With the *Discours de la methode* and the *Principia* the things undreamt of in Horatio's philosophy seem to pass from the world" (Steiner, 193).

That Dewey would be a child of his age is not surprising. While he does not belong at the tip of the continuum dominated by utopians, he is situated well on that end of the continuum. As such, he is a Horatio-type philosopher believing that incrementally we shall come to extend the light of mind over every aspect of reality. This typically nineteenth-century outlook is coupled in Dewey with a commendable drive for social reform. But this drive also reinforces his blindness to the tragic sensibility. This sensibility can be allied to the forces of reaction. Reformers constantly confront opponents who claim reactionaries positively embrace terms associated with the tragic sensibility: inexorability, necessity, inherently natural limitations.

Reformers know that change and improvement are possible. In their haste to improve conditions, however, reformers often fall into the rhetoric of overly sharp dilemmas. Dewey speaks regularly as if there were only two choices. His formulation of these leaves no room for the tragic. One set of alternatives was borrowed from H.G. Wells: that between "education" and "catastrophe" (MW 15:46). He also phrased it as "accommodation" versus "re-action" (LW 9:12), magic versus technological skills (LW 4:9, 20), and "intelligence" versus "subjection to nature" (MW 1:105). Each of these is an echo of the struggle between mind and necessity. Whereas the tragedian realizes that mind will always be in some ways blind to the multifarious workings of necessity, Dewey's reformist faith leads him to lean in the opposite direction. For him mind can come to dominate necessity. This is an attitude central to Dewey's thought at least from the beginning of the century, and lasting until the years just prior to his death. He did come, as the earlier citation from Westbrook noted, to incorporate elements central to the tragic [Westbrook, 416]. But he never made the paradigm switch which would have taken him out of the orbit of Bacon.

4. Sidney Hook's Failed Attempt to Marry Pragmatism and Tragedy

The absence of the tragic sensibility in Dewey can thus be explained by two factors, his coming to maturity during the nineteenth century, a time soaked through with the idea of progress, and his commitment to reform. Such an understanding of why Dewey could not come to abandon his Baconian biases seems to me the best way to deal with the question of Dewey and tragedy. The wrong way to deal with it is that taken by Sidney Hook in his attempt to defend pragmatism as that approach which "is more serious, even more heroic, than any other approach" (Hook, 243). Robert Westbrook describes Hook's essay as "a persuasive argument that there is nothing inherent in Dewey's ethics that is inconsistent with a tragic sensibility" (Westbrook, 163–164, note 10). My own reading of the Hook essay comes to exactly the opposite conclusion. It is upersuasive and misguided.

Hook does the best that is possible for aligning pragmatism and tragedy. Following in the tradition of Hegel he focuses on the Antigone-type conflict between competing goods. "Every genuine experience of moral doubt and perplexity in which we ask: 'What should I do?' takes place in a situation where good conflicts with good" (Hook, 235). Once tragedy is defined in this way, the alliance of pragmatism and tragedy makes sense. Pragmatism is a philosophical tradition which believes that "problems of normative social inquiry—morals in the broad sense—are the primary, not exclusive, subject matter of philosophy, and that reason or scientific intelligence can and should be used to resolve them" (Hook, 232).

This last citation allows us to grasp both the strength and the weakness of Hook's interpretation. It is true that, with its focus on practice, pragmatism may be a more suitable partner for tragedy than philosophies devoted to pure contemplation. However, the last part of the citation undermines any serious attempt to align pragmatism with tragedy. Hook's focus on the centrality of conflict provides the link between tragedy and Deweyan moral philosophy. The lingering optimism about mind together with the failure to appreciate the force of necessity makes any presumed link a forced and artificial one.

Several important ingredients in the tragic sensibility, such as the facts that the genuinely tragic always involves a remainder even after the resolution, and that necessity ever takes on new forms, are not recognized in Hook's interpretation. Instead Hook waxes optimistic about intelligence resolving once and for all some of the pressing problems of humanity. Looking back on Hook's pronouncements they seem to us charmingly naive. "First, given the rapidly expanding horizons of knowledge in our age, there is nothing in the nature of things which requires that the sick, any more than the poor, must always be with us. If scientific medicine develops at the same pace in the next few hundred years as it has in the last century, it is not shallow optimism to anticipate that the most serious forms of sickness will disappear and not be replaced by others" (Hook, 233).

Fortuna is no longer a goddess in Hook's scheme of things. Mind and necessity might battle each other, but mind is destined to emerge triumphant. Its triumph is not precarious and temporary, but a definitive conquest. What is a strong essay describing how the actual challenge of moral deliberation stems from being forced to choose between competing goods or between good and "right" (Hook, 236), is unfortunately blended with one that seeks to forge an alliance which is simply not present. Deweyan pragmatism, properly purged of its Baconian elements, may incorporate the tragic sensibility, but the pragmatism described by Hook has not yet jettisoned this Baconian baggage. A better direction, and a sobering counterpoint to Hook's optimism about the disappearance of "most serious forms of sickness," was recently articulated by John McDermott. "The arrival of the AIDS virus has put an end to any innocence that we might still have with regard to the embattled character of our entwining with the affairings of nature" (McDermott, 1994, 18).

5. Tragedy *Redivivus*

Holding on to the tension between Mind and Necessity is a more uncomfortable task than opting for the ultimate triumph of one or the other. Philosophy's penchant is to elevate Mind to a position of preeminence. Reformers, in their urgency to ameliorate, might forget that it is precisely the presence of Necessity that requires constant vigilance, and ever renewed fervor for reform. The dreams of Machiavelli and Bacon represent a temptation of pride on the part of intellectuals, the one temptation that must be most resisted and yet is the most difficult to resist.

Perhaps developments in the later twentieth century will provide a more suitable soil for a garden which accommodates both Mind and Necessity. The focus on technological advances provided the background for the Modern belief in progress, in the domination of Necessity by Mind. The twentieth century has provided some powerful counterexamples. Mustard gas and trench warfare, nationalistic expansionism, death camps, hopeful social experiments transformed into gulags and killing fields, are the most prominent on the grand historical stage. The difficulties of human love, issues about children, the widening of the gap between rich and poor, increased violence, death-dealing viruses, and a fraying social structure, provide examples closer to our individual lives.

Philosophers might be less inclined to the temptation that Mind will someday overcome Necessity, if they treated the issue analogously to the way they treat critics of philosophy. Anti-philosophy critics have claimed that with each new discipline like psychology, history, or physics, the scope of philosophy became narrower and narrower. But what philosophers know is that the growth of these disciplines is not a zero-sum game. The growth of psychology, for example, does not come at the expense of philosophy. Indeed philosophy expands as a new subdiscipline, the philosophy of psychology, comes into existence.

A similar case could be made for the tension between Mind and Necessity. The advances of Mind do not mean the gradual disappearance of Necessity. Even in the technological realm where one might expect this to be most prevalent, it is not the case. Biomedical questions provide the most appropriate examples. The ability to prolong the life of an aging relative is now coupled with the necessity of making a decision about employing those newly developed means. Amniocentesis does not shrink necessity. It adds

new necessities: those of deciding whether to undergo the procedure, and those of making decisions in light of the results of the
procedure.

Plato was, after all, right. Not the Plato so anachronistically
misread by philosophy professors projecting modern categories back
into his thought. Not the Plato, that is, who emphasized a one-
sided domination of cold reason on the rich world of experience.
But the Plato who in the *Timaeus* did not even make his creating
god superior to the force of Necessity.

Notes

1. Cp. "Nor is the tragic vision for those who, though admitting unsolved questions and the reality of guilt, anxiety, and suffering, would
become quietist and do nothing" (Sewall, p. 5).

2. Cp. "Thus Othello is ensnared in a murderous jealousy by the very
passion of his love for Desdemona" (Niebuhr, 1937, 159).

3. "Specifically, although the personification of fortune as female is
very old, Machiavelli appears to be the first to use that metaphor as a way
of suggesting the sexual conquest of fortune, introducing into the realm of
politics and history concerns about manliness, effeminacy, and sexual prow-
ess" (Pitkin, 144).

4. After explaining that Bacon's projections in the *New Atlantis* earn
him forgiveness for his overly simplistic notion of method, Dewey goes on
to link Bacon to Pragmatism: "When William James called Pragmatism a
New Name for an Old Way of Thinking, I do not know that he was thinking expressly of Francis Bacon, but so far as concerns the spirit and atmosphere of the pursuit of knowledge, Bacon may be taken as the prophet of
a pragmatic conception of knowledge" (MW 12:100).

5. Cp. "The philosophy of the eighteenth-century enlightenment was
animated throughout by conceptions of the prospect of the indefinite perfectibility of man. . . . While one result was an outbreak of utopias and
millennial schemes of all kinds, anarchistic, communistic and socialistic,
nonetheless we owe to this movement of the eighteenth century our present
almost religious faith in the need of progress and in the possibility of
making it the ruling principle of human affairs" (MW 7:332–333).

6. Scheler criticizes theories which, based on such beliefs, interpret
tragedy as a sign of primitive, pre-scientific attitudes toward the world.
"Theories like that which Maeterlinck proposes, basically the theory of
every Rationalism and Pantheism, are totally wrong. According to these

theories the tragic is the result of a false and unstable interpretation of the world. The tragic is attributed to the ways of thinking in uncivilized times with uncontrolled emotions" (Scheler, 251).

7. In another essay of 1949 Dewey imagined what a Galileo might say to a contemporary audience: "It is for you to do for the very life of man what we did for the physical and physiological conditions of that life. Discovery of these conditions was for us the immediate task that determined the end of our search. You possess the results of this search. It is for you to use them as means to carry forward the establishing of a more human order of freedom, equity and nobility" (LW 16:368).

8. Marx's claim is an echo of the Emersonian position cited at the beginning of this essay.

References

Works of Dewey

References to the works of Dewey are from the critical edition:

EW *John Dewey: The Early Works: 1882–1898*, ed. Jo Ann Boydston, 5 vols. Carbondale and Edwardsville: Southern Illinois University Press, 1969–1972.

MW *John Dewey: The Middle Works: 1899–1924*, ed. Jo Ann Boydston, 15 vols. Carbondale and Edswardsville: Southern Illinois University Press, 1976–1983.

LW *John Dewey: The Later Works: 1925–1953*, ed. Jo Ann Boydston, 17 vols. Carbondale and Edwardsville: Southern Illinois University Press, 1981–1990.

Other Works

Abel, Lionel, ed. (1967). *Moderns on Tragedy*. Greenwich Ct.: Fawcett Publications.

Cohen, Morris Raphael (1940). "Some Difficulties in Dewey's Anthropocentric Naturalism." LW 14:379–410.

Coughlan, Neil (1973). *Young John Dewey*. Chicago: The University of Chicago Press.

Emerson, Ralph Waldo (1982). *Selected Essays*. Ed. Larzer Ziff. New York: Penguin.

Hegel, G. W. F. (1832). "Hegel on Tragedy," in Abel 367–416.

168   *Raymond D. Boisvert*

Hook, Sidney (1960). "Pragmatism and the Tragic Sense of Life," in Abel 227–249.

Krutch, Joseph Wood (1929). "The Tragic Fallacy," in *The Modern Temper*. New York: Harvest Books, 79–97.

Machiavelli, Niccolo (1513). *The Prince*. Trans. Harvey C. Mansfield, Jr. Chicago: The University of Chicago Press, 1985.

McDermott, John (1987). "Introduction," in LW11:xi–xxxii.

McDermott, John (1994). "Ill-at-Ease: The Natural Travail of Ontological Disconnectedness." *Proceedings and Addresses of the American Philosophical Association* 67:74-28.

Niebuhr, Reinhold (1937). *Beyond Tragedy: Essays on the Christian Interpretation of History*. New York: Charles Scribner's Sons.

Niebuhr, Reinhold (1954). *The Irony of American History*. New York: Charles Scribner's Sons.

Nussbaum, Martha (1986). *The Fragility of Goodness: Luck and Ethics in Greek Tragedy and Philosophy*. Cambridge: Cambridge University Press.

Pitkin, Hanna (1984). *Fortune Is a Woman: Gender and Politics in the Thought of Niccolo Machiavelli*. Berkeley: University of California Press.

Plato (1961). *Collected Dialogues*. Ed. Edith Hamilton and Huntington Cairns. New York: Pantheon Books.

Ricoeur, Paul (1969). *The Symbolism of Evil*. Trans. Emerson Buchanan. Boston: Beacon Press.

Steiner, George (1961). *The Death of Tragedy*. London: Faber and Faber.

Sewall, Richard B. (1990). *The Vision of Tragedy*, 3d ed. New York: Paragon House.

Scheler, Max (1923). "On the Tragic," in Abel 249–267.

Westbrook, Robert (1991). *John Dewey and American Democracy*. Ithaca: Cornell University Press.

9

The Private and Its Problem: A Pragmatic View of Reproductive Choice

Eugenie Gatens-Robinson

There is an urgent need within contemporary American society to find a means to retain the democratic character of our institutions while we come to grips with the diversity of opinions and conflicting analysis on issues that affect our daily lives. It seems that we have not progressed very far from the time when John Dewey wrote *The Public and Its Problems*[1] in response to Walter Lippmann's pessimistic assessment of the capacity of the public to govern itself.[2] Within and among nations, it is clear that our public will is not univocal. The more and more frequent allusions to the "will of the people" in attempts to forward various political agendas is clearly little more than a political ploy of groups that want to claim that their will is coextensive with the mythic "people's will."

The plurality of voices arises not only from the influx of new populations. It is emergent, as the *different voices* with whom we have hitherto coexisted (women, racial and ethnic minorities, gays, people with disabilities, the aged, and children) have begun to speak publicly of their needs and legitimate political expectations.

This manifest pluralism of the postmodern condition is to be regretted only if it cannot be rendered intelligent in Dewey's sense. For him intelligence is "critical method applied to goods of belief, appreciation and conduct," applied not by the elite expert but by people in face-to-face interaction.[3]

As Dewey clearly saw, the problem of democracy *is* the problem of the public. It is the problem of how a social community of open discourse and face-to-face interaction is to be recovered within the context of a complex nation state like the United States. He readily agreed with Lippmann that such a social community did not exist in the United States as yet, that we had not as yet moved from the great society to the "great community." Unlike Lippmann, however, he believed that an appropriately educated democratic public was possible.

In this essay, I will explore what it would mean to bring a pragmatic Deweyan perspective into the current discussion on the nature of the public and the private. In particular, I will focus on a difficult and often painful contemporary issue that has many of us perplexed, the issue of reproductive choice. Since the state of public discourse in this area has particularly degenerated by incorporating not only an intolerance for free and open expression of difference but overt violence, we might suspect that both sides of the debate are framing the situation badly. It can be argued that the seemingly irremediable conflict between right-to-life and pro-choice voices is due to a mistaken construal of a number of centrally important ideas. These ideas are not to be understood merely as those that arise within the discourse on either side of this issue. They are ideas about the nature of effective democratic deliberation in general.

Dewey, writing in 1922, saw himself in a time of social flux. It is in such periods, he said, that mobility invades society and classes of people who were formerly separated in terms of their vision of virtue and the good life are brought together in ways that are intensely unsettling. "Congealed habits thaw out, and a flood mixes things once separate." At such times,

> Each class is sure of the rightness of its own end and hence not over scrupulous about the means of attaining them. . . . One side proclaims the ultimacy of order—that of some old order conducive to its interests. The other side proclaims its right to freedom, and identifies justice with its submerged claims. . . . The demand of each side treats its opponents as a willful violator of moral principles, an expression of self-interest or superior might. Intelligence which is the only possible messenger of reconciliation dwells in the far land of abstractions. . . .[4]

This description can be borrowed as an apt portrayal of the situation that has faced us for almost three decades now in the conflict between the women's movement and its demands for re-productive choice for women and the antiabortion (and anti-birth control) movement that has arisen in response to the liberalization of abortion laws and the wide availability of birth control. This conflict has deepened continuously since the Roe versus Wade decision of 1973, a decision that removed most legal barriers to medical abortion.

1. Feminist Political Thought and the Problem of the Private Choice

The distinction between the public and the private realm, while getting much play within contemporary political philosophy, is one that is not easily nor clearly made. Feminist political theorists have recognized that the movement from the private to the public is a complex and tricky one, especially while they are simulta-neously trying to critique liberal polity as it now stands. It was the emergence of white middle-class women from the "domestic sphere" of the nuclear family into the public arenas of work and politics that marks one of the greatest social changes in our century. Nev-ertheless this change was not accompanied by the rise of the eco-nomic status of women and children in general. The feminization of poverty and the feminization of labor are phenomena that the existing social and political structures have as yet been unable to assimilate or even to speak of coherently. As Nancy Fraser tells us, the fiscal crisis of the welfare states in Western Europe and the United States has been accompanied by the movement of women and children into the ranks of the poor.[5]

Feminist political theorists have found the definition of the public/private distinction perplexing. It has been used in the past by both liberal democratic and Marxist theorists to submerge ques-tions of domination and exploitation within the space of family and home. At first it seemed clear to many feminist thinkers that the barriers shielding what had been called private from the scrutiny of public deliberation must become more porous. However, the com-monly held feminist definition of the public as *any* sphere of activ-ity lying outside the domestic realm too hastily collapses several very different realms of public deliberation under one label. Follow-ing Fraser, these distinct non-domestic domains include "the ad-ministrative state, the official economy of paid employment, and the arenas of public discourse."[6] To conflate all of these under the one label of the "public sphere," she argues, is to create a confusion with significant consequences. Issues of central concern to sub-merged groups including women are open to an analysis that uncritically follows the logic of the market or of the established administrative state. For example, discussions of parental rights and custody, following hard on the expanded use of *in vitro* fertilization and surrogacy, were structured by market notions of "free enterprise" and by legal notions inherited from an outworn conception of "the family." To this extent, the very terminology in which these awkward dilemmas concerning birth mothers, biological fathers, and adoptive mothers are being framed seems ill suited to their admitting of happy solutions.

There must be a sphere of democratic discourse that can be critical of both market and state *because* it is distinct from them. Thus Fraser follows Habermas in defining the public sphere as an arena of discursive interactions among citizens that is distinct from both the state and the market. This distinction of a sphere of democratic association is one she claims is essential to democratic theory. She says:

> ... something like Habermas's idea of the public sphere is indispensable to critical social theory and democratic political practice ... no attempt to understand the limits of actually existing late capitalist democracy can succeed without in some way or another making us of it.[7]

Since the right of a woman to choose to end a pregnancy has been defended on the basis of privacy and control of the individual over her body, it is of particular relevance to this debate how the interface of the public and the private is delineated. With the movement of women into the spheres of politics and labor, the domains that had formerly been easily classified as domestic and thus private have come under more public scrutiny and regulation. As Seyla Benhabib puts it, "The emancipation of workers made property relationships into a public political issue, the emancipation of women has meant that the family and the so-called private sphere became political issues.... The struggle over what gets included in the public agenda is itself a struggle for justice and freedom."[8] The status of the decision either to become pregnant or to allow a pregnancy to come to term and bear a child has become an issue of public debate for a variety of reasons, appearing on various cultural and social levels from the scientific to the religious. In this essay I will focus primarily on the issues that are woven through these debates as they relate to our shared public life.

With the proliferation of genetic and reproductive technologies, it remains an open question whether it has been in the best interest of women and their families, as members of a complex modern community, to maintain freedom of reproductive choice by submerging these issues again into the private realm where coercion and domination remain publicly invisible. Indeed some have argued that the Roe versus Wade decision has not had the intended results of allowing women an unencumbered freedom to choose whether or not to maintain a pregnancy. Ironically it has served as a springboard for the regulation and surveillance of women's reproductive lives, especially the lives of poor women. In the final section of this essay, I intend to show how Dewey's view of the public and the private connects with the ideas that arise from the struggle of feminist political theory to bring pluralism and liberal democratic thought together in ways that have a hope of enriching and making more intelligent our lived interactions.

2. Dewey's Public and Private

For Dewey the distinction between the public and the private is a fluid and organic one, tied to the changing social, technological, and economic conditions of the environment. What is private are simply those interactions between people that have no significant effects on those outside that particular interaction. *Something becomes public if the activities involve effects of importance beyond the local interaction itself.* As always, Dewey sees us as organisms interacting in an environment. It is the effects of those interactions that can allow us to make a claim about their character as either a matter for private or public deliberation.

Dewey's description of the public/private distinction can be seen as the basis for a kind of political ecology. The boundary is ever changing between what is a private transaction between individuals and what is public, effecting others within the broader context of associated life. Changing technologies or social arrangements, even apparently simple ones, can bring something from one sphere into the other. There is no final definition of what falls within the realm of private transactions or what appropriately falls under the transformative power of state care. Thus, Dewey has a functional and historical account of publics and how they are constituted within the ongoing process of social life. They arise around a common problem: the need for clean air or water, the need for access to education or work, or, in the case being discussed here, the need to enhance or restrict access to safe abortions in order to maintain an environment in which the association of parent and offspring is better maintained than the current situation allows. As historical situations change, different publics arise and others vanish. Dewey says,

> ... the line between public and private is to be drawn on the basis of the extent and scope of the consequences of acts which are so important as to need control, whether by inhibition or by promotion. ... The public consists of all those who are affected by the indirect consequences of transactions and to such extent that it is deemed necessary to have those consequences systematically cared for.[9]

The same individual may belong to many different overlapping publics, viz. Gay activism, NOW, environmentalism, a worker's union, the local parents' association. This pluralism of publics is at the very heart of the experience of democracy for Dewey. Democracy, as the form of community life, is always an experiment. Therefore, it must, like other empirical endeavors, call upon a pluralist experience to go on in an intelligent manner.

The state arises out of a recognized need for the transformation of, and care for, those consequences of activities that affect those beyond the persons immediately involved in them. The public articulates itself into a state by means of appointing officials whose function it is to care for public interests. In this way the state grows organically from the complex of problems arising from associated life. At the same time, certain aspects of state care can become "an affront" when they are no longer an appropriate means to the end of democratic association. Our individual and private activities are transactions within a physical and social environment. They necessarily result in changes within that environment, changes that require a balancing response. Some such changes are benign and have negligible effects on our neighborhoods downstream or across the hedge. But some have significant effects for good or ill. It is on these changes that public attention must focus. This means that the state is not definable in terms of some essential forms. Its form is always relative. The only constant Dewey acknowledges is "the function of caring for and regulating the interests which accrue as the result of the complex indirect expansion and radiation of conjoint behavior."[10] Just as in the realm of ethics, where Dewey argues that there are no pre-existing universal principles that serve to dictate the morally appropriate modes of behavior independently of the context in which moral perplexity arises, so too he argues that it is a mistake to claim that there is some essence of the state which can be determined beforehand and applied. The state and its officials arise from the historical need to control certain consequences of particular instances of associated life. The question in each case is how that is to be done intelligently and cooperatively.

The attribution of intelligence to this process is central for Dewey, but as with many other "ordinary" words, Dewey is using "intelligence" in an extraordinary way. Intelligence is not properly understood as a "property" of an elite few individuals. Rather it is an embodied condition of our associated life.[11] This means that we are intelligent together or not at all. The state and its offices, including that of voter-citizen, are inevitably ever changing. This is not to be regretted. Dewey maintains a pluralistic and dynamic view of publics, and thus of the state. Thomas Alexander argues that Dewey's idea of a social intelligence *requires* a pluralism of perspectives. He says that "this model of democratic rationality requires a number of different communicating points of view in order to work."[12] This is so because social intelligence is based in communication and a capacity for critical consciousness. Alexander says that "To be constructively critical, we must speak from within the framework of shared but different contexts, which can *listen* to each other and search creatively for integrative, mutually sustaining frameworks."[13] Robert Westbrook claims, in addressing Dewey's pluralism, that Dewey might have better titled his book "Publics and Their Problem." He says:

> . . . the State was also a plural phenomenon, a collection of publics organized into representative institutions (though presumably one institution or collection of officials might serve several publics). For this reason Dewey's statement that a new state was created every time a public organized itself was less bizarre than it sounded. For it did not mean that the governing institutions of the state of previous

publics were replaced wholesale but rather that they were supplemented or themselves took on new functions."[14]

Fraser also maintains that both the critical function and the pluralistic character of the public must be recognized. She points out that in *The Structural Transformation of the Public Sphere*, Habermas "stops short of developing a new, post-bourgeois model of the public sphere." Fraser claims that Habermas idealizes the liberal model of the public sphere as a unified space in which differences are bracketed and all participants are *taken* as equal. This public sphere, she argues, has been constructed as much on exclusion as anything else. Fraser points out that contemporaneously with the appearance of the bourgeois public, which claimed to be *the* public, there arises competing counter-publics, viz, popular peasant publics, elite women's publics, working class publics, black feminist publics, gay and lesbian publics. The ideal of a unitary public where rational debate is possible *because* differences are bracketed constitutes a mode of domination which "secures the ability of one stratum of society to rule the rest."[15]

This rubric of *artificial* equality seems to haunt many contemporary views of public discourse from Rawls to Rorty. Fraser suggest, several modifications of the Habermasian analysis that bring it closer to what I would describe as a pragmatic view of the public. She suggests that the presumption that difference can be bracketed and equality presumed only functions to support the idea, an idea which she contests, that democratic interaction is possible in a situation of social inequality. Where inequalities are rendered invisible, they are unavailable for discussion. In such a situation of social inequality, what she calls "subaltern publics" are excluded from the deliberation.

> We should question whether it is possible even in principle for interlocutors to deliberate *as if* they were social peers in specially designated discursive areas when these discursive arenas are situated in a larger societal context that is pervaded by structural relations of dominance and subordination.[16]

Further she suggests that the proliferation of publics is actually a step toward and not away from democracy. She questions the assumption that discussion in the public sphere should focus only on the common good and refrain from discussion of "private issues." In a society of social inequality to presume there is "a common good shared by exploiter and exploited may well be a mystification."[17] Fraser's impulse both to maintain the notion of the public as a source of revision and critique and to reformulate it to accommodate the postmodern plurality of voices that must enter that discussion is remarkably similar to Dewey's characterization of the plural public and its function in relationship to the state. Further criticism of the Habermasian public, that it inappropriately restricts discussion to those topics involving some predefined common good, points to an open and pragmatic construction of the line between private and public concerns.

The power of Dewey's naturalism that pervades his political theory may be missed by some feminist theorists, perhaps because "biology" has been used to define women out of the public spaces at least since Aristotle. In that regard the more abstract arena of critical theory seems a safer, more *neutral* place from which to scrutinize questions involved in bringing "women's questions" into areas of public deliberation. Nevertheless, many of these "women's questions" concern embodied life. For that very reason they are best addressed from an historical and organic perspective rather than from the pretense of abstract and often cynical neutrality. The general question at issue centers on the possibility of finding just, mutually enriching, and appropriately flexible social and political arrangements for a sexually dimorphic and racially diverse species with a long and varied history of customs and habits of association. This is no easy task at least in part because our modes of abstract public discourse have not been constructed to take in the messy details of daily domestic experience. Intelligence in this regard "dwells in the far land of abstractions." It is difficult for the "interests" arising from what has commonly been thought of as the private life of home, child care, and sexuality to find a voice of the right tone or pitch to be heard and responded to respectfully within the public sphere. "Women's issues," except this issue of abortion rights, are often left to women-only associations, groups Fraser would call "subaltern publics." Dewey and Fraser would agree that one of the chief problems for the plural publics is in finding ways for those who have been previously silent or silenced to be heard and listened to. For Dewey, "The new public which is generated remains long inchoate, unorganized because it cannot use inherited political agencies. The latter, if elaborate and well institutionalized, obstruct the organization of the new public."[18]

3. The Antiabortion and Pro-choice Publics and Their Problems

The antiabortion movement has organized itself around a specific transaction of human associated life, the medical termination of pregnancy, which it claims has far reaching effects. These organizations claim that the consequences of the use of medical abortion include the devaluing of human life and the undermining of the moral structure of the traditional family. The current antiabortion movement is *a public* that has its roots in the older established order of privately, domestically controlled reproductive decisions. This order was established well before the widespread use of contraceptives, the liberalization of abortions laws, or the movement of the majority of women with children into the work force. It is a public that remains unsettled by the egalitarian consequences of the movement of women into the public arenas. One such consequence has been that pregnancy and child rearing have become a burden to women and men in different ways than they ever were before.

The antiabortion public seeks to institute, by means of a constitutional amendment, an official governmental mechanism for drastically limiting abortion. This public seeks in general to criminalize abortion as an act of violence by controlling the access to medically safe means to end an unwanted pregnancy. They would argue that the circumstances of abortion are radically unlike the private circumstance where I, in consultation with my physician, choose to remove a gall bladder or appendix that is causing me difficulties. In such a case I am deciding privately what is required to lead a "good" life from the perspective of an informed personal judgment. They argue that the decision to undergo the medical termination of a pregnancy is not private and must fall under the control of public officials. Providing such service, they claim, should be deemed a criminal offense, as it has been in the past. Yet there appears to be an interesting anomaly here. One might presume that seeking such service would be a punishable criminal act as well, analogous to seeking a hit man. Nonetheless, controlling the activity of the pregnant woman or girl is not usually proposed via criminal sanctions, presumably because casting a young pregnant woman as a criminal is unappealing and incongruous with other beliefs and agendas held by such publics. Her condition and her reaction to it, they might argue, are appropriately maintained within the private spheres of family and religion. She is to be counseled, chastised, or forgiven, but her actions in relationship to her pregnancy are, as in the past, the province of the private realm. This "old" private realm is one clearly structured in patriarchal terms where the activities of women and children are under the benign control of the male head of household or religious authority.

The antiabortion movement has been more and more successful in making abortions difficult to obtain by initiating legal regulations that control where abortions can be performed, how long one must wait before having the abortion performed, permission and consent laws for minors, and regulations on how federally funded agencies are to "talk about options." Funding by government agencies for abortions for poor women has also been limited, in some cases even when the pregnancy is the result of rape. Some of these groups have also used unofficial means of limiting access to medical abortion by harassing women going to women's health clinics. Some have used threats and actual violence against health providers so that fewer and fewer physicians are willing to take on the risk of providing abortions. The result of this is that fewer and fewer medical schools are providing adequate training for physicians in abortive techniques, and more and more regional hospitals are refusing to allow abortions to be performed within their walls. The result has been that large geographical areas in the United States have no abortion services available, not even for therapeutic purposes. This affects the rural poor disproportionally because they cannot afford to travel long distances and stay for the required waiting periods. Ironically, the decrease in the availability of abortions is simultaneous with a decrease in prenatal and birthing facilities in the same areas of rural America. As Dewey has pointed out, simply removing formal conditions of limitation is merely a negative freedom. What is always required for positive freedom as an activity are "methods and instrumentalities for control of conditions."[19] It matters little if one has the "right" to decide to terminate a pregnancy, if the means are very difficult to obtain or simply unavailable.

The pro-choice public might have had no particular center around which to organize if the Roe versus Wade decision had been received with less aggressive response by the antiabortion public. It has been over twenty years since that decision and the conflict between the antiabortion and pro-choice associations has grown ever more contentious and violent. It is worth wondering, since this conflict remains unsettled and increasingly divisive, if the resolution might have been sought in the wrong places all along. Dewey claims that continual conflict is a sign that the problem has been wrongly posed, pointing out that the posing of consequences and

solutions to those consequences are as least as subject to error as
are our perceptions:

> Judgments about what to undertake so as to regulate them
> and how to do it, are as fallible as other plans. Mistakes
> pile up and consolidate themselves into laws and methods
> of administration which are more harmful than the conse-
> quences which they were originally intended to control.[20]

If we accept the hypothesis that this debate over reproductive
freedom has gone astray, how might one proceed to find another
ground to deal with the problems involved? The pragmatic course
would surely involve an attempt to understand historically how we
have come to this impasse. There is a way of telling the story that
perhaps might lead us to a higher discursive space than is available now. Even though an adequate overview of this history cannot
be offered here, I would like to point out that the deep emotional
responses surrounding this topic lie close to the heart of the very
notion of human community. Obviously the social, religious, and
legal control of decisions of a woman of reproductive age have a
very long history. These controls constitute one of the core threads
of history of any community, as much as do war and conquest. The
question of how we bear our young into the next generation, under
what social arrangements, and how they are to be educated and
nurtured, is connected with possibly every other important question within both our actual public life and the ideal of a "good life"
in general. It is a contemporary social tragedy that issues in areas
of reproductive choice are ones that most of us fear to raise except
in circles where we are sure our views are shared. The language
that has evolved on both sides of the issue of reproductive choice
has functioned not as a means to establish some shared meaning,
but to actively negate that possibility. The discursive space has
been occluded for a variety of reasons. Thus the questions must
arise of how we are to open it.

4. A Story in Need of Changing: Replotting the Means

First of all, I want to be clear that, in criticizing the way things
have gone in our public discussion since Roe versus Wade, I am not
suggesting that we ought to restrict women's reproductive choices
in ways they were restricted before that decision. Nor do I mean to

imply that *radical* change in this arena is not needed. I totally agree with Dewey when he claims that liberalism must be radicalized if it is to accomplish its task. Radical in this context means an articulation of the necessity of thoroughgoing changes in the set-up of institutions and corresponding activity to bring the changes to pass. Thus he says that "the gulf between what the actual situation makes possible, and the actual state itself is so great that it cannot be bridged by piecemeal policies undertaken ad hoc."[21] Rather, genuine reform requires the envisioning of an aim, an end-in-view, that allows each present reform to act as an appropriate means to that fuller picture. With that reassurance of my "liberal" and radical intent, I want to proceed to examine how, since 1973, we have reached our current impasse.

Roe verus Wade was a decision based on what is called a penumbral or shadow right of privacy. A shadow right is one that is implied, but not explicitly stated in the Constitution. The cases that preceded Roe, and acted as precedents for it, included one, Griswald versus Connecticut (1965), that deemed unconstitutional a state law that made it a crime to distribute birth control information even to married couples. Following this and like decisions, Roe ruled that a decision to end a pregnancy was a private one between a woman and her doctor.

Ruth Bader Ginsberg,[22] now a Supreme Court justice, has argued in a number of places that this decision was too precipitant to be fully assimilated, given the social conditions at that time. Instead, it resulted in immediate and continued violent opposition, on both a political and social level. Rather than being based on a necessarily ambiguous notion of privacy, she claims that the ruling should have been based on a notion that had already been successfully used in states on gender issues, including weakening existing abortion restrictions. That basis lay in equal access unencumbered by gender discrimination. The focus, Ginsberg claims, should have been a woman's right not to be disadvantaged socially or economically by virtue of her sex or conditions related specifically to her sex. Instead of taking this course with its already well-established precedents and strong constitutional support, the court used the notion of privacy and then laid down detailed guidelines in terms of trimesters and conditions of pregnancy that allowed for abortion based on the private decision of a woman and her physician.

Ginsberg points out that if things had proceeded as they had been going from the mid-1960s onward, when state laws concerning abortion had become increasingly more liberal, the resulting furor and immense breach of communications might have been greatly diminished. At the very least, the plausibility of the anti-abortion argument would have had far less appeal to the general public:

> ... in my judgment, Roe ventured too far in the change it ordered. The sweep and detail of the opinion stimulated the mobilization of a right-to-life movement and an attendant reaction in Congress and state legislatures. In place of the trend "toward liberalization of abortion statutes" legislatures adopted measures aimed at minimizing the impact of the 1973 rulings, including notification and consent requirements, prescriptions for the protection of fetal life, and bans on public expenditures for poor women's abortions."[23]

Ginsberg advocated a more local and gradualist strategy that would have continued the trend already present in the laws of many states. She points out that the Constitution "armed the Court with no swords to carry out its pronouncements ... the Justices generally follow, they do not lead, changes taking place elsewhere in society."[24] As it was, the Supreme Court decision simultaneously rendered unconstitutional all state laws as they then stood, even those in the most progressive states. Even if liberalization of abortion restrictions had been based on claims of equality of access, deeply held opinions on the morality of abortion would have resulted in conflict and debate. However, Ginsberg claims that arguing on these grounds allows the clearer articulation of the view that reproductive choice in a circumstance of a problem pregnancy does not simply involve a conflict between the interests of an individual fetus and those of an individual woman. "Also in the balance is a woman's autonomous charge of her full life's course—her ability to stand in relation to man, society and the state as an independent, self-sustaining equal citizen."[25]

It is interesting to note that Ginsberg's judicial strategy in her work in the area of gender discrimination is itself pragmatic in a Deweyan sense. She specifically has chosen to take cases involving gender discrimination that have male plaintiffs put at a disadvantage in terms of collection benefits from spouses *because* they were male. This allows her to "teach" the legal structure from a stance internal to it, a stance which maintains that gender discrimination in our current contexts has consequences that are damaging to both men and women and thus constitute a threat to the common good.

If we follow Ginsberg's reasoning, the Roe verus Wade decision amounted to what Dewey calls "a short-cut revolution."[26] Dewey points out that changes in overt action that are accomplished by what he calls "muscular tricks" without an accompanying change in habits of thought are bound to have a long lag time in actually being incorporated into the moral habits of feeling and response of the institutions in question. There must be corresponding changes in the objective arrangement of institutions for such "legal" changes to be fully accepted. In the case of women's reproductive choice, necessary changes, such as a reorganization of working conditions for caregivers, restructuring of health care for women and children, child care options, and appropriate educational structures, have yet to appear.

Dewey's analysis of how habit effects action is a powerful tool for understanding what has gone wrong in this area. He claims that we cannot command that a customary mode of habituated human response simply change, as if it were a matter of individual wills. Will *is* habit in Dewey's view. Habits must intervene between wish and moral action. If there is no habit of respectful attention to voices that are attempting to describe the difficult conditions for working women and poor women which children in an increasingly violent and misogynistic welfare state, then those voices that are raised will be heard as shrill and strident and "selfish." Dewey might point out that if we have established conditions within our society in which more and more women, if given that option, forgo motherhood for a variety of reasons, then we have an environment in which having a child has become "fearful."

One might say that Ginsberg, like Dewey, is engaging in a social psychology of a pragmatic sort. In a Deweyan spirit, she might have claimed that not only was the legal precedent for arguing in terms of equality of opportunity well established, but also that our *command habit* of loyalty to that idea was even more deeply entrenched. In a sense, we would have been better able to attend to women's real circumstances, if these had been framed in terms providing equal opportunity for a good life for all citizens, thus avoiding the unfairness of unequal social and economic burdens borne by women in relationship to human reproductive life. This might have been more easily assimilated into our habits of moral and civic thought than the notion of a right to private choice that is too easily constructed as selfish, arbitrary, and antisocial within this area of child bearing and rearing.

Dewey claims that the mistake of those who wish to impose rapid radical reforms upon an existing social context is that they neglect the inertia of our habituated social, emotional, and moral responses. We are creatures of habit "much more than either instinct or reason." Reason is not some personal psychological possession; rather it is a "laborious achievement of habit needing to be continually worked over."[27] Here as elsewhere, Dewey is using the idea of the organism interacting with its environment as his model. He refuses to countenance either a reductionistic social psychology that explains social action only in terms of instinct or one that postulates human behavior as both innately rational and infinitely malleable, ready to jump from one form of associated life into another *tout court*. Democratic life is always an ongoing project.

The model Dewey presumes is one that recognizes that human beings are born into an environment of habits and customs with which they interact and which form their individual expectations and judgments and emotional dispositions. Habits, as Dewey uses the concept, are skills. They are arts of response. So, for Dewey, social psychology is the psychology of habits, that is, the study of how "established interacting arrangements nurture different minds." Of course the minds that are most appropriate to a democratic context are ones that do not allow themselves to be lulled into unreflective, purely repetitive habits that maintain the status quo. Rather, habits are not separated from thought: "Thinking is secreted in the interstices of habit."[28] The distinction or disconnection between habit and thought is one that Dewey has strong reasons to debunk. Habit and thought are intimately and organically connected. But this is not to postulate some form of social determinism, rather the contrary. The very heart of goodness in conduct, and thus of reasonableness, is in the mastery of the conditions that *now* prevail. Habits are the channels that form a place in which to begin thinking about those prevailing conditions. To separate habit from thought is to follow the same course that separates practice from theory. Such separation allows the intellectual to see herself or himself as "free" of the present conditions of conduct and unconcerned about how they have evolved from the past. This amounts to engaging in political theory as if from a vantage point outside of the ongoing processes of life. But from a pragmatic perspective "habit is an ability, an art formed from past experience." For Dewey, "what makes a habit bad is enslavement to old ruts. Habits deprived of thought and thought deprived of habit are two sides of the same fact."[29]

Conflicts, such as the difficult one I am addressing here, are what stimulate thought in the midst of custom and habits. Dewey believed the method of democracy addressed such conflicts:

> Of course there are conflicting interests, otherwise there would be no social problems. . . . The method of democracy— insofar as it is that of organized intelligence—is to bring these conflicts out into the open where their special claims can be seen and appraised, where they can be discussed and judged in the light of more inclusive interests than those represented by either of them separately.[30]

A clue to how we might best proceed in relationship to human reproductive freedom is provided by Dewey's insistence that means and ends be organically connected. There is simply no undemocratic means to a democratic end. When behavior is genuinely intelligent, the means that are part of attaining some end in view are at one with that end.

If we can take that claim as a given, then our course might seem more clearly drawn. It is important to find a means by which a pluralistic public can be heard, not just in some general sense, or by the state, or in some artificial arena of "presumed neutrality," but by one another in face-to-face interaction. The very possibility of community requires the possibility of this form of communication.

First it must be seen that the parties to the conflicting interests in the abortion conflict do indeed hold important ends in common. If things are put in a certain light, it can be argued that, in fact, the parties to this particular conflict hold a number of important ends in common. It takes but a moment of reflection to remember that no one wants there to be as many abortions in our society as there are now. Abortion must be available, one side argues, in case of an emergency, an unwanted pregnancy. This raises the question: how have we created an environment where such *emergencies* are endemic? The large number of abortions and teenage pregnancies is a symptom of social distress, not of individual wills gone astray. In fact, a common end in view for both sides is for abortions to become the rare result of very rare contraceptive accidents or medical emergencies. What are the conditions that have resulted in the escalation of abortions? Increasingly, pregnancy and the duties of motherhood in the present economic and social circumstances are seen as extremely disadvantaging. The troubling escalation of teenage pregnancy, which many relate to the low self-esteem and desperate social and economic conditions of young girls in many areas of our society, adds to this problem enormously.

It is not biology, but social and economic circumstances, that have left women with most of the burden of caring for and, more recently in this country, providing economically for a child. And it becomes increasingly unlikely that a woman alone with her children will be able to provide for them adequately. The increasing number of female-headed households has resulted in the steep increase in the numbers of women and children living below the poverty line. Day care is difficult to find and too expensive for most single parents. Prenatal and postnatal health care is lacking so that the infant mortality rate in some parts of this country reaches the level of the Third World. This is an environment that is not set up to welcome children or to support their caregivers. Why is it expected that a particular woman would, against the very disposition of her environment, welcome the increasing burden of motherhood? The irony is that in the political climate of the 90s, if she does make such an "heroic" choice, she will be blamed and punished for having done so. The members of the New Republican Congress of 1994, especially those who are strongly opposed to access to abortion, found themselves at odds with fellow conservatives. Increasingly, they have come to recognize the serious conflict between their "pro-life" stand and a stand advocating the cutoff of funding for poor women with children.

The aim of decreasing the number of abortions in the United States, if it is to be a function of democratic intelligence, must be connected with creating conditions of equality for women. And equality is not a claim of indistinguishable sameness, not a "mathematical equivalence."[31] Equality is the fruit of community and as an organic entity it must be cultivated so it might grow. Equality is the "unhampered share which each individual member of community has in the consequences of associated life."[32] Such equality recognizes the uniqueness of individuals as well as the difference of living circumstances associated with pregnancy and the care of an offspring who remains in developmental dependence and in need of care and education for twenty or more years.

If the various conflicting voices in this debate could come to see some common end-in-view, the kinds of radical changes that seem to be required as the means to this end might begin to come about. It is not clear how such change ought to begin. But the conditions must be established for the public dialogue to be of such a nature that it effectively brings into existence the consciousness of a communal life, that it allows us to articulate a "we," where we might have been once more inclined to say "them." As this debate stands at the moment, such conditions do not exist except in isolated instances where pro-life and pro-choice groups have deliberately chosen to suspend their debate and work together on those things that they can mutually embrace in the present. One might imagine that as these groups work closely together, they will come to communicate more fully, and that interaction itself will becomes the means to an end of the sort spoken of above. James Campbell points out in his essay in this volume that Dewey's ideal of democratic practice is often criticized in that it does not seem to take into account the importance of political power rather than cooperative democratic communication in our society. It seems naive from that perspective to think that discussions and cooperative inquiry among ordinary people might effect radical change in the institutional structure of our lives. But Campbell says that:

> Dewey's realistic point . . . is that if we ever hope to break out of the problems of our current practice, we need to reconstruct our situation to make more appropriate something like democracy as cooperative inquiry. The political process could then be seen as an educative one in which we all try to grow in our ability to address social problems and in our appreciation of our shared existence.[33]

Social intelligence is not a property of the individual in isolation, but of the individual in a certain sort of community. Thus as long as there are deep and divisive conflicts such as the abortion debate within a society that claims to be democratic, that society cannot be deemed "intelligent," and the "great community" remains elusive. I, as a pro-choice advocate, cannot be intelligent in my responses without listening with care to the concerns of those who oppose my view. The task is one of *re-membering*, as Seyla Benhabib suggests.[34] She says we must look carefully at a fragmented past and rejoin what has been dislocated. Language, she says, is a potent witness to our dislocations and dismemberments. The very words in which we frame our deliberations can betray our efforts: pro-life, pro-choice, antiabortion. They are words of conflict. We are all in some sense pro-life and pro-choice and antiabortion, even if we disguise it from ourselves and others in the heat of rhetoric and

apparent conflicts of ends.[35] It requires the creativity of an aesthetic sense to put things back together well. It requires a "rethinking that sets free the lost postentials of the past."[36] Benhabib
points out that for Hannah Arendt, the political theorist is a story
teller who must "cull from the past a story that can orient the mind
in the future." This is an art, a habit in Dewey's sense, that we can
only learn and practice together. Dewey tells us that:

> Men's conscious life of opinion and judgment often proceeds
> on a superficial and trivial plane. But their lives reach a
> deeper level. The function of art has always been to break
> through the crust of conventionalized and routine con-
> sciousness.[37]

Thus we must learn the habit of listening with respect to the
voices of ordinary women and men and indeed children whose lives
have a deeper level that can only be ascertained if they can come
to express that experience *in their own terms*. It is important to
harbor suspicion of received linguistic categories and theoretical
analyses in an intellectual sphere so willing to separate habit and
custom from thought. It is one of the growing points of feminist
literature, both philosophical and literary, to challenge theory and
the received language. I claim that this strategy is a pragmatic one
in Dewey's sense. It is a strategy deployed not in the elite intellectual interest of deconstructing the world or the text or both, but in
the hope of the possibility of creative communication and thus
democratic life. I cannot imagine what the public sphere will be
like when such arts of communication are in full blossom, but the
means to that end is in the present, embodied in the conflicts that
lead—indeed, press—us to communicate across the gulf of diverse
conceptions of goodness.

Notes

1. John Dewey, *The Public and Its Problems*, vol. 2 of *The Later
Works*, ed. Jo Ann Boydston (Carbondale: Southern Illinois University Press,
1988): 235–375.

2. See Walter Lippmann's *The Phantom Public* (New York: Maxmillan,
1925). For Dewey, Lippmann's sharp criticisms of participatory democracy
were on target and required an adequate response. Lippmann used a language not unlike Dewey's in speaking of the effect of the social environ-

ment on political action. Lippmann thought that most people misrepresented their social and political environment to themselves because their sources of information about that environment were misleading and inaccurate. Their information about the real world was censored in order to simplify it for their consumption. Lippmann did not think that this need to simplify and distort the news was something that could be remedied in such a way as to establish a citizenry capable of intelligent political participation. The majority of citizens, he thought, were not capable of taking in much more. This led him, unlike Dewey, to a political elitism where the governing elite were to be the recipients of expert opinion concerning the problems of associated life and the voice of the average citizen should be heard only on procedural matters. It may be argued that Dewey's reply to Lippmann's political realism was not fully adequate. It is clear that the debate between political realism and the ideals of participatory democracy continues both in this volume and in the public forum generally.

3. John Dewey, *Experience and Nature*, vol. 1 of *The Later Works*, ed. Jo Ann Boydston (Carbondale: Southern Illinois University Press, 1981), 325.

4. John Dewey, *Human Nature and Conduct*, vol. 14 of *The Middle Works*, ed. Jo Ann Boydston (Carbondale: Southern Illinois University Press, 1975): 59.

5. Nancy Fraser, *Unruly Practices: Power, Discourse, and Gender* in *Contemporary Social Theory* (Minneapolis: University of Minnesota Press, 1989): 144.

6. Nancy Fraser, "Rethinking the Public Sphere," in *Habermas and the Public Sphere*, ed. Craig Calhoun (Cambridge: MIT Press, 1992): 111.

7. Ibid., 111.

8. Ibid., 79.

9. Dewey, *The Public and Its Problems*, LW 2:245–246.

10. Ibid., 265.

11. Dewey, "Renascent Liberalism," in *The Later Works*, vol. 11, ed. Jo Ann Boydston (Carbondale: Souther Illinois University Press, 1987): 38.

12. Thomas Alexander, "John Dewey and the Roots of Democratic Imagination," in *Recovering Pragmatism's Voice*, ed. Lenore Langsdorf and Andrew R. Smith (Albany: State University of New York Press, 1995): 132.

13. Ibid., 134.

14. Robert Westbrook, *John Dewey and American Democracy* (Ithaca: Cornell University Press, 1991): 305.

15. Fraser, "Rethinking the Public Sphere," 111.

16. Ibid., 120.

17. Ibid., 131.

18. Dewey, *The Public and Its Problems*, LW 2:234–235.

19. Ibid., 340.

20. Ibid., 254.

21. Dewey, "Renascent Liberalism," LW 11:45.

22. See Ruth Bader Ginsberg, "Some Thoughts on Autonomy and Equality in Relation to Roe versus Wade," *North Carolina Law Review* 63 (1985): 375–386, and "Speaking in a Judicial Voice," *New York University Law Review* 67 (1992): 1185–1208.

23. Ginsberg, "Some Thoughts," 381.

24. Ginsberg, "Speaking in a Judicial Voice," 1208.

25. Ginsberg, "Some Thoughts," 382.

26. Dewey, *Human Nature and Conduct*, MW 14:77.

27. Ibid., 137.

28. Dewey, *The Public and Its Problems*, LW 2:335.

29. Dewey, *Human Nature and Conduct*, MW 14:49.

30. Dewey, "Renascent Liberalism," LW 11:56.

31. Dewey, *The Public and Its Problems*, LW 2:329.

32. Ibid.

33. James Campbell, "Dewey and Democracy," in this volume.

34. Seyla Benhabib, "Models of Public Space: Hannah Arendt, the Liberal Tradition and Jürgen Habermas," in *Habermas and the Public Space*, ed. Craig Calhoun (Cambridge: MIT Press, 1992). Also see her *Situating the Self: Gender, Community and Postmodernism in Contemporary Ethics* (New York: Routledge), 1992.

35. I am including here an exercise in my attempt to listen to the interests of a public that I do not consider myself personally a part of, the antiabortion public. I have listed some of the deep concerns that the antiabortion public expresses. I have tried to voice them in a way that allows a connection and a sharing of ends with those within the pro-choice public. This is a tentative listing, and the connections I try to make here are at best a tenuous beginning. I recognize that the meanings given to some of the ideas included are contested. Nonetheless, I offer them as an example of the kind of work we must begin to do in order to be able to listen and respond to one another in a constructive and democratic manner.

Concerns Frequently Voiced by the Antiabortion Public:

1. Life is sacred.
Connection: Most feminist and especially feminist environmentalists assert the sacredness of life and of all living things.

2. We have a special responsibility for the young and the vulnerable among us.
Connection: The feminist ethics of care is based on a recognition of responsibility, arising from historical connections and relationships, that goes beyond duties entailed by the recognition of individual rights.

3. The frequent use of abortion trivializes the violence that it entails.
Connection: Violence is endemic in women's lives. Pregnancy is not infrequently the result of either overt violence or the coercion of young girls into early sexual activity. Abortion can be seen as an extension of that violence. The desensitization to violence creates a growing danger to women and children in this society.

4. Making abortion too easily available undermines the impulse to commit to the nurturing and education of the young.
Connection: The maintenance of a long-term committed relationship within which one can find a good life and perhaps raise children is much harder to establish in the post-industrial welfare state. The nurturing and economic commitment to the young is often left to women living without a partner.

5. There is concern for the physical and psychological effects of abortion on women.
Connection: Women have become increasingly aware of the medicalization of normal female physiology and of the false options presented by advances in reproductive medicine. The use of abortion in countries like India to limit the birth of female children is one such use. Minority women in this country have good reason to be suspicious of medical interventions of any sort in their lives.

6. There is concern for the interest of third parties who will be affected in a deep way by the decision to have an abortion: The sexual partner of the woman, her parents, her children.
Connection: Feminists have often rejected the ethical and political orientations that depict them as individualistic utility maximizers in their decision making; they insist that women have always manifested concern in their deliberations for the network of connections in which we all exist. Thus the connection between the concerns of the pro-life and pro-choice publics can be seen as going much deeper than merely the shared end of reducing the number of abortions.

36. Benhabib, *Situating the Self*, 76.

37. Dewey, *The Public and Its Problems*, LW 2:349.

10

Dewey on Experience: Foundation or Reconstruction?

Richard Shusterman

I

Dewey is rightly hailed as America's major prophet of antifoundationalism, the view that philosophy should break with its traditional project of trying to guarantee our knowledge by grounding it on fixed, unquestionable foundations. These were long sought in self-evident first principles, primal essences, necessary categories, and privileged primary certainties: in notions like the *cogito*, the Kantian categories, sense-data, and the *a priori* laws of thought. Such indubitable, incorrigible foundations, Dewey argued, are neither available nor required for human knowledge and social practices.

Richard Rorty, who has done the most to champion Dewey's value for contemporary philosophy, shows how Dewey shares this attack on foundationalism with Wittgenstein and Heidegger. But in contrast to these later thinkers, Dewey's aim in freeing philosophy from its search for foundations was to employ it for concrete practical reform. Post-foundationalist philosophy, for Dewey, was neither mere Wittgensteinain therapy to relieve linguistic cramps and itches nor was it a Heideggerean attempt to recapture a pre-Socratic experience of Being or attain a higher realm of Thinking. The aim was rather to transfer and apply philosophy's critical acumen and imaginative energy to the resolution of concrete socio-cultural problems. Some of these, however, can be so deeply entrenched and structured by the ideology of past philosophies that new philosophical thinking is needed to resolve them; for instance, by making room for new solutions that do not fit with our current presumptions by revising those presumptions. Philosophy should be transformational instead of foundational. Rather than a metascience for grounding and justifying our current cognitive and cultural activities, it should be a form of cultural criticism which aims to redescribe our experienced world and reconstruct our practices and institutions so as to improve the quality of our lives. Improved experience, not originary truth, is the ultimate philosophical goal and criterion.

Experience is surely the heart of Dewey's philosophy, yet ironically it is also where Rorty thinks Dewey's philosophy is most vulnerable and dangerous since foundationally retrograde. With characteristic bluntness, he argues that "Dewey should have dropped the term 'experience'" rather than making it the center of his philosophy.[1] Pragmatism must replace this central notion with that of language and insist on a radical discontinuity between linguistic and sub-linguistic behavior which the term experience can only blur. Since the value of "experience" represents the major divide between Deweyan (and Jamesian) pragmatism and the post-linguistic-turn pragmatism advocated by Rorty and others,[2] the question of Dewey's use and abuse of this concept warrants further scrutiny.

This paper will probe the extent of Dewey's experiential foundationalism in order to see whether, *pace* Rorty, the idea of experience still has a vital role to play in pragmatism. I think it does; and its value lies in precisely that notion of experience—immediate, nondiscursive experience—which seems most vulnerable to charges of foundationalism and which, in any case, is most repugnant to contemporary philosophers who have made the linguistic turn. I shall therefore be concentrating on Dewey's notion of immediate experience to see whether it can be stripped of its foundationalist function and still have a point.

My view is that in emphasizing nondiscursive experience and its cognitive role, Dewey was on to something valuable which he unfortunately confused and devalued by treating it in traditional epistemological terms. This nondiscursive dimension is what Rorty refuses to countenance in philosophy, and the easiest way to discredit it is through identification with already discredited foundationalism, with which it is, in fact, typically linked. My goal is to separate them better than Dewey did, so as to avoid Rorty's criticisms and my own. We should start, then, by considering these criticisms.

II

One of Dewey's major goals in deploying his concept of experience was to advance a "naturalistic humanism" which would overcome the traditional dualisms of metaphysics and epistemology, dualisms which ultimately stemmed from the primal dualism of mind and matter. Given this dualism and secular culture's acceptance of the scientific materialist world-picture, the metaphysical question was how to find room in objective reality for the spiritual phenomena of consciousness, knowledge, and value without trying to justify them as "superimposed" from a superior, extra-natural world and without trying to reduce them to purely mechanistic networks of neurophysiology. There was also the epistemological question, at least as old as Descartes, of how material reality could be known by a mind defined as its radical other.

Dewey's naturalistic thesis of continuity and emergence answered both these questions. Inspired by Darwin, it argued that the higher human expressions of life emerge naturally from more simple organic forms through increasingly greater organization and more discriminating behavior. Mind was not an outside observer of the natural world but an emergent part of it; knowledge and value were not transcendental imports but emerging products (and tools) of natural interactions. Experience, Dewey thought, was the best general notion to bridge these different but continuous dimensions of nature. Since "experience" could cover both what was experienced and the specific how of experiencing, it could span the object/subject split which spurs epistemology; and since it could also be attributed to lower animals, it could bridge the gap between human thought and cruder forms of existence. To affirm such continuity is surely one (but not, in my view, the best) reason why Dewey insists that experience be conceived more widely than its standard philosophical construal as conscious, intellectual experience:

> When intellectual experience and its material are taken to be primary, the cord that binds experience and nature is cut. That the physiological organism with its structures, whether in man or in the lower animals, is concerned with making adaptations and uses of material in the interest of

life process, cannot be denied. The brain and nervous system are primarily organs of action-undergoing; biologically, it can be asserted without contravention that primary experience is of a corresponding type. Hence, unless there is breach of historic and natural continuity, cognitive experience must originate within that of a non-cognitive sort. And unless we start from knowing as a factor in action and undergoing we are inevitably committed to the intrusion of an extra-natural, if not supernatural, agency and principle.[3]

Rorty cites this passage in repudiating its notion of experience. Though sympathetic to Dewey's naturalism and critique of dualisms, he argues that experience is not only unnecessary for realizing Dewey's aims, but also renders these aims suspect by contamination with foundationalist confusions and myths: confusions of justifying knowledge through appeal to original causes, and myths of an immediate given. Experience is unnecessary because its target of dualism can be overcome through other means:

Dewey . . . confuses two ways of revolting against philosophical dualisms. The first way is to point out that the dualism is imposed by a tradition for specific cultural reasons, but has now outlived its usefulness. This is the Hegelian way— the way Dewey adopts in "An Empirical Study of Empiricisms." The second is to describe the phenomenon in a nondualistic way which emphasizes "continuity between lower and higher processes." This is the Lockean way—the way which led Locke to assimilate all mental acts to raw feels, thus paving the way for Humean skepticism.[4]

Rorty sees Dewey's notion of experience as representing the second way and misleading us back into Lockean foundationalist epistemology, blurring the line between cognitive and non-cognitive existence so that the latter can ground the former. Rather than eliminating "epistemological problems by eliminating the assumption that justification must repose on something other than social practices and human needs," Dewey tries "to solve" them by finding "'continuities' between nervous systems and people, or between 'experience and nature'." But "one does not need to justify our claim to know that, say, a given action was the best we could take by noting that the brain is an 'organ of action-undergoing'" (DM 82).

Certainly we should not try to justify specific knowledge claims by mere appeal to the causal conditions of knowing. But Rorty never really shows that Dewey commits this confusion in asserting the continuity of cognitive and non-cognitive experience. To make his case Rorty cites Dewey's view that language gives meaning to more primitive qualities of organic experience, thus rendering them conscious, definite feelings.

> This "objectification" is not a miraculous ejection from the organism or soul into external things, nor an illusory attribution of psychical entities to physical things. The qualities never were "in" the organism; they always were qualities of interactions in which both extra-organic things and organisms partake (EN 211–212).

Rorty then rightly critiques this notion of experience's "qualities of interaction" for simply dodging the standard questions of dualistic epistemology, e.g. "Is my *interaction* with this table brown, rather than, as I had previously thought, the *table* being brown" (DM 83). But this ambiguous use of experience and its failure to resolve the debate between idealism and realism surely do not amount to using non-cognitive experience as justificational evidence for our conscious cognitive claims. In asserting the general continuity of cognitive and non-cognitive experience, Dewey is not claiming that the latter functions cognitively as a criterion for the truth of the former. In fact, on the very page Rorty cites, Dewey effectively denies this by asserting that primitive non-cognitive experience is simply *had* but not *known*.[5] And since not even known as "had," it is unavailable for use as evidence to support specific knowledge claims. Moreover, in insisting that only language constitutes feelings or sensations as objects of meaning and knowledge, Dewey has already taken the linguistic turn which requires that the realm of cognitive justification (what Rorty, after Sellars, calls "the logical space of reasons") be entirely linguistic. This should suggest that Dewey's claims for noncognitive, nonlinguistic experience in *Experience and Nature* are ultimately motivated by something other than the quest for epistemological foundations, a suggestion I later develop in terms of aesthetic and practical uses of such experience.

The closest Dewey comes to foundationalism here is to suggest that though any particular knowledge claim may be questioned, we can't take global scepticism seriously because we are linked to the world in a primal way before the question of knowledge claims can even arise. For even the formulation of sceptical doubts presupposes a behavioral background and use of world materials, organs and language. There can be no total, unbridgeable gulf between subject and object (or mind and world) since both are only constituted as distinct terms through experiential interaction. Rorty himself often employs the same kind of anti-sceptical strategy through his preferred notion of language. Rather than a continuum of experience (extending from the pre-cognitive hence pre-sceptical), we have a continuum of linguistic behavior ranging from merely practical, pre-cognitive use to the making and justification of knowledge claims. Since we can have no sense of the world apart from how it is used, determined, and known through language, there is no wedge for a radical scepticism that language is completely out of touch with the world. Here the subject/object dualism is dissolved not in the common solvent of experience but in the network of language as a social practice through which particular minds and particular objects are constituted as individuals.

Rorty is right that language works much better than experience for such epistemological purposes; not only because language is a much clearer notion but because epistemology is a distinctively linguistic enterprise. But this does not mean that non-cognitive experience is intrinsically a foundational notion, while language is intrinsically immune to such uses. Protocol sentences have been used foundationally, and even the Wittgensteinian linguistic line which I share with Rorty is open to such misconstrual.

Consider Wittgenstein's claim that justifications must come to an end and the way he typically ends them by invoking the fact that *"this language game is played,"* that this is how we were taught to use words and to live our "forms of life."[6] While Wittgenstein was seeking therapy from philosophy's quest for ultimate foundations, his remarks are easily read instead as substituting empiricism's myth of the given with an allegedly non-mythical *linguistic* given. The huge project of analytic metaphysics through philosophy of language constitutes such a foundational reading.

However, even if pre-cognitive, non-linguistic experience does not entail foundationalism, philosophy has most often used it for precisely this purpose. Dewey himself does not always resist such temptations. Let us see precisely where he succumbs and whether immediate experience can be stripped also of Dewey's foundationalist use and still be philosophically important. For if not, Rorty is essentially right that contemporary pragmatism must renounce it.

III

Dewey's most thorough accounts of how immediate experience relates to knowledge occur in his essay "Qualitative Thought" (1930) and in his culminating treatise *Logic: The Theory of Inquiry* (1938).[7] Here, as elsewhere, he firmly eschews the standard foundationalist strategy of using the qualities of immediate experience as indubitable, incorrigible evidence for particular claims of knowledge. They could not possibly have such a role since they are simply had rather than known and would have to be reconstructed and formulated in order to serve as a justificational foundation of truth.

But Dewey courts a different, more subtle variety of foundationalism when he argues that experience of immediate, nondiscursive quality not only underlies but must guide all discursive thought. Here immediate experience is invoked not to justify particular truth claims but to ground the coherence of any thinking from which such claims emerge. Dewey claims that even if such experience is unknowable and ineffable, its existence and functioning can be recognized by introspection and, moreover, can be inferred as necessary in all our thinking. For it performs five logical functions needed for thought which, Dewey maintains, are otherwise not provided.

In sharp contrast to the atomism of traditional empiricism, Dewey's argument for experiential foundations rests on good holist premises:

> we never experience nor form judgements about objects and events in isolation, but only in connection with a contextual whole. This latter is called a "situation" . . . ; *an* object or event is always a special part, phase or aspect of an environing experienced world . . . [and] stands out conspicuously because . . . of some problem of use or enjoyment which the *total* complex of environment presents. (L 72)

1. All thinking, then, is contextual, but what determines the relevant context or situation? What constitutes it as the single context it is, and gives it the unity, structure, and limits necessary for providing thought with an effective framework? Dewey's answer is *immediately experienced quality*: "a situation is a whole in virtue of its immediately pervasive quality" (L 73). It is "held together, in spite of its internal complexity, by the fact that it is dominated by a single quality," "constituted by a pervasive and

internally integrative quality" (Q 97). "The pervasively qualitative is not only that which binds all constituents into a whole but it is also unique; it constitutes in each situation an *individual* situation, indivisible and unduplicable" (L 74).

2. In constituting the situation, this immediate quality also controls the distinctions and relations of objects which reflective thought will identify and employ as parts of the situation (e.g. whether we notice a sound as a message or disregard it as background noise).

> Confusion and incoherence are always marks of lack of control by a single pervasive quality. The latter alone enables a person to keep track of what he is doing, saying, hearing, reading, in whatever explicitly appears. The underlying unity of qualitativeness regulates pertinence or relevancy and force of every distinction and relation; it guides selection and rejection and the manner of utilization of all explicit terms. . . . For the latter are *its* distinctions and relations. (Q 98–9)

Hence, for Dewey, "A universe of experience is a precondition of a universe of discourse. Without its controlling presence, there is no way to determine the relevancy, weight, or coherence of any designated distinction or relation" (L 74). Yet this controlling immediate quality lies below the level of thematized consciousness and language. It "surrounds and regulates the universe of discourse but never appears as such within the latter" (L 74); and when we bring it into speech and awareness we are transforming it into an object of a new situation defined by its own immediate and ineffable unifying quality.

3. Apart from unifying the context of judgment and determining the relations of its terms, immediate quality provides a sense of what is adequate in judgment, what level of detail, complexity, or precision is sufficient to render the contextual judgment valid. Is the earth really round? Is running good for your health? Does water boil at 100 degrees centigrade regardless of other factors? We can always make our judgments more detailed and precise. "But enough," as Dewey says, "is always enough, and the underlying quality is itself the test of the 'enough' for any particular case" (Q 108).

4. A fourth function of immediate quality is to determine the basic sense or direction of the situation and to sustain it over time,

despite the confusing general flood of experience. Although the quality is non-discursively "dumb," it has "a movement or transition in some direction" which provides the needed sense of unity and continuity in ongoing inquiry (Q 107).

> This quality enables us to keep thinking about one problem without our having constantly to stop to ask ourselves what is it after all that we are thinking about. We are aware of it not by itself but as the background, the thread, and the directive clue in what we do expressly think of (Q 99).

> It is this unique quality that not only evokes the particular inquiry engaged in but that exercises control over its special procedures. Otherwise, one procedure in inquiry would be as likely to occur and to be as effective as any other. . . . Were not the sequence determined by an inclusive situation, whose qualitative nature pervades and holds together each successive step, activity would be a meaningless hop-skip-jump affair (L 109, 126).

5. Finally, Dewey argues that immediate experience's integrative quality is the only adequate way to explain the association of ideas. The standard explanations of physical contiguity and similarity are insufficient to make the link, because "there is an indefinite number of particulars contiguous to one another in space and time" and because everything in some respect is similar to everything else. Mere spatio-temporal proximity cannot explain, for example, why I associate an empty nest with a bird I never saw rather than with "the multitudinous leaves and twigs which are more frequently and more obviously juxtaposed" to the nest. And why should mere similarity lead my thought from this hammer to a nail rather than to another nearly identical hammer in the store? Something else is needed to make the connections of associative thinking, and Dewey's answer is that it can only be the ineffable quality of immediate experience which binds through its sense of relevance: "What alternative remains save that the quality of a situation as a whole operates to produce a functional connection?" Association must be "an intellectual connection" produced through "an underlying quality which operates to control the connection of objects thought of"; "there must be relevancy of both ideas to a situation defined by unity of quality" (Q 111).

For a non-foundational philosopher like Dewey, this account of immediate quality as the underlying guide of all thought and discourse seems very much out of character. Had he simply argued that immediate quality can sometimes effectively ground or direct our thinking, his position would be convincing. Unfortunately, however, such quality is affirmed as what determines, *in every particular situation*, the coherence of our thinking, the structure of discourse, and the measure of adequacy in judgment. Moreover, it does all this without being a distinct object of awareness or term of discourse. We can never really analyse it, because doing so transforms it into something else. Yet, Dewey argues , we know it must exist and function as described, since otherwise coherent thought would be impossible. Here Dewey's radical empiricism forsakes him for a foundational metaphysics of presence justified by transcendental argument, a qualitative presence which, though mute, is the logically efficacious factor directing all thought.

There is good reason not to follow Dewey in embracing this ineffable experiential foundationalism, particularly since he elsewhere provides the means to avoid it. His pragmatism typically emphasizes how thought and action are governed by habit, purpose, needs of the organism, and the specific saliencies of the situation (as shaped by the organism's habits, purposes, and needs). Such factors, which typically function unreflectively, can perform all the necessary tasks for which immediate qualitative experience was invoked as thought's indispensable foundational guide.

The basic structural unity of situation which thought requires is provided by the practical unity of purpose and the continuity and direction of habit. It need not be qualitatively determinate presence of unity but simply a vague, presumptive unity of purposive behavior toward a particular end.[8] A pursued purpose binds together the situational elements enlisted in its pursuit, and a habit already implies an internal organization of activity which projects itself on further organization. Habit and purpose can also provide the basis for our distinctions of objects and relations within the situation and our judgments of their relevance and importance. For Dewey, "habits are abilities" that are "conditions of intellectual efficiency," not only by focussing perception and thought within productive limits and patterns but by refining and developing it through repeated but varied practice. They provide the initial, prereflective structure for "all the perceiving, recognizing, imagining, recalling, judging" we perform.[9] If our habits of perception and classification initially structure the situation, our specific purposes further shape it. "The operations that institute a 'this' as a subject are always selective—restrictive of something from out of a larger field," the constituting of a situational focus from an indefinite experienced background. But, Dewey continues, this "selective-restriction [is always] made for a definite purpose" (L 131). So given the structuring of habit and purpose, there is no need to appeal to a special unifying quality, a felt presence, to organize the situation as an organized whole.

The function of giving the situation a definite, sustained direction is similarly met by habit and purpose. Since "all habit has continuity," is "projective" by its very nature, our thinking habits naturally continue their directional course (without needing to reflect to do so) and tend to resist interruption or distraction (HN 31, 168). Purpose also clearly provides direction and stimulates continuity of action for its realization, its desired end calling forth a series of coordinated means to reach it. These factors, rather than a mysterious qualitative presence, are what bind and control the successive steps of inquiry.

Purpose is also a better explanation of what is deemed adequate in judgment. Indeed, after advancing immediate quality as the criterion of adequacy, when it comes to clarifying his idea, Dewey reverts to purpose: "Any proposition that serves the purpose for which it is made is logically adequate" (Q 108). Finally, habit and purpose can explain our association of ideas without invoking a mysterious ineffable quality to link them. "When I think of a hammer," Dewey asks, "why is the idea of nail so likely to follow?" (Q 111). The obvious answer is not the qualitative glue of immediate experience, but the entrenched habit of their functional association for practical purposes of construction. Dewey's argument for the necessity of immediate experience as the guiding ground for all thinking is thus as unconvincing as it is inimical to his antifoundationalist agenda.

IV

Why then does Dewey affirm non-discursive experience as an epistemological foundation? His real aim, I believe, was not to provide such foundations but to celebrate the importance of non-discursive immediacy. Its importance was first of all *aesthetic*, central to the realm of experienced value. He always insisted that our most intense and vivid values are those of on-the-pulse experienced quality and affect, not the abstractions of discursive truth. For Dewey, aesthetic satisfaction takes privilege over science, which is simply "a handmaiden" providing the conditions for achieving such satisfaction more frequently, stably, and fully (EN 290). Yet he further saw that non-discursive somatic experience also played an important role in cognition and action. Proprioceptive discriminations beneath the level of thematized consciousness structure our perceptual field, just as unformulated feelings ("expansions, elations, and dejections") influence our behavior and orient our thinking.[10]

Wanting to celebrate the importance of this nondiscursive experience, Dewey did so in the way philosophers have habitually emphasized factors they thought primary and essential—by erecting it as a theoretical foundation. This was a bad confusion of what was (or should have been) his true aim—to establish and improve the quality of immediate experience as a practical end and useful tool. Dewey wanted philosophers to see that nondiscursive experience could be used to improve knowledge as well as the felt quality of living. Even if philosophers were trained to dwell instead on discursive reason, their task of giving an account of human reality required recognition of the role of nondiscursive experience.[11] Moreover, given pragmatism's aim of not merely explaining reality but improving it, the value of nondiscursive experience seemed still more important as a project to be realized, and its crucial but much neglected locus was the body.[12]

A major inspiration here was F. Matthias Alexander, the renowned body therapist and founder of "Alexander Technique," whose influence on Dewey has not been adequately recognized.[13] A long-devoted student of Alexander, not simply of his texts but of his somatic exercises, Dewey wrote encomiastic introductions to three of his books, defending Alexander's work against sceptical reviewers and praising it as having "demonstrated a new scientific principle with respect to the control of human behavior, as important as any principle which has ever been discovered in the domain of external nature."[14]

Alexander argued that many of the physical and mental ills that we suffer in the modern world result from disharmony between our more advanced intellectual behavior and our more basic bodily functions. While the efforts of millennia have been devoted to developing the intellect, bodily functioning—long scorned as belonging to the base realm of sense or unchangeable instinct—has been left to entrenched habits and instincts inherited from ancient times when the body worked in different conditions. Contemporary civilized conditions are unsuited to the inherited forms of somatic expression and moreover subject us unconsciously to new customs and regimes of body control (like Foucauldian disciplines of biopower). The result "is the larger number of physical disorders which inflict themselves exclusively upon civilized man [e.g. the modern form of back trouble], and the large number of neuroses which express themselves in intellectual and moral maladies."[15] Yet no serious inquiry had been devoted to develop somatic functioning so as to make it not only better coordinated and more suited to the contemporary world, but to render it an effective stimulus for improving that world to answer human needs of psycho-somatic fulfilment.

Alexander therefore urged a reeducation of our somatic functioning which required a reeducation for somatic awareness, a new attention to bodily experiences. More importantly, he offered a concrete method of such reeducation, one which worked by extending conscious control over bodily actions formerly abandoned to unconscious habit, by bringing into conscious focus experiences previously unnoticed and unattended. This insistence on *thinking* through the body, to achieve more conscious control and more acute perception of its condition, clearly distinguishes Alexander's approach from standard physical culture and body building. In fact, he vehemently attacked them for dealing only with externals by means of brute drill rather than bringing greater sensitivity and quality to inner experience by means of heightened consciousness (SI 13–28).

Dewey's emphasis on immediate nondiscursive experience and its continuity with higher intellectual activity is most fruitfully understood in this Alexandrian context: not as foundational epistemology but as a panegyric to the somatic in the face of centuries of denigrating philosophical scorn. In his 1918 introduction to Alexander's *Man's Supreme Inheritance*, seven years before advancing his theory of experiential and mind-body continuity in *Experience and Nature* (in which Alexander's work is twice invoked and his terminology appropriated), Dewey writes:

> Men are afraid, without even being aware of their fear, to recognize the most wonderful of all the structures of the vast universe—the human body. They have been led to think that a serious notice and regard would somehow involve disloyalty to man's higher life. The discussions of Mr. Alexander breathe reverence for this wonderful instrument of our life, life mental and moral as well as that life which

somewhat meaninglessly we call bodily. When such a religious attitude toward the body becomes more general, we shall have an atmosphere favorable to securing the conscious control which is urged. (SI 351)

Recognizing that body-functioning influences the mind, Alexander likewise grasped the mind's potential for the body. His project was to improve somatic (and consequently mental) functioning by using the mind, employing a method of "constructive conscious control" directed by the individual on his body.[16] Our bad bodily habits (e.g. bad posture or poorly coordinated movement) are usually performed without thinking and are taken for granted. Moreover, when we do focus on them, they seem right because they are familiar as our habits. When asked to stand or move differently we may be unable to, not because we are anatomically impaired but simply because we cannot yet feel ourselves into an alternative way.

To improve our bodily habits and psycho-somatic integration we need to bring our somatic functioning and its attendant feelings into greater consciousness, so we can learn both to detect subtly different modalities of posture and movement and to assess the quality of their coordination and their attendant affectivity. Without detecting these modalities we could never learn how to perform different somatic actions which could be developed into better habits; without qualitative appreciation we would not learn which somatic behavior should be rendered habitual so as to provide a better background of unconscious psycho-somatic functioning. For example, we need to become conscious both of how to hold the head in different positions and of which position gives us the best felt quality and case of breathing in order to select this position over others for a new habituation. Once the habit has been reconstructed through this concentrated attention, the now improved habit can well be returned to its unreflective character in order to allow consciousness to concentrate on other tasks.

Such an improved habit, even if it functions unconsciously, can also enhance our conscious thought, since better breathing can mean better awareness and more steady concentration. We must recall, however, that conscious attention was required to improve this unconscious functioning; and so, by the way, is language—as the means for designating body parts, movements, and feelings on which we are instructed to concentrate. The interdependent continuity of mind and body can be seen as reflected in the similar continuity of conscious thinking and the nondiscursive background which orients thought, an often unconscious somatic background which can however be brought into consciousness.[17]

We can now understand what Dewey's experiential foundationalism was concerned with, and how it erred. He was wrong to think that an unconscious, non-discursive immediate quality was the necessary grounding guide or regulatory criterion of all our thinking, though he was right to insist that nondiscursive background experience influences our conscious thought. Rather than such unnoticed quality being the guide for conscious thought—the controlling criterion which binds thought together—it is instead the noticing of experiential quality, the bringing of it into consciousness, which can help us give greater unity and richness to our thought, better coordination and affect to thought's nondiscursive experiential background, and greater integration of the psychosomatic and the intellectual. Dewey's mistake is not in emphasizing the unifying quality of experience, but only in positing it as an antecedent foundational fact rather than regarding it as an end and means of reconstruction.

Through the Alexandrian perspective we can also see the limits of Rorty's critique. *Pace* Rorty, the dominant pragmatist aim of Dewey's philosophy of experience is not the metaphysical goal "of obtaining continuity between us and the brutes" by our "sharing something called 'experience'—something not the same as consciousness or thought but something of which consciousness or thought are more developed forms." Nor is it the epistemological goal of ensuring that our perceptions are not "'out of touch' with nature" since both belong to the unity of experience (DHD 10).[18] Instead, Dewey's prime purpose was the aesthetic and practical one of improving experience by making it the focus of our inquiry, of enriching and harmonizing our experience, for example, by affirming and enhancing the continuity between soma and psyche, between nondiscursive experience and conscious thought. The aim, as he presents it in advocating Alexander's technique, is "to integrate into harmonious coordination our animal inheritance and our distinctively human capacities of intelligence" (RR 355).

So even if Rorty is right that experience cannot solve the theoretical problems of metaphysical and epistemological continuity, this does not nullify the point of Dewey's philosophy of experience. For his philosophy is not so much directed at proving theoretical continuity but instead at enhancing continuity *in practice*, at healing the painfully (though often unconsciously) experienced fragmentation of human life. This, he believed, could be achieved only by recognizing the crucial somatic dimension of experience, a recognition which he occasionally misconstrued in foundational terms.

V

But what does it mean for philosophy to recognize this somatic dimension? Simply to say that it exists, even as a necessary feature of human existence, seems an empty gesture that goes nowhere. The importance of nondiscursive experience in actual living does not entail that it is *philosophically* important. And how could it be, since philosophy, as traditionally practiced, can apparently do nothing with it except misuse it discursively for foundationalist fantasies? The somatic, so central to the pragmatist thought of Dewey and James, is therefore rejected by Rorty as a philosophically outdated and troublesome notion which contemporary pragmatism (not only his own but Davidson's and Putnam's) has justly jettisoned. Endorsing the linguistic turn, pragmatism should eschew the Deweyan—Jamesian stress on experience as a useless vestige of turn-of-the-century panpsychism. Instead it should insist that language exhausts the realm of philosophy, following Peirce's cue that "my language is the sum total of myself" (DHD 3).[19]

Though appreciative of the linguistic turn, I am also wary of its totalizing tendencies and reluctant to abandon pragmatism's traditional concern with the somatic and nondiscursive (which even Peirce recognized in his notion of Firstness). Before burying the body, we need to assess more critically philosophy's resistance to nondiscursive experience. Such resistance is based not only on arguments but on deeply entrenched biases and agendas which work, most effectively, beneath the level of conscious thought.

The reason Rorty most frequently gives for banishing nondiscursive experience from the domain of philosophy is that it involves us in the foundationalist myth of the given. In our search to base knowledge on something immune to error, we retreat to a brute experiential immediacy whose nondiscursivity makes it immune even to linguistic error. But this appeal to a nondiscursive given is mythical, because for such experience to function as justificational evidence it must be conceptualized or rendered discursive.

The case against the myth of the given is impeccable; but it does not follow that philosophy should never concern itself with the nondiscursive. Drawing this conclusion means assuming that philosophy's only possible use for nondiscursive experience is in justificational epistemology, and that assumption is neither self-evident nor argued for. To find more fruitful ways for philosophy to treat the nondiscursive presents a vital task for pragmatism. Prefigured in Dewey's confused advocacy of immediate experience, it is today more urgently demanded by our culture's increasing devotion to techniques of somatic transformation yet continuing failure to give them sympathetic philosophical study.[20]

This somatic option is implicitly denied by Rorty's second argument for banishing the nonlinguistic: that introducing somatic experience into our philosophical concerns undermines philosophy's distinctive role and logical space by confusing between causes and reasons. This argument forms part of his attack on the myth of the given. For in this myth, nondiscursive physical sensation—which may be the antecedent *cause* of knowing something (e.g. a burning sensation resulting in awareness that the plate is hot)—is falsely taken for a *reason* that justifies such knowledge, a reason that seems evident and irrefutable by its brute immediacy. But, as we saw, nondiscursive experience cannot, as such, play a role in the language game of epistemological justification, whose regimentation has always been philosophy's distinctive task. Such experience may be "a causal condition for knowledge but not a *ground* for knowledge."[21] Since philosophy is concerned with the rational justification of our beliefs, not their psychological or physiological causes, it should therefore resist trafficking with things like somatic experience which belong to the nondiscursive domain of causes; it should remain within "the logical space of reasons." For "nothing is to be gained . . . by running together the vocabularies in which we describe the causal antecedents of knowledge with those in which we offer justifications of our claims to knowledge" (PMN 182, DM 81).

Nothing gained, that is, for epistemology, from whose standpoint Rorty attacks the nondiscursive. But why should philosophy be confined to its standard role of justifying by reasons rather than modifying through causes, of merely legitimating beliefs and practices rather than creating or transforming them? Such justificational restriction seems particularly foreign to pragmatism, and Rorty himself boldly rejects it when he comes to his own central philosophical topic—language. Here Rorty advocates a philosophy of causation rather than legitimation. The aim is to create new vocabularies and transform our ways of speaking, not to ground those already in place.[22] He even insists on blurring the very distinction he elsewhere strictly defended: "once we raise the question of how we get from one vocabulary to another, from one dominant metaphoric to another, the distinction between reasons and causes begins to lose utility," for there is insufficient common ground to provide decisive reasons for change (CIS 48).

Building on Rorty's own example, we can argue as follows: if philosophy takes for its pragmatist goal not the grounding of knowledge but the production of better lived experience, then it need not be confined to the realm of discursive truth and the language-games of their justification. Philosophy can aim more directly at the practical end of improving experience by advocating and embodying practices which achieve this. And if the practice of linguistic invention provides one such tool, why can't the practice of somatic disciplines focussing on the nondiscursive provide a complementary other?

This option is never admitted, however, because the dominant philosophical ideology of textualism represses the nonlinguistic. This ideology, common to analytic and continental philosophy, insists that language exhausts the scope of experience, since whatever lies outside of language cannot be thought or given content, and so cannot function as a term for us. Hence Sellars claims that "*all* awareness is a linguistic affair"; Gadamer stresses "the essential linguisticality of all human experience of the world"; Rorty asserts that we humans are "nothing more than sentential attitudes"; and Derrida declares that there cannot be a "hors-texte," "a reality . . . whose content could take place, could have taken place outside of language."[23]

Textualist ideology has been extremely helpful in dissuading philosophy from misguided quests for absolute foundations outside of our contingent, changing linguistic and social practices. But in making this therapeutic point by stressing what Rorty terms "the ubiquity of language,"[24] textualism also encourages an unhealthy idealism that identifies human being-in-the world with linguistic activity and so tends to neglect, minimize, or over-textualize other somatic experience. As "the contemporary counterpart of [nineteenth century] idealism," textualism not only inherited idealism's rejection of the supremacy of natural science, but also idealism's disdain for nondiscursive materiality, hence for the corporeal. Idealism, we should remember, was an attempt to secure, through consciousness, a realm of spirituality after natural science had displaced religion's authority and secularized the world; and it inherited, by and large, the Christian impulse to depreciate the body.[25] After

Freud's disenchantment of consciousness, language has become the new representative of soul in contrast to corporeal nondiscursivity. The whole project of policing the borders between "the logical space of reasons" and the realm of physical causes so as to confine philosophy to the former can be seen as just one more assertion of the old dualism of separating the concerns of the superior soul from the corruption of the material body, whose study is consigned not to the human but the natural sciences.

Textualism's resistance to the nondiscursive soma goes far beyond its recent idealist heritage. Such resistance is built into the very project of philosophy as a saliently linguistic discipline devoted to the *logos*. Ever since the Greeks, the *alogon* was at once the nonlinguistic and the irrational. Two factors thus tend to repress philosophy's treatment of the nondiscursive. The first is simply structural censorship by the philosophical field through disciplinary inertia. Despite a fine heritage of materialist thinkers, philosophy's long dominant tradition of spiritual logocentrism and its entrenched practice as a linguistic form have structured the discipline in a way that automatically tends to exclude serious focus on the nondiscursive.[26] There is no allocation for it in Western philosophical space, no sub-discipline of "philosophy of body" to complement philosophy of mind (as hatha yoga serves the more spiritual raja yoga in Indian thought). The result is that non-discursive somatic experience is either ignored, relegated to other fields like psychology or neuroscience, or instead subsumed under clearly discursive projects like that of epistemological justification or genealogical accounts of reading the body as a social text on which a society's practices of subjugating power are inscribed.

A second reason for ignoring the nondiscursive involves what might be called the disciplinary fallacy: the idea that what a discipline does not treat (or treat seriously) cannot be important for that discipline. Such reasoning precludes disciplinary growth and would have denied chemistry's importance for botany or the central role of the unconscious for psychology. This fallacy is especially dangerous in philosophy which sees itself both as a specialized profession (with a technical literature and strictly regimented questions) and also as a basic, time-honored human enterprise of universal significance and scope. Through the former self-conception it materially reproduces itself as a professional institution, while the latter affords it a charismatic aura of deep relevance and wisdom (painfully lacking in its actual institutional expression) which helps legitimate its institutional reproduction. By the professional conception (especially as understood through textualism), nondiscursive somatic experience has no place in philosophy. But by the latter, if it has no place, it cannot be important for understanding human experience and so no new place should be made for it. The upshot of this equivocation is that philosophy is right to shirk the nondiscursive as unimportant because its very doing so proves this unimportance.

The disciplinary fallacy seems so persuasive because it expresses a compelling pragmatic point. An individual discipline can't do everything, and should therefore concentrate on doing what it does best and avoid doing what it can't do. Since philosophy is strongly centered on language and seems ill-equipped to handle the somatic and nondiscursive, it should not try to treat them. For what, after all, can philosophy do here except embroil itself, as Dewey did, in foundationalist regressions? This question presents a major task for somatic philosophy, and I cannot pretend to give a full answer. But I shall conclude by briefly suggesting three ways that philosophy can productively engage nondiscursive somatic experience.

First and most simply, philosophy can argue for the importance of such experience (as Merleau-Ponty did far better than Dewey) so that it will not be merely acknowledged to exist but will be more vigorously explored as a legitimate object of research and of personal cultivation. Overcoming its *parti pris* against the nonlinguistic, philosophy can lend support and analytic skills to scientific inquiries into the nondiscursive features of human experience (e.g., Daniel Stern's groundbreaking work on the prelinguistic understanding of infants).[27] And it might launch its own inquiries into the role of nonverbal experience in aesthetics and ethics as well as in cognition.

Secondly, contemporary popular culture displays an intense preoccupation with the body. Apart from the proliferation of gyms and centers for aerobics, massage, and body building, there is a growing number of somatic therapies which promise not merely relief from physical ailments but improved psychosomatic integration, or, more simply, better harmony of lived experience. Since the work of Alexander, we have been offered Rolfing, Bioenergetics, Eutony, Feldenkrais Method, Somatics, Ideokinesis, to name just a few. There is also the greatly heightened interest in older practices like yoga and T'ai chi. We philosophers are prone to dismiss these things as New Age quackery or simply ignore them as none of our business. (Are you not quick, dear reader, to condemn this part of my paper as irrelevant bunkum?)

But Dewey's attention to Alexander should give us pause. If philosophy sees itself most broadly as culture criticism, then somatics is an increasingly significant dimension of our culture that is ripe for philosophical critique. Philosophy here can have the role of critically examining such body practices and their attendant ideologies to see what sense or nonsense they make, what good or harm they do, and whether they could profit from a better formulation of aims and methods.[28] It might helpfully disentangle useful technique from misguided theory so as to make these practices more convincing and effective.

Finally, the most radical and interesting way for philosophy to engage somatics is to integrate such bodily disciplines into the very practice of philosophy. This means practicing philosophy not simply as a discursive genre, a form of writing, but as a discipline of embodied life. One's philosophical work, one's search for truth and wisdom, would not be pursued only through texts but also through somatic exploration and experiment. By acute attention to the body and its nonverbal messages, by the practice of body disciplines which heighten somatic awareness and transform how one feels and functions, one discovers and expands self-knowledge by remaking one's self. This quest for self-knowledge and self-transformation can constitute a philosophical life of increasing embodied enrichment that has irresistible aesthetic appeal, for one's life becomes a developing work of art.

Such a vision of philosophy as a thoughtfully disciplined, somatically-centered way of life was powerfully revived by Foucault in his very last lectures at the Collège de France (1984), inspired in large part by the example of Diogenes the Cynic. However alien it seems to today's academy, the idea of philosophy as a way of life, an embodied practice, was important to the *logos*-loving Greeks. It was also central to the American thought of Emerson and Thoreau, from which Dewey and pragmatism derive inspiration. Scorning the academic philosophy of his day, Thoreau wrote in *Walden*, "There are nowadays professors of philosophy, but not philosophers. Yet it is admirable to profess because it was once admirable to live."[29]

"The *bios philosophicos*," Foucault explains of Diogenes, "is the animality of being human, renewed as a challenge, practiced as an exercise—and thrown in the face of others as a scandal."[30] But the somatically-focussed, aesthetically engaging philosophical life need not be as scandalous as Foucault preferred to see and practice it. Thoreau's exercises in simple living, labor, and purity of diet—or Dewey's explorations through the Alexander method (to which he attributed his improved capacities for attention and awareness, and even his longevity)—present alternative models of embodied philosophical life that seem equally informative, transformative, and aesthetically enriching, though of course less dramatic and spectacular than Foucault's violent experiments in drugs and sado-masochistic sex.

His dazzling, but also daunting, example reaffirms the need for critical attention to the variety of somatic practices through which we can pursue our quest for self-knowledge and self-creation, for wisdom and beauty, for the reconstruction of immediate experience into improved living. Experience, in at least this sense, remains the vital heart of philosophy.

Temple University

Notes

Earlier drafts of this paper have profited from the comments of Richard Bernstein, James Miller, Chuck Dyke, Marx Wartofsky, David Seiple, and Vincent Colapietro. They have my thanks.

1. Richard Rorty, "Dewey Between Hegel and Darwin," published in French as "Dewey Entre Hegel et Darwin," *Rm Descartes*, 5 6 (1993). I quote from page 12 of the English manuscript, henceforth referred to as DHD. The paper is forthcoming in Dorothy Ross (ed.), *Modernism and the Human Sciences* (Baltimore: Johns Hopkins University Press, 1994).

2. Rorty underlines this point in his *Objectivity, Relativism, and Truth* (Cambridge: Cambridge University Press, 1991), 16–17.

3. John Dewey, *Experience and Nature* (LaSalle: Open Court Press, 1929), 23; henceforth EN.

4. Richard Rorty, "Dewey's Metaphysics" in *Consequences of Pragmatism* (Minneapolis: University of Minnesota Press, 1982), 82; henceforth referred to as DM.

5. EN 211. Moreover, in the following paragraph Dewey goes on to deny the empiricist idea of immediate non-discursive knowledge: "The notion that sensory affections discriminate themselves, apart from discourse, as being colors and sounds, etc., and thus *ipso facto* constitute certain elementary modes of knowledge, even though it be only knowledge and their own existence, is inherently so absurd that it would never have occurred to anyone to entertain it, were it not for certain preconceptions about mind and knowledge" (212).

6. Ludwig Wittgenstein, *Philosophical Investigations* (Oxford: Blackwell, 1968), para. 190, 197, 217, 485, 654; pp. 208, 226.

7. John Dewey, "Qualitative Thought," repr. in *Philosophy and Civilization* (New York: Capricorn, 1963), henceforth abbreviated as *Q*; and *Logic: The Theory of Inquiry* (Carbondale: Southern Illinois Press, 1986), henceforth L.

8. Such unity is largely prospective, an impulse or aim of coordinated activity. See John Dewey, *Human Nature and Conduct*, 1922 (Carbondale, IL: Southern Illinois University Press, 1983), 79, 128.

9. Ibid., 47, 121, 124.

10. See EN 244.

11. This point, of course, has been emphasized by Merleau-Ponty, whose philosophy advocates the same attention to the body that I am advocating. His account of the lived body as the experiential unifying ground of perception has many similarities to Dewey's use of the unifying ground of felt quality; and it could be vulnerable to similar criticisms. There is no space to pursue this here, nor to pursue what I think is a more important criticism: Merleau-Ponty's concentration on the theoretical importance of bodily experience and his lack of attention to the project of how to improve this experience rather than simply describe it as it is. This suggests a basic difference between phenomenology and pragmatism as I conceive it.

12. Rejecting dualism to embrace an emergent naturalism, Dewey and I share the view that all experience, even abstract thinking, is body-dependent, just as our bodily functioning is often influenced by thought. Body and mind are functional distinctions of an organic whole Dewey called "body—mind" (EN 203). My ensuing emphasis on the soma should not therefore be taken as implying a new inverted dualism. Nor should the notion of nondiscursive immediacy be seen as limited to the formalized somatic disciplines I cite (which are themselves body—mind disciplines). Nondiscursive immediacy plays a wide-ranging role in our everyday understanding and praxis. However, while insisting that everyday experience is not an intrinsically inferior realm, pragmatism still advocates that it can be bettered through intelligent means. Somatic disciplines claim to provide such means and so, as Dewey recognized, warrant pragmatist consideration.

13. Robert Westbrook's landmark biography only mentions him once in a footnote; and even there he is mentioned not in terms of his own work or relationship to Dewey but only as an "occasion" for a polemical exchange between Dewey and Bourne. See Robert Westbrook, *John Dewey and American Democracy* (Ithaca: Cornell University Press, 1991), 221n26. This neglect is sadly the norm in Dewey studies. There is, however, a discussion of Alexander's influence on Dewey in Steven Rockefeller, *John Dewey: Religious Faith and Democratic Humanism* (New York: Columbia

University Press, 1991), 333–344. For a deeper account of Dewey's relations with Alexander and of the scientific evidence for Alexander's theories, see F.P. Jones, *Body Awareness in Action: A Study of the Alexander Technique* (New York: Schocken, 1979). For a comparative analysis of Alexander work with other currently popular somatic therapies, see Richard Shusterman, "Die Sorge um den Körper in der heutigen Kultur," in Andreas Kuhlmann (ed.), *Philosophische Ansichten der Kultur der Moderne* (Frankfurt: Fischer Taschenbuch, 1994).

14. John Dewey, "Introduction" to F. Matthias Alexander, *Constructive Conscious Control of the Individual* (New York: Dutton, 1923), reprinted in John Dewey, *The Middle Works*, vol. 15 (Carbondale: Southern Illinois University Press, 1983), 313.

15. John Dewey, "Reply to Reviewer" (R. Bourne) of F. Matthias Alexander, *Man's Supreme Inheritance* (New York: Dutton, 1918), in *New Republic* 15 (1918), repr. in John Dewey, *The Middle Works*, vol. 11 (Carbondale: Southern Illinois University Press, 1982) 354, henceforth abbreviated RR. The same volume also contains Dewey's "Introductory Word" to the book, henceforth abbreviated SI. Dewey also wrote an "Introduction" to a third book by Alexander, *The Use of the Self* (New York: Dutton, 1932), reprinted in John Dewey, *The Later Works*, vol. 6 (Carbondale: Southern Illinois University Press, 1985), 315–20, in which Dewey describes his long experience as a pupil of Alexander.

16. This is reflected in the title of Alexander's book, *Constructive Conscious Control of the Individual* (New York: Dutton, 1923). Dewey's introduction to this book is reprinted in *Middle Works*, vol. 15, 308–315.

17. The question of what exactly qualifies as "conscious" is a complex problem that I should raise but cannot answer here. In describing certain habits or experiences as unconscious, I mean here simply that they are not thematized objects of consciousness or objects of reflection. I am not implying that we are unconscious when they occur, nor that they are not in some way mentally processed or noticed. John Searle, for example, argues that such unthematized events or objects in sentient experience are conscious, though they are not objects of attention. He thinks that "we need to distinguish the conscious/unconscious distinction from the center of attention/periphery distinction." See John Searle, *The Rediscovery of the Mind* (Cambridge: MIT Press, 1992), 138. Certainly we need to distinguish different levels of attention, if we do not distinguish different levels or degrees of consciousness. But the point I am making about the unappreciated somatic background can be made just as easily in terms of the "unattended" as the "unconscious."

18. Rorty's argument against the concept of "experience" as a tool for resolving these ontological and epistemological puzzles of continuity is as follows:

The problem with this way of obtaining continuity between us and the brutes is that it seems to shove the philosophically embarrassing discontinuity back down to the gap between, say viruses and amoeba. Only giving something like experience to protein molecules, and perhaps eventually to quarks—only a full-fledged pan-psychism—will span this gap. But when we invoke pan-psychism to bridge the gap between experience and nature, we begin to feel something has gone wrong. For notions like "experience," "consciousness," and "thought" were originally invoked to *contrast* something which varied independently of nature with nature itself. The philosophically interesting sense—the only sense relevant to epistemology—of experience . . . [applies] to a realm which might well be "out of touch" with nature because it might vary when nature remained the same, and remain the same when nature varied (DHD, 10).

I have some sympathy with the thrust of this argument, but I would resist the idea that our notions of experience, consciousness, and thought were first invoked for philosophical purposes of epistemological contrast with nature rather than with more practical functions of interacting with it. Similarly, I would question the narrow identification of "the philosophically interesting sense of 'experience'" with its traditional epistemological use of contrast. There are other (e.g. aesthetic and ethical) uses of the notion of experience which are interesting and to which Dewey's philosophy of experience is directed (as we can see from his interest in Alexander). For an account of Dewey's aesthetic use of experience, see Richard Shusterman, *Pragmatist Aesthetics* (Oxford: Blackwell, 1992), 25–33, 46–59.

19. The quote is taken from *Collected Papers of Charles Sanders Peirce* (Cambridge Mass. 1933–58), 5:314.

20. In *Dialectic of Enlightenment* (New York: Continuum, 1986, 234), Horkheimer and Adorno save the idea of "remaking the body into a noble object," and the fine recent work of Susan Bordo [*Unbearable Weight: Feminism, Western Culture, and the Body* (Berkeley: Univ. Of California Press, 1993)] provides similar but updated critiques of today's ideals and ideologies of somatic plasticity. However, it is Foucault rather than the Frankfurt school that informs her work. Foucault is an ambiguous ally here. Though very critical of society's use of "biopower" to normalize and subjugate the subject, he was also one of the few to see the emancipatory potential of powerful, immediate somatic experiences. He therefore advocated an experiential somatic plasticity, even though he recognized that the initial forms of such experience are conditioned by society's discursive forms. Another feminist disciple of Foucault, Judith Butler, emphasizes the body's plasticity but concentrates on gender and insists on the wholly socially discursive nature of the body. [See *Gender Trouble: Feminism and*

218   *Richard Shusterman*

the Subversion of Identity (New York: Routledge, 1990)]. There is thus room for a philosophy that takes nondiscursive somatic transformation more seriously, yet discusses it more clearly and soberly than do Deleuze and Gualtari. I try to develop this project in "Die Sorge um den Körper in der heutigen Kultur," and in *Practicing Philosophy: Pragmatism and the Philosophical Life*, forthcoming from Routledge.

21. Richard Rorty, *Philosophy and the Mirror of Nature* (Princeton: Princeton University Press, 1980), 183; hereafter PMN.

22. See Richard Rorty, *Contingency, Irony, and Solidarity* (Cambridge: Cambridge University Press, 1989), henceforth CIS, where Rorty argues that the privileged use of language is not to represent or justify something already there, but to cause something different, "to make something that never had been dreamed of before" (CIS 13).

23. Wilfred Sellars, *Science, Perception, and Reality* (London: Routledge & Kegan Paul, 1963) 60; Hans-Georg Gadamer, *Philosophical Hermeneutics* (Berkeley: University of California Press, 1976), 19; Rorty, CIS 88; Jacques Derrida, *Of Grammatology* (Baltimore: Johns Hopkins University Pres, 1976), 158. I provide a more detailed account and critique of these textualists in "Beneath Interpretation," ch. 4 of *Pragmatist Aesthetics*. A slightly longer version of this paper appears in D. Hiley, J. Bohman, and R. Shusterman, eds., *The Interpretive Turn: Philosophy, Science, Culture (Ithaca: Cornell University Press, 1991)*.

24. See Richard Rorty, "Introduction: Pragmatism and Philosophy," in *Consequences of Pragmatism*, xix. The other citation in this paragraph is from another essay in this volume, "Nineteenth Century Idealism and Twentieth Century Textualism," 140.

25. Although this impulse to depreciate the body was dominant, Christianity included a variety of thinkers and sects who saw the body—despite its material inferiority and even because of it—as a central tool to achieve greater spirituality, notably through somatic asceticism. Jesus, after all, needed incarnation to go through the passion of crucifixion. Origen, in the third century, urges this ascetic route to making the body into a "temple of the Lord" with the following metaphorical injunction: "You have coals of fire, you will sit upon them, and they will be of help to you." For more on this topic, see Peter Brown, *The Body and Society: Men, Women, and Sexual Renunciation in Early Christianity* (New York: Columbia University Press, 1988), citations from 165, 175.

26. This tradition can be traced from Democritus, Epicurus, and Lucretius to Hobbes, La Mettrie, and d'Holbach, to Marx and T.H. Huxley, to R. W. Sellars and others in our century. For all the merit and influence of these thinkers, they obviously do not constitute the core of the academic discipline of philosophy. Hobbes and Marx are, of course, more central, but

this is mainly because of their influential political philosophy, not their materialist metaphysics. Nietzsche in *The Will to Power* can also be seen as a somatic philosopher, but he is obviously foreign and inimical to the dominant logocentric line.

I should further note the strong tradition in ancient Greece and Rome of treating philosophy not just as theoretical *logos* but as an embodied life-practice in which care for the body (often expressed in aestheticism) was essential to progress of the soul. This tradition has, however, been ignored and occluded by aesthetic's modern self-image as a theoretical, academic discipline. I return to this practical embodied tradition at the end of this essay and, much more fully, in my *Practising Philosophy: Pragmatism and the Philosophical Life*.

27. Daniel Stern, *The Interpersonal World of the Infant* (New York: Basic Books, 1985).

28. In a recent article, I take up this project by examining the techniques and ideologies of three popular body practices (Alexander Technique, Feldenkrais Method, and Bioenergetics) as well as trying to explain our culture's growing concern with somatic techniques of self-transformation. See Richard Shusterman, "Die Sorge um den Körper in der heutigen Kultur."

29. Henry Thoreau, *Walden*, ch. 1 ("Economy") in *The Portable Thoreau* (New York: Viking, 1964), 270.

30. From the conclusion of Michel Foucault's College de France lecture of March 14, 1984, the transcript of which I received from his biographer James Miller. Miller provides a full and often lurid account of Foucault's own somatic experiments in sexual sadomasochism in *The Passion of Michel Foucault* (New York: Simon and Schuster, 1993). Foucault's French words are: *Le bios philosophies* comme vie droite, c'est l'animalité de l'éire humain, relevée comme un defi, pratiquée comme un exercice, et jetée à la face des autres comme un scandale."

11

Of Depth and Loss: The Peritropaic Legacy of Dewey's Pragmatism

Daniel W. Conway

When it is acknowledged that under disguise of dealing with ultimate reality, philosophy has been occupied with the precious values embedded in social traditions, that it has sprung from a clash of social ends and from a conflict of inherited institutions with incompatible contemporary tendencies, it will be seen that the task of future philosophy is to clarify men's ideas as to the social and moral strifes of their own day.

—John Dewey, *Reconstruction in Philosophy*[1]

Philosophers could be seen as people who work with the history of philosophy and the contemporary effects of those ideas called "philosophic" upon the rest of the culture—the remnants of past attempts to describe the "generic traits of existences." This is a modest, limited enterprise—as modest and limited as carving stones into new shapes, or finding more basic elementary principles. But it sometimes produces great achievements, and Dewey's work is one of those achievements.

—Richard Rorty, *Consequences of Pragmatism*[2]

Richard Rorty's attention to the philosophy of John Dewey has contributed over the past two decades to a welcome renascence of interest in American pragmatism. The *imprimatur* of a prominent scholar formerly ascendent within the Anglo-American paradigm of analytic philosophy has brought great excitement to the previously quiet world of Dewey studies. According to many Deweyans, however, the interest galvanized by Rorty's attention is not without its costs to pragmatism itself. Indeed, the Dewey who emerges from Rorty's various sketches bears a suspicious resemblance to Rorty himself, especially with respect to the trenchant anti-foundationalism they allegedly share.

In this essay, I wish to treat Rorty's appropriation of Dewey as an occasion for mapping the legacy of American pragmatism. I am especially concerned to illuminate the particular branch of Dewey's legacy that turns back upon itself, thereby subjecting Dewey himself to the critical scrutiny that he regularly applied to others. This is the branch of Dewey's legacy that Rorty most regularly (and more persuasively) claims for himself. This turning back upon a dominant tradition of philosophy—what we might call the *peritropaic* movement of pragmatic thinking—not only serves as the guiding motif of Rorty's interpretation of Dewey, but also distinguishes Rorty's unique articulation of the legacy of Dewey's pragmatism.

In seeking to reconstruct Rorty's peritropaic reception of Dewey, I am not particularly concerned to evaluate Rorty's pragmatist credentials, which task I happily leave to the self-appointed gatekeepers of Deweydom. I am more interested in interpreting Rorty's frosty reception by rival Deweyans as a sign of the times, as symptomatic of a crisis on the horizon for American pragmatists. Indeed, to ostracize Rorty is to violate the "both-and" spirit of inclusivity that Dewey located at the heart of American pragmatism. That pragmatists are so ready and willing to close their thin ranks, to banish the popular (and powerful) outsider who has made them topical once again, suggests that they may have strayed from their primary vocation of bringing intelligence to bear on concrete social problems.

I: Pragmatism and Peritropaic Criticism

After twenty years, Rorty's celebration of his kinship to the giants of American pragmatism still comes as a great surprise to many of Dewey's loyal readers.[3] In fact, the stripped-down Dewey whom Rorty honors as his anti-essentialist predecessor strikes many readers as suspiciously lean—if not anemic, or even emaciated. How is it possible, Rorty's critics have asked, that his Dewey is so uniquely qualified to dispense the anti-foundationalist therapy that Rorty himself now prescribes?

Rorty's general strategy for reading Dewey derives from his conviction that Dewey is "a kind of antiessentialist" who "sees no breaks in the hierarchy of increasingly complex adjustments to novel stimulation."[4] He consequently interprets Dewey's approach to philosophy as "therapeutic" in nature, for Dewey meant to disabuse philosophers and laymen alike of the metaphysical confusions that prevent them from addressing social questions of immediate, quotidian importance.

Rorty is surely correct to locate in Dewey's pragmatism a powerful animus against those metaphysical ideals that typically distract philosophers and laymen from concrete social problems. As he appropriately reminds us,

> Dewey... helped several generations of American intellectuals to avoid ... "philosophical depth" and thus to turn to the detailed, particular dangers of their times.[5]

Notwithstanding his salutary influence on American intellectuals, however, Dewey was neither simply nor consistently the "therapeutic" anti-foundationalist whom Rorty celebrates.[6] Dewey was also an intrepid (if not always resolute) explorer of nature, and his metaphysical forays, particularly in *Experience and Nature*, constitute a strong source of attraction for many pragmatists.[7]

To his credit, Rorty does not attempt to deny the overtly metaphysical aims of Dewey's philosophy. He endeavors instead to demonstrate that these aims are eclipsed by the "larger aim" of Dewey's pragmatism, which Rorty treats as the more enduring focus of his thought:

> Dewey ... was not as good at dissolving philosophical problems as the followers of either the early or the later Wittgenstein—but he had a larger aim in view. He wanted to sketch a culture that would not continually give rise to new versions of the old problems, because it would no longer make the distinctions between Truth, Goodness, and Beauty which engender such problems.[8]

Rorty's interpretation thus follows naturally from his identification of the "larger aim" of Dewey's enterprise.[9] As he explains, his interpretation favors the "syncretic, holistic side" of Dewey's pragmatism, i.e., the side

> that tries to see human beings doing much the same sort of problem-solving across the whole spectrum of their activities (*already* doing it and so not needing to be urged to start doing it).[10]

As we shall soon see, the "larger aim" that Rorty attributes to Dewey is also a distinctly *political* aim, which Rorty believes can justify the sacrifice of pragmatism itself in the service of liberal ideals.

According to Rorty, Dewey's occasional lapses are consequently attributable to his stubborn (and misplaced) insistence that philosophy must have a distinctly constructive mission of its own:

> Dewey never quite brought himself to adopt the Bouwsma-like stance that philosophy's mission, like that of therapy, was to make itself obsolete. So, he thought, in *Experience and Nature*, to show what the discovery of the true "generic traits" of experience could do.[11]

Hence the upshot of Rorty's reception strategy: If Dewey was wrong to insist on a constructive mission for philosophy, then the metaphysical explorations that he hoped would advance this mission can be dismissed in good conscience as harmless deviations from his own best insights.

Dewey's mistaken wish to further the constructive mission of philosophy is repeated within the microcosm of his own pragmatism. Just as he never fully reconciled himself to the self-neutralizing mission of philosophy, so he never completed the self-corrective experiences for which Rorty and others applaud him. Owing to his lingering conviction that philosophy should stake out an intellectual domain of its own, Dewey occasionally issued himself an exemption from the general terms of his otherwise unstinting interrogations. Whereas Dewey stirringly exhorted his readers to neutralize the obfuscatory effects of their own pet dualisms and distinctions, he nevertheless reserved for himself a constructive, metaphysical project that cannot be reduced without remainder to a regimen of therapeutic self-erasure:

But Dewey did his best to help us get rid of [the spirit of seriousness that leads philosophers to attempt to attain an escape from freedom into the atemporal], and he should not be blamed if he occasionally came down with the disease he was trying to cure.[12]

The "disease" in question, here identified by its prime symptom, the "spirit of seriousness," is what Rorty elsewhere calls "the metaphysical urge to find some ultimate, total, final context within which all our activities could be placed."[13] Rorty understands metaphysics as a pathological quest to inflate the limited empirical continuities that inform human experience into trans-historical, perspective-independent verities. Although Dewey was passionately involved in the project of "getting us out from under the metaphysical urge,"[14] he was not entirely successful in liberating himself in the process:

For better or worse, [Dewey] *wanted* to write a metaphysical system . . . Dewey sometimes described philosophy as the criticism of culture, but he was never quite content to think of himself as a kibitzer or a therapist or an intellectual historian. He wanted to have things both ways.[15]

Rorty's favorite example of Dewey's failure in this respect is his scientistic campaign in *Experience and Nature* to unearth and disclose the "generic traits of experience." He thus explains that

Dewey's mistake . . . was the notion that criticism of culture had to take the form of a redescription of "nature" or "experience" or both.[16]

It is Rorty's general belief that a philosophical genius, like a poet, typically outstrips his epoch of origin, formulating untimely insights that even he himself cannot quite digest. Owing to the inertial power of the prevailing prejudices of his day, the genius either quails before his own best insights or presents them in a context that belies their novelty and truth.[17] To the successor generation(s) thus falls the obligation to update the genius in question, to bring him into harmony with his own best insights, and to expose those vestiges of historical prejudice that are fully expendable. Following this general strategy, Rorty thus glimpses in Dewey's personal failure the enormous promise of his pragmatism. As a demonstration of his heartfelt gratitude, in fact, Rorty masterminds a posthumous cure for Dewey's besetting illness. In a signature gambit that is now familiar to Rorty's readers, he executes an immanent, peritropaic critique of Dewey's pragmatism. That is, he rejects the metaphysical dimension of Dewey's thought, but only in the name of Dewey's own anti-essentialism. Rorty thus saves Dewey's pragmatism by rehabilitating the supposedly fatal tension between his vibrant experimentalism and his retrograde metaphysical urge. He "heals" this tension by orchestrating a collision between these competing aims, which in turn yields a consistently anti-metaphysical interpretation of Dewey's pragmatism.

Representative of this self-canceling activity is Rorty's interpretation of Dewey's *Experience and Nature*:

> [I]t is unlikely that we shall find, in *Experience and Nature*, anything which can be called a "metaphysics of experience" as opposed to a therapeutic treatment of the tradition—on the ground that Dewey's own view of the nature and function of philosophy precludes it.[18]

We will not find in *Experience and Nature* what the author intended to place there, Rorty boldly avers, because Dewey's "syncretic, holistic" view of philosophy is stronger than the metaphysical urge at work within it. Rorty consequently applauds Dewey for (unwittingly) conveying the opposite of his intended message in *Experience and Nature*:

> It is easier to think of the book as an explanation of why nobody needs a metaphysics, rather than as itself a metaphysical system.[19]

By reading Dewey against Dewey in this particular way, Rorty directs our attention to what might be called the *performative* dimension of Dewey's philosophy. According to Rorty's interpretation, Dewey did not merely expose the metaphysical prejudices that characterized his epoch. He also enacted some of these prejudices, even (or especially) as he exposed and interrogated them in others. Unbeknownst to himself, Dewey effectively replaced the metaphysical prejudices against which he inveighed with "scientific" prejudices that contributed so integrally to the self-understanding of the age as to elude detection as such. It is Rorty's attention to this unintended performance that enables him simultaneously to salute Dewey for disabusing his readers of the bogus claims of metaphysical depth *and* to criticize Dewey for maintaining a metaphysical investment in divining the generic traits of experience.

But how does Rorty justify his preference for the anti-essentialist Dewey to the metaphysical Dewey?[20] He finds his principle of selection, and its warrant, embedded in the economy of Dewey's own pragmatism. Dewey's "larger aim" not only *can* be opposed to his lesser, metaphysical aims; it also *should* be so opposed, in fidelity to the animating spirit of pragmatism itself. As Rorty sees it, Dewey situated himself squarely in the tradition of the Enlightenment. He exposed the metaphysical confusions that simultaneously held his readers captive and frustrated their progress in addressing emerging social dangers. By liberating philosophy from the shackles of methodicity, Dewey hoped to restore a genuinely pragmatist agenda:

> Dewey emphasizes that this move "beyond method" gives mankind an opportunity to grow up, to be free to make itself, rather than seeking direction from some imagined outside source.[21]

Rather than introduce Dewey into the *terra incognita* of contemporary philosophy, or bend Dewey's insights to his own peculiar ends, Rorty simply extends Dewey's own project of enlightenment to its "natural," self-referential conclusion. Rorty completes Dewey's exposé by reading into it the exposer himself:

> Their pragmatism is antithetical to Enlightenment rationalism, although it was itself made possible (in good dialectical fashion) only by that rationalism. It can serve as the vocabulary of a mature (de-scientized, de-philosophized) Enlightenment liberalism.[22]

Indeed, Rorty apparently understands himself to have been *invited* by Dewey to execute a peritropaic critique of pragmatism, to further Dewey's project even at the expense of disavowing (some of) Dewey's own express wishes. We might confidently locate the source of this invitation in the performative dimension of Dewey's pragmatism. The collision Rorty orchestrates between Dewey's larger and lesser aims thus issues in a result that Dewey wanted but could not effect: the cancellation of his own residual metaphysical

urge. As Rorty sees it, the best way to honor Dewey's legacy is to
conduct this brand of immanent critique, and to employ this
peritropaic strategy to continue to improve (and historicize) pragmatism itself.[23]

More than anything else, it is this capacity for immanent self-
correction that recommends Dewey's pragmatism to Rorty.[24] For
this reason, in fact, Rorty suggests that we see Dewey "as the self-
canceling and self-fulfilling triumph of the Enlightenment."[25] When
endorsing to aspiring pragmatists "the vocabulary offered by Dewey,"
Rorty expressly applauds "its built-in cautions against metaphysics,"[26] which are sufficiently robust as to countenance self-referential
application. These "in-built cautions against metaphysics" not only
protect practicing pragmatists against the prejudices *du jour* to
which they are inexorably drawn, but also galvanize a community
in which each successive generation of pragmatists corrects for the
metaphysical blind spots of its predecessor. Indeed, what is most
valuable here is not *Dewey's* pragmatism, which betrays the historically idiosyncratic metaphysical commitments of its author, but
pragmatism itself, which, in Rorty's charitable reconstruction, comprises a cumulative, inter-generational project of piecemeal political melioration.[27]

Were Rorty's anti-metaphysical reading of Dewey simply an
arbitrary exercise of historical appropriation, then he might readily
concede to his critics that "his" Dewey bears no family resemblance
to "their" Dewey. Yet he firmly believes his reading of Dewey to be
sanctioned by the "larger aim" of Dewey's pragmatism, which sought
to dislodge metaphysical prejudices wherever they might impede
the free, fluid application of intelligence to concrete social problems.
In reading Dewey against Dewey as he does, Rorty merely completes a project of self-correction begun by Dewey himself. To read
Dewey in this way is to honor the legacy of his pragmatism while
refusing to allow Dewey himself to attain the status of historical
monument. To put this point somewhat polemically: Rorty is not so
concerned to get Dewey right—especially if doing so distracts us
from the pressing social problems at hand—as to put him to work.

From Rorty's historicist point of view, a clean break from
metaphysics would have been virtually impossible for Dewey to
accomplish. Indeed, it is quite likely that all pragmatists (Rorty
included) trade on metaphysical ideas and prejudices that they are
simply unable to discern as obstacles to the progress of pragmatism. Dewey's genius lay in outlining a general method of therapeutic critique that could readily be applied even to *him*. Rorty

thus credits Dewey for (indirectly) instructing his readers to perform this self-canceling exercise on him, such that his personal
prejudices would not retard the progress of pragmatism itself. So
although Dewey did not succeed personally in neutralizing his
metaphysical urge, he provided his readers with the opportunity
and the instruments to do so on his behalf, and on his authority.
The amputative violence that Rorty performs on Dewey is therefore faithful to Dewey's legacy.[28] All Rorty does is to complete the
elusive circle of self-reference, banishing Dewey's metaphysical
bogeys much as Dewey banished those of his readers.

In Rorty's eyes, then, he can offer no greater testament to the
power of Dewey's thought than to preside over its peritropaic extension, by subjecting Dewey to the critical, therapeutic gaze that
Dewey trained on others. What may look to unsuspecting readers
like a violent appropriation of Dewey's thought is, in fact, the logical consequence of reading Dewey against Dewey. That Rorty can
attempt an audacious reconstruction of Dewey's philosophy, without fear of dishonoring the Master, thus renews the promise of
Deweyan pragmatism.

II: The Use and Abuse of Pragmatism

Rorty's agenda for the future of pragmatism is conveyed by his
peritropaic *homage* to Dewey. What Rorty does to/with/for Dewey
serves as a model for what contemporary pragmatists must now do
to/with/for themselves. Just as Dewey's ambivalence toward metaphysics tinctures the political articulation of pragmatism, so the
peritropaic cancellation of Dewey's metaphysical urge portends the
immediate future of pragmatism. If the truth of Deweyan pragmatism is captured in its internal opposition between the two Deweys,
then to call for the end of this opposition is to legislate the end of
pragmatism.

As we have seen, Rorty both salutes and extends Dewey's attempt to articulate a "pragmatism without method." Here he takes
his bearings, without apologies, from the Dewey who eschewed the
kind of metaphysical investigation conducted in *Experience and
Nature*:

[I]f we try to have pragmatism without method . . . the more
holistic and syncretic side of Dewey suggest[s] how intellectual life might be . . . pursued without much reference to

the traditional distinctions between the cognitive and the
noncognitive, between "truth" and "comfort," or between
the propositional and the nonpropositional. . . .[29]

In developing his own characterization of pragmatism, Rorty understands himself to be advancing along Dewey's suggested course.[30]
Although Rorty's version of pragmatism is expressly designed to
rule out the kind of quasi-scientific method deployed by Sidney
Hook in his defense of liberalism,[31] it also militates in general
against any attempt to secure for pragmatism a deep methodological anchorage. Let us turn now to examine what this aversion to
method might entail in concrete terms for the "new" pragmatism
that Rorty unveils.

If it is a weakness for method that makes philosophy unaccept-
ably abstract and ahistorical, then a "pragmatism without method"
would be a pragmatism that has become fully historicized and
contextualized. As Rorty thus explains,

> My first characterization of pragmatism is that it is simply
> anti-essentialism applied to notions like "truth," "knowl-
> edge," "language," "morality," and similar objects of philo-
> sophical theorizing.[32]

Such a pragmatism would resist any appeal to trans-historical truths
about human experience. It would restrict its focus to the tools and
resources arrayed throughout any particular historical epoch, in
order that it might respond expeditiously to the local dangers that
impend over the epoch in question. It would appeal to no deep
metaphysical attachments for the purchase of its normative claims.
It would honor no generic, trans-historical structure or traits that
would define it as such. Attempts to enumerate the necessary and
sufficient conditions of a "pragmatism without method" would inevitably fail:

> Dewey . . . asked us to liberate our new civilization by giv-
> ing up the notion of "grounding" our culture, our moral
> lives, our politics, our religious beliefs, upon "philosophical
> bases."[33]

A pragmatism without method, in short, would be no -ism at all.
    This characterization of pragmatism may sound appealingly
historicist and anti-foundationalist. But what remains in this char-

acterization of Dewey's pragmatism?[34] Here we should note that Rorty is far more comfortable explaining what Dewey's pragmatism is *not*, preferring the privative characterizations that convey Rorty's own general understanding of philosophy as a kind of therapy. In the historicist light favored by Rorty, pragmatism is best understood not as the philosopher's trusty toolbox, which, as Dewey imagined it, would shelter the experimental instruments of political melioration. Nor does Rorty figure pragmatism as a handsome guide to the appropriate use and care of tools, for this figure conveys a residual methodicity. Nor does he view pragmatism as an envelope or context of instrumentality, since it is itself an instrument. Indeed, any distinction between pragmatism (*qua* -ism) and the *pragmata* it comprises verges perilously upon metaphysical abstraction and methodological confusion.

What, then, remains of pragmatism? Unimpeded by any intractable metaphysical essence or methodological constraints, Rorty's privative characterizations ultimately reduce pragmatism itself to the status of a tool. In a significant deviation from Dewey's own position, Rorty proposes to treat pragmatism as itself a *pragma*, as an instrument to be deployed in the service of Dewey's "larger aim"—namely, political liberalism. "Pragmatism without method" thus serves as the rallying cry for treating pragmatism itself as one tool among many, with a particular use and function all its own.

Dewey's champions will certainly bristle at this proposal to demote their pragmatism to the rank of a common tool, but this is not the most controversial element of Rorty's reconstruction. His "new" pragmatism is best understood as a tool that destroys or cancels itself upon completing its assigned task. That is, Rorty's orientation to American pragmatism is peritropaic not only with respect to his relationship to predecessor pragmatists, but also with respect to the historical project of pragmatism itself. Like Wittgenstein's oft-borrowed ladder, which is Rorty's favorite image for a "pragmatism without method," pragmatism itself will be retired from use upon successfully completing its assigned task. Pragmatism, Rorty believes, should preside happily over its own eventual disuse and obsolescence in the service of liberal politics. Born of the Enlightenment rationalism that it aims ultimately to reject, pragmatism must neutralize and cancel itself, thereby contributing to the articulation of a fully developed, post-metaphysical liberalism. Rorty's "postmodernist bourgeois liberalism" thus marks a confluence of historical contingencies that summons pragmatism itself into a posture of standing reserve.

Here we discern the true political costs of opposing the "larger aim" of Dewey's pragmatism to its (supposedly) lesser aims. With a clear and happy conscience, Rorty charges pragmatism to fulfill its historical destiny as *pragma* and facilitate the evolution of a post-metaphysical, anti-scientistic version of liberalism. Once it has finally vanquished all other -isms, thereby guiding liberal democracy to its post-metaphysical destination, pragmatism itself, *qua*-ism, will wither away. The cultural labor heretofore performed by philosophers and theorists will be taken up by the poets and mythwrights who will fashion the enabling narratives of a post-metaphysical liberal democracy.[35]

And why not? Once pragmatism has been purged of its residual methodicity, it becomes fair game for strategic implementation as a tool in its own right. Rorty's critics will brand him a traitor to the legacy of Deweyan pragmatism,[36] but what greater honor could he offer to its testament than to call into question the proper use and appropriate value of pragmatism itself? Indeed, this would be the ultimate proof that pragmatism is no -ism at all, that it concerns itself exclusively with solving social problems and not with securing the conditions of its own institutionalization. Pragmatists, who pride themselves on conducting an unsentimental appraisal of the historical resources arrayed before them, have typically exempted themselves and their charger from this interrogation. Arrogating to themselves an evaluative prerogative that smacks of priestly privilege, pragmatists have been quick to separate themselves and their efforts from the tools and implements they mobilize on behalf of the epoch they represent.

On Rorty's interpretation, the hegemony of a priesthood may have been necessary—even crucial—for the historical development of pragmatism, especially in conjunction with an uncertain social experiment in liberal democracy. But times have changed, and so has the political agenda for practicing pragmatists.[37] Having secured the future of liberal democracy, pragmatists must now guide its halting transition to a post-metaphysical incarnation, by protecting the ideals and institutions of liberal democracy from the periodic recrudescence of metaphysical essentialism. As the example of Dewey's own self-cancelation indicates, pragmatists can embrace no greater responsibility, no nobler cause, than a self-consuming assault on the remaining vestiges and strongholds of metaphysical thinking. Just as the "syncretic, holistic side" of Dewey's pragmatism vanquishes the occasional eruptions of his metaphysical urge, so Rorty's "new" pragmatists will douse the metaphysical fires that arise within and without their ranks. These "new" pragmatists will put themselves out of business in the process, but they will thereby seal the truth of pragmatism itself, as a historically-specific philosophical enterprise that was able to gather even itself under the umbrella of its enabling historicism. What grander finale could pragmatists possibly envision for themselves and their enterprise? Indeed, for what future skirmishes are Deweyan pragmatists saving themselves?

Rorty claims to have inherited this interpretation of pragmatism from Dewey, who treated pragmatism as an instrument for advancing the cause of liberal political reform:

> In the form John Dewey gave it, pragmatism is a philosophy tailored to the needs of political liberalism, a way of making political liberalism look good to persons with philosophical tastes. It provides a rationale for nonideological, compromising, reformist muddling-through (what Dewey called "experimentalism").[38]

Although Dewey never expressly assigned to pragmatism the self-canceling role that Rorty now confers upon it, Rorty nevertheless believes that the spirit of Deweyan experimentalism is best realized in an imaginative campaign to banish the metaphysical ghosts that continue to haunt the machine of liberalism. Invoking Dewey's appeal to the plastic power of poetic imagination, Rorty urges pragmatists to preside over the demise of metaphysics and escort liberalism across the threshold of a post-metaphysical utopia. Citing Dewey, he thus maintains that

> [T]he poeticized culture of my liberal utopia would . . . agree with Dewey that "imagination is the chief instrument of the good . . . art is more moral than moralities. For the latter either are, or tend to become, consecrations of the status quo . . . the moral prophets of humanity have always been poets even though they spoke in free verse or by parable."[39]

Rorty thus depicts the self-canceling role of pragmatism as both noble and heroic, and he honors those pragmatists who disenfranchise metaphysics (and themselves in the process) as the poets whom Dewey lauds for calibrating the moral compass of a democratic society.

Rorty's decision to include pragmatism itself within the historical array of *pragmata* accurately reflects the historicist orientation of his political project, but it may also betray an irrecuperable discontinuity between his vision of pragmatism and Dewey's own. In calmly slating pragmatism for historical self-extinction, Rorty approaches pragmatism from the outside, as one who would not necessarily mourn its passing. Rorty's attachment to pragmatism is presumably no different, and certainly no "deeper," than his attachment to any other arbitrary configuration of historical contingencies. Pragmatism is apparently to be regarded like any other passing fad or fashion, its loss simply another (non-teleological) advance along an unsentimental concatenation of incremental historical changes.[40]

Rorty's call for the historical self-cancelation of pragmatism is not exactly callous, but it fails to reflect the kind of deep, enduring attachment to which Dewey-eyed pragmatists often bear witness. Whereas a tool can be taken up or discarded at will by a plucky *bricoleur*, pragmatism itself is not so easily disentangled from the identity of many pragmatists. Rorty has long urged practicing pragmatists to "get over" their metaphysical commitments and ontological attachments, and he has located the promise of Deweyan pragmatism (as well as the warrant for his claim to its legacy) precisely in Dewey's acknowledgment of the need for pragmatism regularly to perform self-purgative ablutions. Here it becomes clear, however, that Rorty intends for his ban on "deep" attachments to extend even to the pragmatist's commitment to pragmatism itself.

Rorty thus extols a pragmatism to which Dewey could (and would) not have pledged allegiance. Dewey positioned himself to become Rorty's hero only by experimenting (albeit unsuccessfully) with a pragmatism without method, only by clinging (despite his "best" insights) to pragmatism as an -ism. He arrived at his own imperfect practice of pragmatism only as a result of wrestling with— though never eliminating—a deep attachment to the metaphysically-inflected mission of philosophy. Rather than exorcise his metaphysical demons (a method that Rorty appears to endorse), Dewey attempted to fortify and expand his thought, in order that it might assimilate these demonic elements and harness their necromantic vitality.

Here, in fact, Rorty's historicism rebounds to challenge his claim to the legacy of Dewey's pragmatism. For a Dewey to engage in something like the self-directed "ironism" that Rorty recommends to contemporary pragmatists is far more perilous and profound than for Rorty to undertake a (formally) similar regimen of self-aversion.[41] Dewey explicitly recognized "self-realization as the ethical ideal" and insisted that attaining this ideal "demands the full development of individuals in their distinctive individuality, "through" growth, learning, and modification of character."[42] For Dewey, that is, something deep and identity-preserving was at stake in his immanent critique of pragmatism, an attachment whose loss he was not likely to "get over" simply by ruminating on the contingency of selfhood. There was a limit to his allegiance to the Enlightenment project he endorsed, a limit measurable in terms of his irrational reliance on identity-preserving metaphysical ideals. The loss of pragmatism, as adumbrated in Dewey's calesthenics of self-cancelation, could not be experienced (or anticipated) by him as the loss of a passing fad or fashion; indeed, this may be one reason for his failure to finish the job of purging his thought of its residual metaphysical ideals. Since Rorty himself never shared this deep attachment to pragmatism, his own immanent critique is not nearly so risky or momentous. He will "get over" the loss of pragmatism, just as he will "get over" the loss of positivism, essentialism, and objective validity.

My point here is not simply to rehearse the familiar debate between metaphysical and historical interpretations of philosophical "depth." I am concerned instead to illuminate the potential differences in scope, ambition, and danger that obtain between the regimens of self-cancelation respectively practiced by Dewey and Rorty. Even if Dewey was confused about the ultimate depth of his deep attachments, he nevertheless attempted to interrogate the meaning and value of attachments (e.g., his commitment to the constructive mission of philosophy) that he sincerely believed to be identity-preserving. He was resolutely engaged, that is, in a regimen of self-cancelation that he believed could have resulted in the loss not only of those deep attachments that secured his very identity, but also the experience he held so dear.[43]

Dewey may very well have been mistaken about the likely results of his regimen of self-correction, but his mistake nevertheless signifies an intensity and resolve that Rorty cannot claim for his own ironism. Because Rorty "knows" that his identity is merely the transient confluence of contingent historical currents,[44] he also "knows" that his regimen of self-cancelation cannot possibly entail the loss of anything that anchors his experience of the world. His privately-practiced ironism is intended to subvert a previously functional final vocabulary, with which he will describe his experience of the world in equally satisfying terms.[45] Whereas for Dewey the loss of one's final vocabulary might entail the loss of one's ownmost identity, Rorty attaches to his private ironism no such possibility of radical, irrecuperable loss.[46]

In fairness to Rorty, we now must entertain a familiar rejoinder: *historical*, not metaphysical. The alleged "depth" of Dewey's attachment to pragmatism bespeaks a quirk of history rather than an intimation of Being. *Of course* Rorty views Dewey's pragmatism "from the outside"; he has no choice in the matter. This reflects a failure neither of character nor of will, but simply a difference between their respective historical epochs.[47] While some readers might wish Rorty to identify some essential, history-recalcitrant property of pragmatism, shared in common by his rendition and Dewey's, his anti-essentialism precludes his recourse to any such gambit. The fidelity of his pragmatism to Dewey's is established not by appeal to necessary and sufficient conditions of pragmatic inquiry, but simply by the sturdiness of a narrative bridge he constructs to connect the two:

> For pragmatists, telling stories about how one's favorite and least favorite literary texts hang together is not to be distinguished from—is simply a species of—the "philosophical" enterprise of telling stories about the nature of the universe which highlight all the things one likes best and least. The misguided attempt to be "scientific" is a confusion between a pedagogical device—the device of summarizing the upshot of one's narrative in pithy little formulae—and a method of discovering truth.[48]

If we refuse to entrust our footfalls to the narrative bridge he constructs, then Rorty has nothing more to offer us in defense of his claim. Nor does he believe that anything more *could* be offered to appease skeptical critics.

Rorty does not question or ridicule the alleged depth of deep attachments; he merely denies that this depth admits of metaphysical measure. Attachments that one experiences (and that philosophers formerly described) as anchored in the ontological bedrock of the World are now easily explained as enmeshed in the historically-specific webs of beliefs that we weave in concert with the epoch we represent. Strictly speaking, of course, Rorty's "perspectivalism" should restrict the scope of this claim to *his* pragmatism. Rorty may be right about the depthlessness of his own deep attachments, but about Dewey's he can at best hazard a guess.

III: Pragmatism and Politics

In the books and essays that followed the publication of *Philosophy and the Mirror of Nature*, Rorty has gradually developed a distinctly political articulation of his anti-foundationalism. Here too he invokes Dewey's influence, which has enabled him to clarify his own thoughts about the linkages between philosophy and politics, between pragmatism and liberalism:

> Dewey seems to me to have given us the right lead when he viewed pragmatism not as grounding, but as clearing the ground for, democratic principles.[49]

Rorty thus believes that he inherits from Dewey the project of yoking pragmatism to the particular exigencies of liberal politics:

> That shift from epistemology to politics, from an explanation of the relation between "reason" and reality to an explanation of how political freedom has changed our sense of what human inquiry is good for, is a shift which Dewey was willing to make.[50]

As Rorty's broad-brushed sketch of Dewey gradually comes into focus, we discover that Rorty reveres Dewey as a precursor of the post-modernist, anti-essentialist approach to philosophy that Rorty himself now champions. Rorty thus advertises his "postmodernist bourgeois liberalism" as continuous with Dewey' liberalism, claiming to advocate the

> idea of a community which strives after both intersubjective agreement and novelty—a democratic, progressive, pluralist community of the sort of which Dewey dreamt.[51]

Rorty thus credits Dewey with correctly identifying the proper relationship between political action and philosophical (i.e., discursive) justification. In fact, Dewey's therapeutic efforts helped to free philosophers from the impossible demands of epistemic justification, enabling them to divert their productive energies from epistemology to pragmatism. According to Rorty, then, Dewey

would happily grant that a circular justification of our practices, a justification which makes one feature of our culture
look good by citing still another, or comparing our culture
invidiously with others by reference to our own standards,
is the only sort of justification we are going to get.[52]

This pragmatic relationship between philosophical narrative
and political institution also informs Rorty's reckoning of his debts
to Dewey's political philosophy. Rorty boldly opines that the "final"
revolution in political theory has already transpired, as articulated
in the liberal privatism espoused by John Stuart Mill and Isaiah
Berlin.[53] Indeed, the bottom line for Rorty is captured in Berlin's
impassioned warning against even well-intentioned public cam-
paigns to enhance the positive liberty of private citizens. Following
Mill and Berlin, Rorty insists that we can cherish, protect, and
even welcome the achievement of private self-realization without
actively and publicly promoting it in others. Indeed, we *must* so
refrain from shaping the political sensibilities of our fellow citizens, since every attempt to manage the cultivation of self-realization
culminates in unwanted tyranny. Hence the basic principle of Rorty's
liberal utopia: All regimens of self-realization are restricted to the
private sphere, which is tenaciously defended on liberal principles
from public incursion.

But Rorty's bottom line in politics does not correspond to
Dewey's. Like many philosophers of the twentieth century, Dewey
failed to appreciate fully the triumph of liberal privatism as the
final revolution in political theory.[54] He famously believed that
philosophy might play an active, constructive role in creating the
informed, responsible citizenry required to manage a thriving democracy. Rorty acknowledges that Dewey (and others) reserved for
pragmatism an extra-instrumental designation and status, but he
treats this view as reflecting the heady (and misguided) optimism
of the day, when philosophers still considered themselves agents of
progressive social reform:

> [M]ost American intellectuals in Dewey's day still thought
> their country was a shining historical example. They
> identified with it easily. The largest single reason for their
> loss of identification was the Vietnam War.[55]

Rorty hastens to add that Dewey would never have pursued
his "constructive mission" had he believed it to be deleterious to

liberal freedoms.[56] Rorty consequently updates Dewey's position in order to reflect our hard-earned understanding of the non-negotiable perils involved in implementing progressive social reforms:

> For Dewey, communal and public disenchantment is the price we pay for individual and private spiritual liberation, the kind of liberation that Emerson thought characteristically American. Dewey was as well aware as Weber that there is a price to be paid, but he thought it well worth paying. He assumed that no good achieved by earlier societies would be worth recapturing if the price were a diminution in our ability to leave people alone, to let them try out their private visions of perfection in peace.

Dewey may have had good historical reasons to attempt to fuse the personal and the political, but we do not. To continue Dewey's public promotion of private self-realization would constitute for us a historical mismeasure of potentially egregious proportions.

Having learned well this historical lesson, Rorty's "new" pragmatists no longer believe that they can or should prosecute progressive social reforms, especially those that aim to fuse the personal and the political. Indeed, if these "new" pragmatists retain at all the imagery of a toolbox or context, within which the instrumentality of *pragmata* is cataloged, then they would appeal not to some philosophical -ism or method that might re-awaken their dormant metaphysical urges, but to the historical epoch itself, whose peculiar constellation of needs and exigencies determines the nature and range of implements to be marshalled in the defense of political liberalism. In fact, Rorty's "new" pragmatism, fully historicized and purged of its residual methodicity, is simply whatever the "new" pragmatists decide that it is:

> [Pragmatism] is the doctrine that there are no constraints on inquiry save conversational ones—no wholesale constraints derived from the nature of the objects, or of the mind, or of language, but only those retail constraints provided by the remarks of our fellow-inquirers.[57]

The big gamble involved in undertaking this reconstruction is that Dewey's pragmatism will survive in some recognizable form the corrective surgery that Rorty prescribes for it. Rorty hopes to eliminate the (bogus) metaphysical depth of Dewey's philosophy without also sacrificing what might be called the human depth of his pragmatism. Anticipating this possible line of objection to his project, Rorty assures his readers that a culture

> in which doubts about the public rhetoric of the culture are met not by Socratic requests for definitions and principles, but by Deweyan requests for concrete alternatives and programs . . . could . . . be every bit as self-critical and every bit as devoted to human equality as our own familiar, and still metaphysical, liberal culture—if not more so.[58]

With respect to this delicate operation, however, we might legitimately worry that Rorty has misidentified the engine of Deweyan pragmatism. Perhaps it derives its dynamism not from the self-corrective mechanism that successor pragmatists sequentially engage, but from the constant tension transacted between the opposing poles of his thought. In other words, the genuine testament to Dewey's pragmatism may lie not so much in eliminating this tension through a peritropaic cancellation of Dewey's atavistic metaphysical prejudices, but in reinforcing—even amplifying—this tension. The elimination of this metaphysical tension may deliver a leaner, less troubling Dewey, but it also may deprive pragmatism of the personal, psychological depth that many pragmatists prize above all else. Indeed, Dewey's allegiance to the Enlightenment may not have been as unwavering as Rorty wishes us to believe. What we call "Enlightenment" may derive its internal dynamism from the resistance provided by the moments of stubborn disenlightenment studded throughout its sprawling empire. It may be the case, then, that Dewey's "mistake" is better left uncorrected. Metaphysical depth and human depth may be inseparably symbiotic, two sides of the only valuable coin we possess.

Dewey is a valuable ally, as Rorty claims, in the campaign against false appeals to metaphysical depth. But has Rorty satisfactorily established that pragmatism can sustain commitments admitting of personal, human depth without the metaphysical depth that he wishes to abjure? To be sure, he expresses confidence that a society without metaphysical depth can nevertheless shelter the human depth of solidarity. Defending the central thesis of his *Contingency, Irony, and Solidarity*, he explains,

> I have been urging in this book that we try *not* to want something which stands beyond history and institutions.

> The fundamental premise of the book is that a belief can
> still regulate action, can still be thought worth dying for,
> among people who are quite aware that this belief is caused
> by nothing deeper than contingent historical circumstance.[59]

Persuasive as it may be, this statement seems more a promissory note than anything else, and we cannot expect old-fashioned, Dewey-eyed pragmatists to give up their depth simply on the promise of post-modern solidarity.[60] Indeed, questions like these lead many pragmatists to suspect that Rorty's peritropaic criticism may have thrown out the baby with the bathwater.

IV: Conclusion

Some pragmatists have objected strenuously to Rorty's claim to the legacy of Dewey's pragmatism. His claim is variously judged by critics to be presumptuous, insincere, uninformed, or simply erroneous. In at least one important sense, however, Rorty is entirely faithful to Dewey's legacy, for he extends Dewey's celebrated experimentalism along unprecedented planes and vectors.[61] He thereby refuses to invest in Dewey himself the kind of magisterial authority that could transform "pragmatism" into yet another diversion from the pressing social problems of the day. Surely Dewey's legacy is sufficiently rich and ramified to include Rorty's pragmatism among others.[62] Indeed, I see no good reason to dispute his claim to be one heir (among many) to the complex legacy of Dewey's pragmatism.[63]

Rorty thus pursues one ramification of Dewey's densely-thicketed legacy. But his greatest value for successor pragmatists may lie in his serving as an occasion for illuminating the internal limitations of the prevailing academic disposition of American pragmatism. In the "both-and" world of Deweyan pragmatism, Rorty is neither a hijacker to be thwarted nor a pretender to be exposed, but a sign of the times, an indicator of the reconstructive work that remains to be done. Indeed, the wisdom of Rorty's suggestion that pragmatists "get out from under" an anachronistic conception of authority is (ironically) confirmed by the vitriolic response that Rorty's pragmatism has drawn from some orthodox Deweyans. Rorty need be attacked in this way only if he commands the privileged authority of the priest or philosopher. But this is an authority that can be invested in him only by his critics.[64] Rorty himself nowhere claims to have uttered the last word on Dewey, and he never boasts of having consolidated a monopoly in the cottage industry of American pragmatism.

The guiding question is not whether Rorty is faithful to Dewey, but whether pragmatists who disagree with Rorty can disengage themselves sufficiently from their squabbles to articulate their own versions of pragmatism. Indeed, if Rorty is not the sybilline guardian of the Deweyan mysteries, then his version of pragmatism need neither be debunked nor discredited by rival Deweyans. Rorty-bashing may pay modest academic dividends; it may even be entertaining in certain circles of resentful, disaffected intellectuals; but it contributes nothing to the progress of pragmatism itself.[65] to discredit Rorty in skirmishes of strictly academic interest is to postpone indefinitely the task of bringing intelligence to bear on the concrete problems that face liberal democracy at the turning of the millennium. Rival pragmatists should respond not with spitting contests, but with alternative experiments in democratic practice.

There would seem to be a vast middle ground to be explored between the quasi-scientific ontology that Rorty associates with positivism and the historical contingency he embraces. In fact, any particular orientation to experience would seem to presuppose at least residual intimations of ontological anchorage. Rorty seems to treat ontology as a slippery slope, however, on which unwitting pragmatists quickly slide from an attunement to the continuities that inform human experience to a myopic campaign to discover the Truth of the Real World. As evidence of this slippery slope, Rorty points to Dewey's misguided campaign to divine the "generic traits of experience."

In addition to contesting Rorty's estimation of the grade and glide of this alleged slope, pragmatists might also devote their energies to the articulation of alternative models of experience. The important point for pragmatists is not to wrangle with Rorty over whether or not a non-positivistic ontology of experience is possible, but actually to chart and convey the deep resonances—ontological or otherwise—that characterize their ownmost experiences. Indeed, if experience alone warrants the pragmatic truth of the webrous narratives that connect the present to the past, then pragmatists (Deweyan or otherwise) gain nothing by challenging the richness or depth of Rorty's own experience. Their prodigious talents are much better employed in the service of an alternative version of pragmatism, one that more accurately reflects the wealth and plenitude of their experiences.[66] If nothing else, in fact, the perceived impoverishment of the experience to which Rorty's pragmatism speaks would provoke rival pragmatists to produce as compelling a sketch as his of the experience to which they cleave. Those pragmatists who claim a deeper or richer sense of experience need simply fashion complementary narratives that reflect their respective modalities of ontological attunement.

Notes

1. John Dewey, *Reconstruction in Philosophy* (Boston: Beacon Press, 1948), p. 26.

2. Richard Rorty, *Consequences of Pragmatism* (Minneapolis: University of Minnesota Press, 1982), pp. 86–87.

3. For a critical evalution of Rorty's Deweyan credentials, see James Gouinlock, "What Is the Legacy of Instrumentalism? Rorty's Interpretation of Dewey," in *Rorty and Pragmatism: The Philosopher Responds to His Critics*, ed. Herman J. Saatkamp, Jr. (Nashville, TN: Vanderbilt University Press, 1995), pp. 72–90. Gouinlock speaks for many Deweyans when he observes tht "Pre-Rortian students of Dewey's thought will be astonished to learn that Dewey was 'beyond method,' and their astonishment is justified" (75).

4. Richard Rorty, *Objectivity, Relativism, and Truth: Philosophical Papers, Volume 1* (Cambridge: Cambridge University Press, 1991), p. 109.

5. Rorty, *Objectivity, Relativism, and Truth*, p. 77.

6. Rorty thus claims, for example, that "[T]he 'therapeutic' conception of philosophy" is displayed in "Dewey's *Reconstruction in Philosophy*" (*Objectivity, Relativism, and Truth*, p. 3).

7. For an appreciation of the metaphysics propounded by Dewey in *Experience and Nature*, see Gouinlock, "What Is the Legacy of Instrumentalism," pp. 85–87.

8. *Consequences of Pragmatism*, p. 86.

9. Konstantin Kolenda suggests that "It is this broadly humanistic consequence of pragmatism that Rorty finds congenial and with which he would like to join forces." *Rorty's Humanistic Pragmatism: Philosophy Democratized* (Tampa: University of South Florida Press, 1990), p. 26.

10. *Objectivity, Relativism, and Truth*, pp. 75–76.

11. *Consequences of Pragmatism*, p. 83.

12. *Consequences of Pragmatism*, p. 88.

13. *Objectivity, Relativism, and Truth*, p. 72.

14. *Objectivity, Relativism, and Truth*, p. 72.

15. *Consequences of Pragmatism*, p. 73.

16. *Consequences of Pragmatism*, p. 85.

17. For an account of Rorty's articulation of a similar interpretation of Nietzsche, see my essay "Thus Spoke Rorty: The Perils of Narrative Self-Creation," *Philosophy and Literature*, Volume 15, no. 1, Spring 1991, pp. 103–110.

18. *Consequences of Pragmatism*, p. 77.

19. *Consequences of Pragmatism*, p. 72.

20. For a criticism of Rorty's preference, see Frank J. Macke, "Pragmatism Reconsidered: John Dewey and Michel Foucault on the Consequences of Inquiry," in *Recovering Pragmatism's Voice: The Classical Tradition, Rorty, and the Philosophy of Communication* (Albany: SUNY Press, 1995), pp. 155–176. According to Macke, "It is not at all clear in reading Dewey, especially in tracing the development of his metaphysics of experience and in his unique perspective on science and art, that his political writings (on liberal culture) and his theory of progressive education best describe the nucleus of his philosophy" (170).

21. *Consequences of Pragmatism*, p. 204.

22. Richard Rorty, *Contingency, Irony, and Solidarity* (Cambridge: Cambridge University Press, 1989), p. 57.

23. For a thorough reckoning of the misuses and misinterpretations of Dewey that are sanctioned by Rorty's interpretive strategy, see John J. Stuhr, *Genealogical Pragmatism: Philosophy, Experience, and Community* (Albany, NY: SUNY Press, 1997), especially chapter 6. Stuhr persuasively shows that many resources that Rorty might use to bolster his own "timid political agenda" (123) could be derived from a more sympathetic and less appropriative engagement with Dewey.

24. Gouinlock points out that this "self-corrective, progressive" element of pragmatism is attributable precisely to the pragmatic *method* that Rorty wishes to discard (75).

25. *Contingency, Irony, and Solidarity*, p. 57.

26. *Objectivity, Relativism, and Truth*, p. 188.

27. Rorty thus argues that "When Dewey talked politics, as opposed to doing philosophy, he offered advice about how to avoid getting hung up

on traditional ways of doing things, how to redescribe the situation in terms which might facilitate compromise, and how to take fairly small, reformist steps." In "Remarks on Deconstruction and Pragmatism," in *Deconstruction and Pragmatism*, ed. Chantal Mouffe (London: Routledge, 1996), p. 17.

28. For a thoughtful and sympathetic account of Rorty's *"strong misreading"* of Dewey, see David L. Hall, *Richard Rorty: Prophet and Poet of the New Pragmatism* (Albany: State University of New York Press, 1994), pp. 80–89.

29. *Objectivity, Relativism, and Truth*, pp. 75–76.

30. For a critical response to Rorty's characterization of Dewey's pragmatism as "beyond method," see Gouinlock (75–76).

31. *Objectivity, Relativism, and Truth*, p. 64.

32. *Consequences of Pragmatism*, p. 162.

33. *Consequences of Pragmatism*, p. 161.

34. This question is raised (and answered in the negative) by Thelma Z. Levine, in "America and the Contestations of Modernity," in Saatkamp, *Rorty and Pragmatism*, pp. 37–49. Levine suggests that Rorty's attempt to purge Dewey's pragmatism of its methodicity involves a *"displacement of the father by the Oedipal son"* (49). See also Richard Bernstein, *The New Constellation: The Ethical/Political Horizons of Modernity/Postmodernity* (Cambridge: MIT Press, 1992), pp. 250–251.

35. For my understanding of the extremity of Rorty's demands upon contemporary pragmatism, I am indebted to discussions with my colleague Douglas R. Anderson and to his unpublished essay, "Pragmatic Intellectuals: Facing Loss in the Spirit of American Philosophy."

36. According to Gouinlock, for example, "Unwittingly but inexorably, Rorty threatens to undo Dewey's work, rather than carry it forward" (87).

37. A compelling case to this effect is made by Richard Shusterman in *Practicing Philosophy: Pragmatism and the Philosophical Life* (London: Routledge, 1996), especially pp. 79–81.

38. *Objectivity, Relativism, and Truth*, p. 211.

39. *Contingency, Irony, and Solidarity*, p. 69. Rorty cites from John Dewey, *Art as Experience* (New York: Capricorn Books, 1958), p. 348.

40. According to Richard Bernstein, Rorty cleaves to an "aestheticized pragmatism" that effectively distances him from "Dewey's primary concerns" (233).

41. *Contingency, Irony, and Solidarity*, pp. 73–82.

42. John Dewey, *Ethics* (MW:S) pp. 302, 305, 348.

43. For an extension of this point to the respective political projects of Dewey and Rorty, see Larry A. Hickman, "Liberal Irony and Social Reform," collected in *Philosophy and the Reconstruction of Culture: Pragmatic Essays After Dewey*, ed. John J. Stuhr (Albany: SUNY Press, 1993), pp. 223–239. For similar reasons, Hickman thus insists that Rorty's "liberal ironist is timid by comparison [to the Deweyan pragmatist]. The focus of her attention lies not in social institutions but in a change of heart— a conversion experience on the part of each individual" (237). Citing Ralph Sleeper, Hickman observes that "What rankles is Rorty's insouciant reductionism. Pragmatism—at least Dewey's sort—had seemed to offer us more than that" (238).

44. *Contingency, Irony, and Solidarity*, pp. 23–43.

45. *Contingency, Irony, and Solidarity*, pp. 80–81.

46. *Contingency, Irony, and Solidarity*, pp. 73–88.

47. For a sympathetic treatment of "the historically different societies that Rorty and Dewey inhabit and the role these societies accord the philosopher," see Shusterman, pp. 73–74.

48. *Objectivity, Relativism, and Truth*, p. 79.

49. *Objectivity, Relativism, and Truth*, p. 13.

50. *Contingency, Irony, and Solidarity*, p. 68.

51. *Objectivity, Relativism, and Truth*, p. 13.

52. *Contingency, Irony, and Solidarity*, p. 57.

53. As Rorty explains, "Indeed, my hunch is that Western social and political thought may have had the last *conceptual* revolution it needs" (*Contingency, Irony, and Solidarity*, p. 63).

54. For a Deweyan critique of Rorty's defense of liberal privatism, see Thomas M. Alexander, "The Human Eros," Stuhr, ed., *Philosophy and the Reconstruction of Culture*, pp. 203–222. According to Alexander, "Rorty's view of the incommensurability of private self-creation with any public concern abandons seeing how public affairs are really implicated in our private worlds or how our private actions may have broad public consequences. He thus encourages the retreat into the private world of aesthetic description with the hope that it eventuates in a 'sentimental education' which somehow bolsters the project of liberal democracy" (211).

55. *Objectivity, Relativism, and Truth*, p. 201.

56. See Shusterman, pp. 80–81.

57. *Objectivity, Relativism, and Truth*, p. 194.

58. *Consequences of Pragmatism*, p. 165.

59. *Contingency, Irony, and Solidarity*, p. 87.

60. *Contingency, Irony, and Solidarity*, p. 189.

61. Charles Hartshorne thus asks, "Why should we give up all efforts to satisfy such natural curiosity as that about the eternal or necessary aspects of reality, in contrast and relation to which the contingent and emergent aspects alone have their full sense and definition?" (20). "Rorty's Pragmatism and Farewell to the Age of Faith and Enlightenment," in Saatkamp, ed., *Rorty and Pragmatism*, pp. 16–28.

62. David L. Hall thus observes that "Rorty seems far less a prophet crying in the wilderness than a lead-tenor backed by an (often involuntary) chorus of reasonably harmonious voices. Rorty's is, indeed, a *new* pragmatism, as we shall see. But, as Rorty himself continues to insist, this pragmatism is a plausible consequence of its parent tradition" (854-86).

63. For the opposing viewpoint—namely, that Rorty is no heir to (and perhaps an enemy of) Dewey's legacy, see Susan Haack, "Vulgar Pragmatism: An Unedifying Prospect," in *Rorty and Pragmatism: The Philosopher Responds to His Critics* (Nashville, TN: Vanderbilt University Press, 1995), pp. 126–27; Levine, p. 49; Gouinlock, p. 87.

64. For a sympathetic reckoning of Rorty's debts to Dewey, see H.O. Mounce, *The Two Pragmatisms: From Peirce to Rorty* (London: Routledge, 1997). The "two pragmatisms" in question refer, respectively, to that of Peirce and James and that of Dewey and Rorty. Mounce maintains that Dewey and Rorty share the same *Weltanschauung*—namely, that of the modern world and its rejection of "the view that the world has an intelligible order which transcends the human mind but to which the human mind is in some measure akin" (174).

65. Hall, for example, attributes to Rorty the "motivation . . . to win the mantle of the Prince of Pragmatists" (84). While Rorty enthusiastically champions the cause of pragmatism, I detect no evidence of this motivation in his work. Perhaps Hall is (partially) responsible for locating it there?

66. Here I follow Shusterman, who argues that "historical purism is false to the forward-looking spirit of pragmatism" (68).

67. Here I agree with Bernstein, who argues that "The pragmatic legacy (which Rorty constantly invokes) will only be recovered and revitalized when we try to do for our time what Dewey did in his historical context—to articulate, texture, and justify a vision of a pragmatically viable ideal of communal democracy" (253). As a friendly amendment to this sage

observation, I would add that Rorty should not be blamed for the failure of other pragmatists to attend to the concrete social problems that beset liberal democracy. Rorty may be the occasion for an academic diversion of pragmatism's focus and energies, but he is not its cause.

Contributors

Douglas R. Anderson is Associate Professor of Philosophy at Pennsylvania State University. He is the author of *Creativity and the Philosophy of C.S. Peirce* and essays on pragmatism, aesthetics, and religion.

Raymond D. Boisvert is Professor of Philosophy at Siena College. He is the author of *Dewey's Metaphysics* and *John Dewey*.

James Campbell is Professor of Philosophy at the University of Toledo. He is the author of *Understanding John Dewey* and of numerous articles on the history of pragmatism.

Vincent M. Colapietro is Professor of Philosophy at Pennsylvania State University. He is the author of *Peirce's Approach to the Self: A Semiotic Perspective on Human Subjectivity* (1989) and *A Glossary of Semiotics* (1993).

Daniel W. Conway is Professor of Philosophy at the Pennsylvania State University. He is co-editor of *The Politics of Irony* and *Nietzsche und die Antike Philosophie* and author of articles on Nietzsche and pragmatism.

Steven Fesmire is Assistant Professor of Philosophy at East Tennessee State University. He has published articles on metaphor, rationality, and pragmatist ethics.

Eugenie Gatens-Robinson is Associate Professor of Philosophy at Southern Illinois University at Carbondale. She is author of

Progress, Precursors and the Relevance of History to the Philosophy of Science, and of articles on pragmatism, epistemology, medical ethics, and the philosophy of science.

Casey Haskins is Associate Professor of Philosophy at the State University of New York, College at Purchase. He is the author of articles on the history of aesthetics and the history of pragmatism, and of a forthcoming book on the autonomy debate in modern aesthetics.

Victor Kestenbaum is Professor of Philosophy at Boston University. He is the author of *The Phenomenological Sense of John Dewey* and the forthcoming *Some Unknown But Still Reasoning Thing: John Dewey and the Intangible*, and editor of *The Humanity of the Ill: Phenomenological Perspectives*.

David I. Seiple is an educational consultant in New York and the WebEditor of Philosophy's Labyrinth (www.dseiple.com). His articles include contributions to the *Oxford Encyclopedia of Aesthetics* and *The Dictionary of Literary Biography*.

Richard Shusterman is Professor of Philosophy at Temple University. He is the author of *Pragmatist Aesthetics, T. S. Eliot and the Philosophy of Criticism*, and *Practicing Philosophy: Pragmatism and the Philosophical Life*, editor of *Analytic Aesthetics*, and co-editor of *The Interpretive Turn: Philosophy, Science, and Culture*.

J. E. Tiles is Professor of Philosophy at the University of Hawaii at Manoa. He is the author of *Dewey* (in the Routledge Arguments of the Philosophers series), co-author of *An Introduction to Historical Epistemology*, and editor of *John Dewey: Critical Assessments*.

Index

251